URBANIZATION AND CONFLICT
IN MARKET SOCIETIES

URBANIZATION AND CONFLICT IN MARKET SOCIETIES

Edited by
Kevin R. Cox
The Ohio State University

Maaroufa Press, Inc.
Chicago

Copyright © 1978 by Maaroufa Press, Inc.
All rights reserved
Library of Congress Catalog Card Number: 77-76158
ISBN: 0-88425-007-5
Manufactured in the United States of America

Designed by First Impression

Contents

INTRODUCTION

The major focus of this collection of essays is the impact of market relationships on urban political processes, in general, and on conflict in cities, in particular. The book, therefore, is concerned with urban problems. But the ideas developed emerge from a growing dissatisfaction with those social science paradigms presently constituting an orthodoxy in the examination of these problems. To a very important degree, the essays represent gropings—some more structured, some less so—towards a more satisfactory paradigm.

For an increasing minority of economists, geographers, and city planners there is a growing unease with that neoclassical paradigm which has been so influential hitherto in urban economies and location theory.[1] In geography and economics this dissatisfaction originated specifically with the sort of questions the neoclassical paradigm posed. Questions of system efficiency were paramount, while distributional issues received only limited attention. In both disciplines, therefore, there is an earlier, more descriptive literature focussing on inequalities.[2] Within a paradigm, however, there is a necessary and close relationship between the sort of questions it asks of the world and the conceptual apparatus it brings to bear on answering those questions. Challenging the relevance of the questions generated by a paradigm was consequently bound to lead to a growing sense of its inadequacy as a conceptual tool and a search for something more adequate.

Parallel developments are evident in other social sciences. In political science, although urban politics has never been a particularly popular subfield of the discipline,[3] there has been a clear shift in focus towards distributional issues.[4] Likewise, there are similar dissatisfactions at the conceptual level. Just as some geographers and economists find the social harmonies implicit in the neoclassical paradigm inadequate for the new questions they are asking, so in urban politics is there increasing doubt about the harmony of interests created by the politics of democratic pluralism.[5]

These probings towards a new paradigm for the study of urban problems are expressed in all social science disciplines and, at a very general level, are shown by a shift in paradigmatic emphasis: a shift *away* from paradigms based on the idea of a fundamental harmony of interests linking one individual to another in society and *towards* paradigms based on the idea of fundamental conflicts of interest between them. In other words, there is a shift from images of a world of reciprocal relations in which the fundamental questions concern improving system performance (increased spatial efficiency, more democracy, increased gross national product per capita, etc.) to images of a world of antagonistic relations in which the fundamental questions concern who gets what and why.

All the papers in this book represent this paradigmatic shift. For at least five of the papers (Harvey, Roweis and Scott, Agnew, Walker, and Cox), one can be even more specific: the shift has been not simply to paradigms based on assumptions of social dissensus, but also towards paradigms deriving from a distinctly Marxist tradition. In these papers, the inner logic and dynamics of price-fixing markets,[6] and the private property rights on which they are based are assumed as absolutely central for an understanding of urban development and the conflicts which it generates.

In the case of the other five papers, it is probably fairer to say that the "market societies" rubric in the title of this book contains more of a descriptive than an analytic imperative. Nevertheless, there are significant complementarities between the two sets of papers. Moreover, further insights can be extracted from this second group of papers by viewing them more from the perspective of a paradigm in which the social, economic, and political relations of market society occupy a central position. It is these complementarities and insights which I have attempted to identify in the introductory comments prefacing each of the three major sections of the book.

The first section sets forth the general conditions underlying conflict in cities in market societies: Some sense of the variety of conflicts involved, their interrelationships, and their broad basis in market society is provided in this section. In the second section, three papers look at a manifestation of urban conflict that has been of particular interest to geographers: controversy over the location of different land uses or public facilities, or what we call here "locational conflict." The final section is more concerned with the outputs of the conflict process: the specific geographical forms which arise from the resolution of ongoing conflicts in cities in market societies: residential segregation, suburbanization, the actual geographical patterns of public housing, and the like.

The circumstances under which this book was put together may also be of some interest. Four of the papers were originally presented (with the same titles as in this volume) in a session at the World Congress of the International Political Science Association held in Edinburgh in August, 1976.[7] Some publisher interest in adopting the papers as the nucleus for a larger collection with the same theme had already been shown; contributions from a number of geographers and political scientists were, therefore, solicited. Apart from David Harvey's paper, a slightly different version of which has appeared in *Politics and Society,* none of the papers has been published elsewhere.

Finally, I would like to thank all the contributors to this volume: first, for bothering at all; second, for living with an extremely tight manuscript preparation schedule; and, not least, for submitting, in a manner that occasionally bordered on the masochistic, to the whims and fancies of a rather unsubtle editorial style.

Worthington, Ohio
February, 1977

Notes

1. For the case of geography, see Kevin R. Cox, "American Geography: Social Science Emergent," *Social Science Quarterly* 57, no. 1 (June 1976): 198–201; symptomatic in urban economics is the establishment of a new journal, *The Review of Radical Political Economics,* and the appearance of readers such as David M. Gordon's *Problems in Political Economy: An Urban Perspective* (Lexington, Mass.: D. C. Heath, 1971).

2. In geography this took the form of a documentation of spatial inequalities. Earlier issues of the journal *Antipode* are representative in this regard. Also of interest is the attempt to project the social indicator concept onto the spatial plane: see David M. Smith, *The Geography of Social Well-Being in the United States* (New York: McGraw-Hill, 1973).

3. A brief perusal of the most prestigious of American political science journals *The American Political Science Review* would quickly convince one of the validity of this assertion.

4. Representative titles include Michael Danielson's recent book, *The Politics of Exclusion* (Princeton: Princeton University Press, 1976); and, a pioneer in this field, Oliver P. Williams et al., *Suburban Differences and Metropolitan Policies* (Philadelphia: University of Pennsylvania Press, 1965). Also indicative is the recent establishment of journals catering more to a consideration of urban problems from a distributional viewpoint: *The Urban Affairs Quarterly, The Journal of Social Policy,* and *Policy and Politics,* for example.

5. Instances of this include the influential book by Peter Bachrach and Morton Baratz: *Power and Poverty* (New York: Oxford University Press, 1972).

6. By price-fixing markets we signify markets in which prices are determined by the intersection of supply and demand curves fixed by the competitive bids and offers of buyers and sellers, respectively.

7. Specifically, these were earlier versions of the papers by Agnew, Cox, Dear and Long, and Harvey.

PART 1

The Conditions
for Conflict
in Market Societies

Overview

In this initial section, four papers attempt to establish the general conditions under which conflict occurs in cities in market societies and the variety of ways in which it expresses itself. The first paper, by David Harvey, attempts to set out a theoretical framework for understanding, in cities in advanced capitalist societies, those class conflicts relating to the production and use of the built environment. In the second paper, Shoukry Roweis and Allen Scott adopt the more general terms of discussing the nature of contemporary urban land development and the characteristic problems associated with it. It would probably be fair to say that, while Harvey's focus is quite demonstrably on distributional issues, Roweis and Scott are somewhat more concerned with the inefficiencies associated with the urban development process. Nevertheless, there are strong continuities between the two papers.

The third and fourth papers, on the other hand, *assume* the sort of conceptual frameworks developed by Harvey and Roweis and Scott. Their major contribution is to go on and examine the question of why class conflicts over the built environment within cities either do not always receive expression in the formal political process; or are transmuted into conflicts assuming more of an intra- rather than interclass character. Kenneth Newton, therefore, examines some major institutions of local government in the United States to see how they have contributed to a defusing of the conflicts latent in the situations described by Harvey and by Roweis and Scott. Kevin Cox, on the other hand, examines the locally competitive political processes— among neighborhood groups and also among local governments—into which class conflict, particularly in American cities, has been transmuted.

As Roweis and Scott indicate, underlying capitalism is an ongoing socio-political conflict over the division of the surplus between capitalists, landowners, and labor. These conflicts, as Harvey argues, bifurcate into work place-related conflicts involving wage rates, hours of work, safety conditions, etc.; and community-related conflicts involving rents, traffic safety, physical amenity, health, and the like. It is, of course, community-related conflicts that are of major concern in this book. While work place-related and community-related conflicts assume surficially different forms, however —and with important implications for class consciousness—they are both basically involved in labor's struggle to control its conditions of existence.

Some of these conflicts revolve around the landlord-tenant relationship. They involve not only levels of rent and the housing commodity received in exchange for rent, but also security of tenure, leases, and compensation in the context of urban renewal.[1]

5

Still other conflicts derive from the relationship between a property development interest which sees the city, in general, and the built environment, in particular, as fields for accumulation; and residents, who see them as a source of use values. Included in the property development interest would be not only property development companies, but also construction companies, builders, realtors, and land companies. As Roweis and Scott point out, it is easy to shift from the identification of this group to what they call "a manipulated city hypothesis" and a misleading concept of urban development as conspiracy and theft[2]; nevertheless, the imperatives of a market society will be revealed in the continual struggle to accumulate and to create a built environment in harmony with the needs of capital, rather than with those of labor. In the Canadian context, therefore, downtown commercial development has created conflicts with low-income residents, not only as a result of the displacements stemming from urban renewal and highway projects,[3] but also as a result of the gentrifications accompanying the increasing role of the central business district as a focus of white-collar employment. More generally, as Cox emphasizes, conflict can stem from the localized welfare impacts resulting from the attempts of capital to use the city as an arena for accumulation: these will range all the way from growth controversies between residents and the development interest in suburbs to conflicts over steering, blockbusting, and partition of owner-occupied housing for apartments in older parts of the city.

Conflicts of these types, quite evidently, generate public intervention at both local and national levels. Nevertheless, the policies introduced provoke certain adjustments by the protagonists which either counteract the effects of the policy or simply reproduce, in a slightly different form, the problem underlying the conflict. A classic case of this is rent control. Frequently called into being to control the so-called profiteering of landlords in times of housing shortage, its usual effect is to drive capital out of the housing market and exacerbate, rather than solve, that shortage. Other cases include housing code enforcement. As Harvey has shown elsewhere, housing codes are enforced in those neighborhoods where they are least necessary, and unenforced in those neighborhoods where they are most necessary; i.e., where the housing stock, by all standard indicators, is severely dilapidated.[4] The reason for this is fairly plain: enforcement in poorer areas of the city would simply drive many landlords out of business, encourage them to disinvest, or, in the eventuality of gentrification, convert to middle-class use and force the evicted tenants to double up in the remaining units.

The failure of these policies, it is argued, stems from their failure to confront the source of the problem: reliance upon the private market and the property relations accompanying it for production and allocation of the built environment. As Roweis and Scott affirm, they are policies which deal with the symptoms, rather than with the fundamental causes, of urban land problems. This is perhaps especially apparent in the recent debate on the effects of busing for racial balance. Resegregation at the interschool district level suggests that the initial analysis underlying the policy was almost entirely devoid of an awareness that the real estate market is a potent weapon for negating such a policy.[5]

There are a variety of a priori grounds, therefore, for expecting class conflict over the built environment of the city to provide a major focus for the urban political process. Paradoxically, this does not seem to occur to the extent we might anticipate. Rather, these conflicts, which we regard as such fundamental manifestations of the urban development process, tend to become defused, and even transmuted, into intraclass, rather than interclass, conflicts: residential households, as Harvey argues in chapter 1, are often more conscious of community than they are of class.

Undoubtedly, Harvey has also pointed to a major source of this defusing and transmutation: the extension of homeownership to larger and larger sections of the general population. Not only does homeownership help to wed labor to the general principle of private property rights; but the tying up of assets in the immobile form of a house and the land on which it stands also sensitizes the owner to neighborhood events and their likely impact on the value of those assets. The result, Cox demonstrates, is conflict among local groups of homeowners, each group attempting to deflect the "obnoxious" products of the urban land development process away from its own turf and to attract, onto the same turf, the "salutary" products of that process.[6]

Newton's paper is also concerned with this defusing process. He draws attention to institutional forces which have tended to limit the inputs of labor into the local political process and separate the antagonistic groups, so that they no longer confront each other in the same political arena. Newton ascribes particular significance to the electoral institutions of the reform movement: the shift from partisan, ward organization to nonpartisan, at-large elections which tend to favor those who are prominent in the life of the city and who can afford to bankroll a citywide—as opposed to a wardwide—campaign.

In addition, there is the combination of jurisdictional fragmentation and home rule so apparent in American metropolitan areas. As a result of fragmentation, conflicting groups frequently do not confront each other. Attempts at redistribution at the local level can be easily frustrated by residential relocation. At the same time, jurisdictional boundaries tend to separate labor into localized factions competing, for example, for state or federal largesse.

On the other hand, it is apparent that transmutation of class conflict into community conflict or competition takes place to varying degrees in different national contexts. Harvey, for example, suggests that community consciousness is more apparent in the U.S., while in Western European countries class consciousness is stronger. It is to this contrast in the transmutation of class conflict into community conflict and competition that the final paper in this section (by Cox) addresses itself.

Competition between neighborhood groups and local governments, for example, is much more prevalent in the U.S. than in Britain. The starting point for an explanation is that the activities of local governments and neighborhood organizations are a species of housing-market management: attempts to deflect the flows of residents—

with their various behavioral and fiscal implications—to local advantage. This goal follows from what was said above regarding the interest of homeowners in neighborhood events.

Critical to an understanding of these localized welfare impacts is the nature of residential preferences in market societies. Market society has been remarkably effective in homogenizing preferences for co-residents. Unfortunately, not all co-residents are equally desirable as newcomers to a community: Middle-class households prefer to live in middle-class neighborhoods, and so would lower-class households; but, if the preferences of the latter are satisfied, then the neighborhoods to which they gain entrance will no longer be middle class. Clearly these residential preferences are basic not only to a vigorous housing market as the impacted try to get away from "them," but also to an understanding of the severity of the localized welfare impacts which the housing market, in turn, induces.

The intensity of these residential preferences, however, can be hypothesized as a variable. To the extent that they are more intense, there will be stronger housing-market pressure to satisfy the demands of the less desirable co-residents. The effect of satisfying those demands will be more severe welfare impacts on households in the middle-class neighborhoods and jurisdictions affected, and a greater incentive to forestall these effects by managing the housing market to local benefit. This suggests that the prevalence of community competition and conflict in the U.S. might be related to more intense preferences for co-residents. The intensity of these preferences is, in turn, related to the impact of certain culture-specific characteristics of the U.S. and Britain.

NOTES
1. For examinations of landlord-tenant conflict, see Michael Lipsky, *Protest in City Politics* (Chicago: Rand McNally, 1970); and Gerald Popplestone, "Collective Action Among Private Tenants," *British Journal of Social Work* 2 (1973).
2. An excellent instance of the "manipulated city hypothesis" is provided by James Lorimer's *A Citizen's Guide to City Politics* (Toronto: James Lewis and Samuel, 1972).
3. On the emergence of an antihighway lobby, see Michael A. Kemp and Melvyn D. Cheslow, "Transportation," in *The Urban Predicament*, ed. William Gorham and Nathan Glazer (Washington, D.C.: The Urban Institute, 1976), pp. 300–304.
4. David Harvey et al., *The Housing Market and Code Enforcement in Baltimore* (Baltimore: The Baltimore Urban Observatory, 1972).
5. On the resegregation phenomenon, see James S. Coleman, Sara D. Kelly. and John A. Moore, *Trends in School Segregation, 1968–73* (Washington, D.C.: The Urban Institute, 1975).
6. For the concepts of obnoxious and salutary land uses, see David R. Reynolds and Rex Honey, "Conflict in the Location of Salutary Public Facilities," chapter 7 of this volume.

Chapter 1

LABOR, CAPITAL, AND CLASS STRUGGLE AROUND THE BUILT ENVIRONMENT IN ADVANCED CAPITALIST SOCIETIES

DAVID HARVEY

In this paper I will seek to establish a theoretical framework for understanding a facet of class struggle under advanced capitalism. The conflicts which will be scrutinized are those which relate to the production and use of the built environment, by which I mean the totality of physical structures: houses, roads, factories, offices, sewage systems, parks, cultural institutions, educational facilities, and so on. In general, I shall argue that capitalist society must of necessity create a physical landscape—a mass of humanly constructed physical resources—in its own image, broadly appropriate to the purposes of production and reproduction. But I shall also argue that this process of creating space is full of contradictions and tensions and that the class relations in capitalist society inevitably spawn strong crosscurrents of conflict.

I shall assume for purposes of analytic convenience that a clear distinction exists between: (1) a faction of capital seeking the appropriation of rent either directly (as landlords, property companies, and so on) or indirectly (as financial intermediaries or others who invest in property simply for a rate of return); (2) a faction of capital seeking interest and profit by building new elements in the built environment (the construction interests); (3) capital "in general," which looks upon the built environment as an outlet for surplus capital and as a bundle of use values for enhancing the production and accumulation of capital; and (4) labor, which uses the built environment as a means of consumption and as a means for its own reproduction. I shall also assume that the built environment can be divided conceptually into *fixed capital* items to be used in production (factories, highways, railroads, offices, and so on) and *consump-*

I am much indebted to Dick Walker for critical comments upon an earlier draft of this paper. Also I should add that his thought and work have contributed in many ways (some of which certainly I am unaware) to my understanding of the issues raised in this paper.

tion fund items to be used in consumption (houses, roads, parks, sidewalks, and the like).[1] Some items, such as roads and sewer systems, can function both as fixed capital and as part of the consumption fund, depending on their use.

I will restrict attention in this paper to the structure of conflict as it arises in relation to labor's use of the consumption fund, rather than to its use of fixed capital in the immediate process of production. An analysis of this aspect of class struggle will do much to shed light, I believe, on the vexing questions which surround the relationship between community conflict and community organizing, on the one hand, and industrial conflict and work-based organizing, on the other. In short, I hope to be able to shed some light on the position and experience of labor with respect to *living*, as well as *working*, in the historical development of those countries which are now generally considered to be in the "advanced" capitalist category. The examples will be taken from the United States and Britain. Some preparatory comments on the general theme to be pursued are in order.

The domination of capital over labor is basic to the capitalist mode of production; without it, after all, surplus value could not be extracted and accumulation would disappear. All kinds of consequences derive from this, and the relation between labor and the built environment can be understood only in terms of it. Perhaps the single most important fact is that industrial capitalism, through the reorganization of the work process and the advent of the factory system, forced a separation between place of work and place of reproduction and consumption. The need to reproduce labor power is thus translated into a specific set of production and consumption activities within the household, a domestic economy which requires use values in the form of a built environment if it is to function effectively.

The needs of labor have changed historically, and they will be met in part by work within the household and be procured in part through market exchanges of wages earned against commodities produced. The commodity requirements of labor depend upon the balance between domestic economy products and market purchases, as well as upon the environmental, historical, and moral considerations which fix labor's standard of living.[2] In the commodity realm, labor can, by organization and class struggle, alter the definition of needs to include "reasonable" standards of nutrition, health care, housing, education, recreation, entertainment, and so on. From the standpoint of capital, accumulation requires a constant expansion of the market for commodities, which means the creation of new social wants and needs and the organization of "rational consumption" on the part of labor. This last condition suggests theoretically what is historically observable: that the domestic economy must steadily give way before the expansion of capitalist commodity production. "Accumulation for accumulation's sake, production for production's sake," which jointly drive the capitalist onward, therefore, entail an increasing integration of labor's consumption into the capitalist system of production and exchange of commodities.[3]

The split between the place of work and the place of residence means that the struggle of labor to control the social conditions of its own existence splits into two seemingly independent struggles. The first, located in the work place, is over the conditions of work and the wage rate which provides the purchasing power for consumption goods. The second, fought in the place of residence, is against secondary forms of exploitation and appropriation represented by merchant capital, landed property, and the like. This is a fight over the costs and conditions of existence in the living place. And it is on this second kind of struggle that we focus here, recognizing of course, that the dichotomy between *living* and *working* is itself an artificial division which the capitalist system imposes.

Labor Versus the Appropriators of Rent and the Construction Interest

Labor needs living space. Land is, therefore, a condition of living for labor in much the same way that it is a condition of production for capital. The system of private property which excludes labor from land as a condition of production also serves to exclude labor from the land as a condition of living. As Marx puts it, "The monstrous power wielded by landed property, when united hand in hand with industrial capital, enables it to be used against laborers engaged in their wage struggle as a means of practically expelling them from the earth as a dwelling place."[4] Apart from space as a basic condition of living, we are concerned here with housing, transportation (to jobs and facilities), amenities, facilities, and a whole bundle of resources which contribute to the total living environment for labor. Some of these items can be privately appropriated (housing is the most important case), while others have to be used in common (sidewalks) and, in some cases (such as the transportation system), even used jointly with capital.

The need for these items pits labor against landed property and the appropriation of rent, as well as against the construction interest which seeks to profit from the production of these commodities. The cost and quality of these items affect labor's standard of living. Labor, in seeking to protect and enhance its standard of living, engages, in the living place, in a series of running battles over a variety of issues which relate to the creation, management, and use of the built environment. Examples are not hard to find: community conflict over excessive rental appropriation by landlords; over speculation in the housing market; over the siting of "noxious" facilities; over inflation in housing construction costs; over inflation in the costs of servicing a deteriorating urban infrastructure; over congestion; over lack of accessibility to employment opportunities and services; over highway construction and urban renewal; over the "quality of life" and aesthetic issues—the list seems almost endless.

Conflicts which focus on the built environment exhibit certain peculiar characteristics because not only does the monopoly power conferred by private property arrangements generate the power to appropriate rent, but it also yields to the owner's command over a "natural monopoly" in space.[5] The fixed and immobile character of the built environment entails the production and use of commodities under conditions of spatial monopolistic competition with strong "neighborhood" or "externality" effects.[6] Many of the struggles which occur are over externality effects. The value of a particular house is, in part, determined by the condition of the houses surrounding it; and each owner is, therefore, very interested in seeing to it that the "neighborhood" as a whole is well maintained. In bourgeois theory, the appropriation of rent and the trading of titles to properties set price signals for new commodity production in a way such that a "rational" allocation of land to uses can be arrived at through a market process. But because of the pervasive externality effects and the sequential character of both development and occupancy, the price signals suffer from all sorts of serious distortions. There are, as a consequence, numerous opportunities for appropriators *and* the construction faction, for developers, speculators, and even private individuals to reap windfall profits and monopoly rents. Internecine conflict within a class and faction is, therefore, just as common as conflict between classes and factions.

We are primarily concerned here, however, with the structure of the three-way struggle between labor, the appropriators of rent, and the construction faction. Consider, as an example, the direct struggle between laborers and landlords over the cost and quality of housing. Landlords typically use whatever power they have to appropriate as much as they can from the housing stock they own, and they will adjust their strategy to the conditions in a way to maximize the rate of return on their capital. If this rate of return is very high, then new capital will likely flow into land-lordism; and if the rate of return is very low, then we will likely witness disinvestment and abandonment. Labor will seek by a variety of strategies (for example, moving to where housing is cheaper or imposing rent controls and housing codes) to limit appropriation and to ensure a reasonable quality of shelter. How this struggle is resolved depends very much upon the relative economic and political power of the two groups, the circumstances of supply and demand which exist at a particular place and time, and the options available to each group.[7]

The struggle becomes three dimensional when we consider that the ability of appropriators to gain monopoly rents on the old housing is, in part, limited by the capacity of the construction interest to enter the market and create new housing at a lower cost. The price of old housing is, after all, strongly affected by the production costs of new housing. If labor can use its political power to gain state subsidies for construction, then this artificially stimulated new development will force downwards the rate of appropriation on existing resources. If, on the other hand, appropriators can check new development (for example, by escalating land costs), or if, for some reason, new development is inhibited (planning permission procedures in Britain have typically functioned in this way), then the rate of appropriation can rise. On the other hand, when labor manages to check the rate of appropriation through direct rent controls, then the price of rented housing falls, new development is discouraged, and scarcity is produced. These are the kinds of conflicts and strategies of coalition that we have to expect in these situations.

But the structure of conflict is made more complex by the "natural monopoly" inherent in space. For example, the monopoly power of the landlord is in part modified by the ability of labor to escape entrapment in the immediate environs of the work place. Appropriation from housing is very sensitive to changes in transportation. The ability to undertake a longer journey to work is, in part, dependent on: the wage rate (which allows the worker to pay for travel); the length of the workday (which gives the worker time to travel); and the cost and availability of transportation. The boom in the construction of working-class suburbs in late nineteenth-century London, for example, can in large degree be explained by the advent of the railways, and the provision of cheap "workman's special" fares and the shortening of the workday, freeing at least some of the working class from the need to live within walking distance of the work place.[8] The rate of rental appropriation on the housing close to the employment centers had to fall as a consequence. The "streetcar" suburbs of American cities and the working-class suburbs of today (based on cheap energy and the automobile) are further examples of this phenomenon.[9] By pressing for new and cheap forms of transportation, labor can escape geographical entrapment and thereby reduce the capacity of landlords in advantageous locations to gain monopoly rents. The problems which attach to spatial entrapment are still with us, of course, in the contemporary ghettos of the poor, the aged, the oppressed minorities, and the like. Access is still, for these groups, a major issue.[10]

The struggle to fight off the immediate depredations of the landlord and the continual battle to keep the cost of living down does much to explain the posture adopted by labor with respect to the distribution, quantities, and qualities of all elements in the built environment. Public facilities, recreational opportunities, amenities, transportation access, and so on are all subjects of contention. But underlying these immediate concerns is a deeper struggle over the very meaning of the built environment as a set of use values for labor.

The producers of the built environment, both past and present, provide labor with a limited set of choices of living conditions. If labor has slender resources with which to exercise an effective demand, then it has to put up with whatever it can get: shoddily built, cramped, and poorly serviced tenement buildings, for example. With increasing effective demand, labor has the potential to choose over a wider range; and, as a result, questions concerning the overall "quality of life" begin to arise. Capital in general and its faction that produces the built environment seek to define the quality of life for labor in terms of the commodities which they can profitably produce in certain locations. Labor, on the other hand, defines quality of life solely in use-value terms and, in the process, may appeal to some underlying and fundamental conception of what it is to be human. Production for profit and production for use are often inconsistent. The survival of capitalism, therefore, requires that capital dominate labor not simply in the work process, but with respect to the very definition of the quality of life in the consumption sphere. Production, Marx argued, not only produces consumption; it also produces the mode of consumption and that, of course, is what the consumption fund for labor is all about.[11] For this reason capital in general cannot afford the outcome of struggles around the built environment to be determined simply by the relative powers of labor, the appropriators of rent and the construction faction. It must, from time to time, throw its weight into the balance to effect outcomes favorable to the reproduction of the capitalist social order. It is to these concerns that we must now turn.

The Interventions of Capital in Struggles over the Built Environment

When capital intervenes in struggles over the built environment, it usually does so through the agency of state power. A cursory examination of the history of the advanced capitalist countries shows that the capitalist class sometimes throws its weight to the side of labor and sometimes to the side of other factions. But history also suggests a certain pattern and underlying rationale for these interventions. We can get at the pattern by assembling the interventions together under four broad headings: private property and homeownership for the working class; the cost of living and the value of labor power; managed collective consumption of workers in the interest of sustained capital accumulation; and a complex, but very important, topic concerning the relation to nature, the imposition of work discipline, and the like. A discussion of the pattern will help us to identify the underlying rationale; and, in this manner, we can identify a much deeper meaning for the everyday struggles in which labor engages in the living place.

Private Property and Homeownership for Labor

The struggle which labor wages in the living place against the appropriation of rent is a struggle against the monopoly power of private property. Labor's fight against the principle of private property cannot be easily confined to the housing arena and "the vexed question of the relation between rent and wages ... easily slides into that of capital and labor."[12] For this reason, the capitalist class as a whole cannot afford to ignore it because they have an interest in keeping sacrosanct the principle of private property. A well-developed struggle between tenants and landlords—with the former calling for public ownership, municipalization, and the like—calls the whole principle into question. Extended individualized homeownership is, therefore, seen as advantageous to the capitalist class because it promotes: the allegiance of at least a segment of the working class to the principle of private property; an ethic of "possessive individualism"; and a fragmentation of the working class into "housing classes" of homeowners and tenants.[13] This gives the capitalist class a handy ideological lever to use against public ownership and nationalization demands because it is easy to make these proposals sound as if their intent were to take workers' privately owned houses away from them.

The majority of owner-occupiers, however, do not own their housing outright. They make interest payments on a mortgage. This puts finance capital in a hegemonic position with respect to the functioning of the housing market: a position of which it is in no way loathe to make use.[14] In reality, the apparent entrance of workers into the petty form of property ownership in housing is, to large degree, its exact opposite: the entry of money capital into a controlling position within the consumption fund. Finance capital not only controls the disposition and rate of new investment in housing, but also controls labor, as well, through chronic debt encumbrance. A worker mortgaged up to the hilt is, for the most part, a pillar of social stability, and schemes to promote homeownership within the working class have long recognized this basic fact. And, in return, the worker may build up, very slowly, some equity in the property.

This last consideration has some important ramifications. Workers put their savings into the physical form of a property. Obviously, they will be concerned with preserving the value of those savings and, if possible, enhancing them. Ownership of housing can also lead to petty landlordism, which has been a traditional and very important means for individual workers to engage in the appropriation of values at the expense of other workers. But, more importantly, every homeowner, whether he or she likes it or not, is caught in a struggle over the appropriation of values because of the shifting patterns of external costs and benefits within the built environment. A new road may destroy the value of some housing and enhance the value of other, and the same applies to all new development, redevelopment, accelerated obsolescence, and so on.

The way in which labor relates to these externality effects is crucial, if only because the housing market is in quantitative terms by far the most important market for any one particular element in the built environment. It would be very difficult to understand the political tension between suburbs and central cities in the United States without recognizing the fragmentation which occurs within the working class as one of its sections moves into homeownership and becomes deeply concerned with preserving and, if possible, enhancing the value of its equity. The social tensions omnipresent within the "community structure" of American cities are similarly affected. In short, homeownership invites a faction of the working class to wage its inevitable fight over the appropriation of value in capitalist society in a very different way. It puts them on the side of the principle of private property and frequently leads them to appropriate values at the expense of other factions of the working class. With so glorious a tool to divide and rule at its disposal, it is hardly surprising that capital in general sides with labor against the landed interest in this regard. It is, rather, as if capital, having relied upon landed property to divorce labor from access to one of the basic conditions of production, in the face of class struggle preserves the principle of private property intact by permitting labor to return "to the face of the earth" as a partial owner of land and property as a condition of consumption.

The Cost of Living and the Wage Rate

Marx argued that the value of labor power was determined by the value of the commodities required to reproduce that labor power. This neat equivalence disappears in the pricing realm; but, nevertheless, there is a relation of some sort between wages and the cost of obtaining those commodities essential to the reproduction of the household.[15]

An excessive rate of appropriation of rent by landlords will increase labor's cost of living and generate higher wage demands which, if won, may have the effect of lowering the rate of capital accumulation. For this reason, capital in general may side with labor in the struggle against excessive appropriation and attempt, also, to lower the costs of production of a basic commodity like housing. Capitalists may themselves seek to provide cheap housing, as in the "model communities" typical of the early years of the industrial revolution, or they may even side with the demands of labor for cheap, subsidized housing under public ownership, provided that this permits the payment of lower wages. For the same reason the capitalist class may seek to promote, through the agency of the state, the industrialization of building production and the rationalization of production of the built environment through comprehensive land-use planning policies, new town construction programs, and the like. Capitalists tend to become interested in such programs, however, only when labor is in a position, through its organized collective power, to tie wages to the cost of living.

These considerations apply to all elements in the built environment (and to social services and social expenditures, also) which are relevant to the reproduction of labor power. Those which are publicly provided (which means the bulk of them outside of housing and, until recently, transportation) can be monitored by a cost-conscious municipal government under the watchful eye of the local business community. And perhaps, in an emergency situation (such as that experienced in New York both in the 1930s and in the 1970s, they can even be placed under the direct supervision of finance capital. In the interests of keeping the costs of reproduction of labor power at a minimum, the capitalist class, as a whole, may seek collective means to intervene in the processes of investment and appropriation in the built environment. In much the same way that the proletariat frequently sided with the rising industrial bourgeoisie against the landed interest in the early years of capitalism, so we often find capital in general siding with labor in the advanced capitalist societies against excessive appropriation of rent and rising costs of new development. This coalition is not forged altruistically but arises organically out of the relation between the wage rate and the costs of reproduction of labor power.

"Rational," Managed, and Collective Consumption

Workers mediate the circulation of commodities by using their wages to purchase means of consumption produced by capitalists. Any failure on the part of workers to use their purchasing power "correctly" and "rationally" from the standpoint of the capitalist production and realization system will disrupt the circulation of commodities. In the early years of capitalist development, this problem was not so important because trade with noncapitalist societies could easily take up any slack in effective demand. But, with the transition to advanced capitalism, the internal market provided by the wage-labor force becomes of greater and greater significance. Also, as standards of living rise, in the sense that workers have more and more commodities available to them, so the potential for a breakdown from "irrationalities" in consumption increases. The failure to exercise a proper, effective demand can be a source of crisis. And it was, of course, Keynes' major contribution to demonstrate to the capitalist class that, under certain conditions, the way out of a crisis (manifest as a falling profit rate) was not to cut wages, but to increase them and thereby to expand the market.

This presumes, however, that workers are willing to spend their wages "rationally." If we assume, with Adam Smith, that mankind has an infinite and insatiable appetite for "trinkets and baubles," then there is no problem; but Malthus voiced another worry when he observed that the history of human society "sufficiently demonstrates" that "an efficient taste for luxuries and conveniences, that is, such a taste as will properly stimulate industry, instead of being ready to appear the moment it is required, is a plant of slow growth."[16] Production may, as Marx averred, produce consumption and the mode of consumption, but it does not do so automatically, and the manner in which it does so is the locus of continual struggle and conflict.[17]

Consider, first of all, the relationship between capitalist production and the household economy. In 1810 in the United States, for example, "The best figures available to historians show that ... about two-thirds of the clothing worn ... was the product of household manufacture, ..." but by 1860 the advent of industrial capitalism in the form of the New England textile industry had changed all that: "... household manufactures had been eclipsed by the development of industrial production and a market economy."[18] Step by step, activities traditionally associated with household work are brought within the capitalist market economy: baking, brewing, preserving, cooking, food preparation, washing, cleaning, and even child-rearing and child socialization. And, with respect to the built environment, house building and maintenance become integrated into the market economy. In the nineteenth century in the United States, a substantial proportion of the population built their own homes with their own labor and local raw materials. Now, almost all units are built through the market system.

The advent of the factory system was a double-edged sword with respect to the household economy. On the one hand, it extracted the wage earner(s) from the home. In the early years of industrial capitalism, it did so for twelve to fourteen hours a day and, under particularly exploitative conditions, forced the whole household—women and children as well as men—into the wage labor force (in this manner the wages of the *household* could remain stable in the face of a falling wage rate). Of these early years E. P. Thompson writes:

> Each stage in industrial differentiation and specialization struck also at the family economy, disturbing customary relations between man and wife, parents and children, and differentiating more sharply between "work" and "life." It was to be a full hundred years before this differentiation

was to bring returns, in the form of labor-saving devices,
back into the working woman's home.[19]

This "return" of commodities to the household is the other edge of the
sword. The factory system produced use values for consumption more
cheaply and with less effort than did the household. The use values may
be in the form of standardized products, but there should at least be more
of them and, therefore, a material basis for a rising standard of living for
labor. In the early years of industrial capitalism this did not generally
happen. Laborers certainly worked longer hours and probably received
less in the way of use values (although the evidence on this latter point is
both patchy and controversial).[20] But the rising productivity of labor which
occurs with accumulation, the consequent need to establish an internal
market, and a century or more of class struggle have changed all of this.
Consumer durables and consumption fund items (such as housing) have
become very important growth sectors in the economy, and the political
conditions and the material basis for a rising standard of living for labor
have indeed been achieved.

The experience of labor in substituting work in the factory for work in
the household has, therefore, both positive and negative aspects. But
these substitutions are not easily achieved because they involve the nature
and structure of the family, the role of women in society, culturally entrenched traditions, and the like. The substitutions are themselves a focus
of struggle. The "rational" consumption of commodities in relation to the
accumulation of capital implies a certain balance between market purchases and household work. The struggle to substitute the former for the
latter is significant because its outcome defines the very meaning of "use
values" and the "standard of living" for labor in its commodity aspects.
The construction of the built environment has to be seen, therefore, in the
context of a struggle over a whole way of living and being.

Techniques of persuasion are widely used in advanced capitalist societies to ensure "rational" consumption. Moral exhortation and philanthropic enterprise are often put to work "to raise the condition of the
laborer by an improvement of his mental and moral powers and to make
a rational consumer of him."[21] The church, the press, and the schools can
be mobilized on behalf of rational consumption at the same time as they
can be made vehicles for genuinely autonomous working-class development. And then, of course, there are always the blandishments of the
admen and the techniques of Madison Avenue.

It would be idle to pretend that "the standard of living of labor" has
been unaffected by these techniques. But, again, we are dealing with a
double-edged sword. They may, in fact, also exert what Marx called a
"civilizing influence" on labor and be used by labor to raise itself to a new

condition of material and mental well-being which, in turn, provides a new and more solid basis for class struggle.[22] Conversely, the drive by labor to improve its condition may be perverted by a variety of strategems into a definition of use values advantageous to accumulation, rather than reflective of the real, human needs of labor. The human demand for shelter is turned, for example, into a process of accumulation through housing production.

"Rational" consumption can also be ensured by the collectivization of consumption primarily, although not solely, through the agency of the state.[23] Working-class demands for health care, housing, education, and social services of all kinds are usually expressed through political channels, and government arbitrates these demands and seeks to reconcile them to the requirements of accumulation. Many of these demands are met by the collective provision of goods and services, which means that everyone consumes them whether he or she likes it or not. Capitalist systems have moved more and more towards the collectivization of consumption because of the need, clearly understood in Keynesian fiscal policies, to manage consumption in the interests of accumulation. By collectivization, consumer choice is translated from the uncontrolled anarchy of individual action to the seemingly more controllable field of state enterprise. This translation does not occur without a struggle over both the freedom of individual choice (which generates a strong, antibureaucratic sentiment) and the definition of the use values involved (national defense versus subsidized housing for the poor, for example).

The built environment has a peculiar and important role in all of this. The bundle of resources which comprise it—streets and sidewalks, drains and sewer systems, parks and playgrounds—contains many elements which are collectively consumed. The public provision of these public goods is a "natural" form of collective consumption, which capital can easily colonize through the agency of the state. Also, the sum of individual, private decisions creates a public effect because of the pervasive externality effects which in themselves force certain forms of collective consumption through private action: "If I fail to keep my yard neat then my neighbors cannot avoid seeing it." The built environment requires collective management and control, and it is therefore almost certain to be a primary field of struggle between capital and labor over what is good for people and what is good for accumulation.

The consumption fund has accounted for an increasing proportion of gross aggregate investment in the built environment in both Britain and the United States since around 1890.[24] The housing sector, in particular, has become a major tool in macroeconomic policy for stabilizing economic growth, particularly in the United States, where it has openly been used as a Keynesian regulator (not always, we should add, with success). And there are also strong multiplier effects to be taken into account. Housing construction, for example, requires complementary investments in other aspects of the built environment, as well as in a wide range of consumer durables. The multipliers vary a great deal according to design and other considerations, but in all cases they are substantial.

These multipliers assume an added importance when we consider them in relation to the "coercive power" which the built environment can exercise over our daily lives. Its longevity and fixity in space, together with its method of financing and amortization, mean that once we have created it, we must use it if the value which it represents is not to be lost. Under the social relations of capitalism, the built environment becomes an artifact of human labor which subsequently returns to dominate daily life. If our cities are built for driving, for example, then drive we must, regardless of our preference, in order to live "normally." The built environment can, therefore, be constructed by capital as a coercive force in the interests of sustained accumulation. The highway lobby in the United States—the automobile, oil, and rubber industries and the construction interests—changed the face of America and used the coercive power of the built environment to ensure "rational" growth in the consumption of their products.[25] But labor is not oblivious to such pressures. The configurations of use values which capital urges upon labor may be resisted or transformed to suit labor's purposes and labor's needs—the automobile becomes, for example, a means of escape—and we will consider from what very shortly.

Insofar as capitalism has survived, we have to conclude that capital dominates labor—not only in the place of work, but also in the living space—by defining the "standard of living of labor" and the "quality of life" through the creation of built environments which conform to the requirements of accumulation and commodity production. To put it this strongly is not to say that labor cannot win on particular issues, nor does it imply that there is one, and only one, definition of use values for labor which fits the need for accumulation. There are innumerable possibilities, but the limits of tolerance of capital are, nevertheless, clearly defined. For labor to struggle within these limits is one thing; to seek to go beyond them is where the real struggle begins.

The Socialization of Labor and the Relation to Nature

Work and living cannot be divorced. What happens in the work place cannot be forgotten in the living place. Yet, we have a very poor understanding of their relationship.[26] The definition of "a use value for labor in the built environment" cannot, therefore, be independent of the work experience. Below we will consider two elemental aspects of this.

We tend to forget that the advent of the factory system required an extraordinary adaptation in social life. It transformed the rural peasant and the independent artisan into mere cogs in a system designed to produce surplus value. The laborer became a "thing," a mere "factor of production," to be used in the production process as the capitalist desired. But the new economic order also required that "men who were non-accumulative, non-acquisitive, accustomed to work for subsistence, not for maximization of income, had to be made obedient to the cash stimulus and obedient in such a way as to react precisely to the stimuli provided." The habituation of the worker to the new mode of production, the inculcation of the work discipline and all that went with it were and still are no easy matter. Consequently, "The modern industrial proletariat was introduced to its role, not so much by attraction or monetary reward, but by compulsion, force, and fear. It was not allowed to grow as in a sunny garden; it was forged, over a fire, by the powerful blows of a hammer."[27] The consequences of this for the manner and forms of subsequent class struggle were legion. And, as Braverman points out, "The habituation of workers to the capitalist mode of production must be renewed with each generation."[28]

The inculcation of the work discipline could be accomplished in part by training, threats, incentives, and cajolery in the work place. These were effective but not, in themselves, sufficient. In the early years of industrial capitalism, the problems were particularly severe because capitalism had not yet woven the "net of modern capitalist life that finally makes all other modes of living impossible."[29] And so originated the drive on the part of capital to inculcate the working class with the "work ethic" and "bourgeois values" of honesty, reliability, respect for authority, obedience to laws and rules, respect for property and contractual agreements, and the like. The assault on the values of the working class was, in part, conducted through religious, educational, and philanthropic channels, with the paternalism of the industrialist often thrown into the balance. But there is another component to this that is of special interest to us here. The early industrialists, in particular, had to deal with workers both inside and outside the factory:

> The efforts to reform the whole man were, therefore, particularly marked in factory towns and villages in which the total environment was under the control of a single employer. Here some of the main developments of the industrial revolution were epitomized: these settlements were founded by the industrialist, their whole raison d'être his quest for profit, their politics and laws in his pocket, the quality of their life under his whim, their ultimate aims in his image.... Great though the outward difference was between the flogging masters and the model community builders, "from the standpoint of control of labour both

types of factory management display a concern with the enforcement of discipline."[30]

This need to socialize labor to a work process through control in the living place is endemic to capitalism, but it is particularly noticeable when new kinds of work processes are introduced. Henry Ford's five-dollar, eight-hour day for assembly line workers (introduced in 1914) was accompanied by much puritanical rhetoric and a "philanthropic" control system which affected nearly every facet of the workers' lives:

> A staff of over thirty investigators ... visited workers' homes gathering information and giving advice on the intimate details of the family budget, diet, living arrangements, recreation, social outlook and morality.... The worker who refused to learn English, rejected the advice of the investigator, gambled, drank excessively, or was found guilty of "any malicious practice derogatory to good physical manhood or moral character" was disqualified from the five-dollar wage ...[31]

Gramsci's comments on "Fordism" are perceptive.[32] There arose at that point in the history of capitalist accumulation a "need to elaborate a new type of man suited to the new type of work and productive process." This transformation, Gramsci argued, could be accomplished only by a skillful combination of force and persuasion, the latter including high wages, "various social benefits, extremely subtle ideological propoganda." Ford's puritanical and social control initiatives had the purpose of "preserving, outside of work, a certain psychophysical equilibrium which prevent[ed] the physiological collapse of the workers, exhausted by the new method of production." Workers had to spend their money "rationally, to maintain, renew, and, if possible, to increase [their] muscular nervous efficiency." The fierce attack on alcohol and sexual activities was also a part of the comprehensive effort to inculcate "the habits and customs necessary for the new systems of living and working." The events which surrounded the introduction of Fordism are a classic example of the attempt by capital to shape the person in the living place to fit the requirements of the work place.

Our interest here is, of course, to understand the manner in which industrialists, in general, and the community builders, in particular, defined the quality of life for their workers and used the built environment as part of a general strategy for inculcating bourgeois values and a "responsible" industrial work discipline. We have already noted a modern version of this in the promotion of working-class homeownership as a means of ensuring respect for property rights and social stability, a connection which was recognized early in the nineteenth century in the United States.[33] But we are here concerned with the more direct forms of control of the living space. Bender suggests, for example, that, in the 1820s, the boardinghouses constructed to house the mill girls of Lowell "served as a functional equivalent of the rural family" and operated as "an effective adaptive mechanism" for the girls being drawn from the New England farms into the factory system.[34] This same point was made most effectively in the design and functioning of those institutions dealing with those who could not, or would not, adapt to the new style of life. As early as Elizabethan times, for example, madness and unemployment were regarded as the same thing, while the advent of industrial capitalism had the effect of defining physical sickness as inability to go to work. Both Pollard, in the British context, and Rothman, in the American, point out the connection between major social institutions—asylums, workhouses, penitentiaries, hospitals, and even schools—and the factory systems, which they closely resembled in layout and in internal disciplinary organization. The rehabilitation of the convict in Jacksonian America, for example, meant the socialization of the convict to something akin to an industrial work discipline.[35]

That there is a relationship of some sort between working and living, and that by manipulating the latter a leverage can be exerted on the former, has not escaped the notice of the capitalist class. A persistent theme in the history of the advanced capitalist countries has been to look for those improvements in the living place which will enhance the happiness, docility, and efficiency of labor. In the model communities this kind of program is explicit. In 1880, George Pullman, in his ill-fated experiment, built the town that bears his name in order to:

> ... attract and retain a superior type of workingman, who would in turn be "elevated and refined" by the physical setting. This would mean contented employees and a consequent reduction in absenteeism, drinking, and shirking on the job. Furthermore, such workers were expected to be less susceptible to the exhortation of "agitators" than [were] the demoralized laborers of the city slums. His town would protect his company from labor unrest and strikes.[36]

And, we should add, the whole enterprise was supposed to make six percent on the capital invested. The Pullman Strike of 1894 was a fitting epitaph to such a dream, demonstrating that a direct, unified control by the capitalists over the lives of labor in both the work place and the living place is an explosive issue.

The Pullman strike, in any case, merely confirmed what had been slowly dawning upon the capitalist producers throughout the nineteenth century. The direct confrontation between capital and labor in the living place exacerbates class tensions and conflict markedly because labor can easily identify the enemy, whether it be in company housing, the company store, company social services, or a factor in the work place itself. It was no accident that some of the fiercest strikes and confrontations—such as Homestead in 1892 and Pullman in 1894—occurred in company towns. Under these conditions it is advantageous for the capitalist producers to seek out mediating influences which diffuse the target of labor's discontent. The privatization of housing provision, the creation of a separate housing landlord class, the creation of innumerable intermediaries in the retail and wholesale sector, and government provision of social services and public goods—all help to accomplish this. These measures also serve to socialize part of the costs of the reproduction of labor power and to facilitate the mobility of labor. For all of these reasons, the industrial capitalists seek to withdraw entirely from any direct involvement in provision or management of the built environment.

The general proposition which Pullman had in mind, divorced from its paternalism and its tight, unified, and direct control aspects is still important. The breakdown of the binding links of the old social order was clearly necessary if the new industrial work discipline was to be imposed upon the reluctant peasant or artisan. But this breakdown posed its own problems for social control and threatened the economic and social stability of the new order in a variety of ways. Bourgeois reformers sought to counter the threats and have long argued that proper housing, health care, education, and the like are essential if workers are to become satisfied, virtuous, and solid citizens capable and willing to perform tasks efficiently and, thereby, to do their bit to enhance the accumulation of capital.[37] Conversely, the typical industrial city, with its slums and overcrowding, its war of all against all, its signs of "moral degeneration" and vice, its dirt and grime and disease, was regarded as unconducive to the formation of a respectable working-class citizenry. Sometimes the reform strategy rests on a rather simpleminded environmental determinism: The idea that good housing creates good workers periodically appears on the stage of bourgeois reform thought, usually without very effective consequences. But, in its more sophisticated form, it proved capable of tapping and organizing that relation between working and living in a manner which indeed did contribute to the reestablishment of social stability and to the creation of a relatively well-satisfied work force. And, in the course of this effort, the reformers in a certain way defined for labor the meaning of a use value in the built environment. Capital seeks to intervene—this time indirectly through bourgeois reform and by means of ideological and political mechanisms—because to do so serves its own purposes and strengthens its hand in its historic struggle with labor. But, as the Pullman strike epitomizes, labor is not always a willing and docile partner in these manipulations.

This brings us to the second aspect of the connection between working and living in capitalist society. Marx's materialist posture led him to regard the relationship to nature as perhaps the most fundamental relation ordering human affairs. This relationship is itself expressed primarily through the work process, which transforms the raw materials of nature into use values. The mode of organizing this work process—the mode of production—is, therefore, the basis upon which Marx builds his investigations. To put it this way is not to engage in a simplistic economic determinism; it merely advances the thesis that the relation to nature is the aspect most fundamental to human affairs. Industrial capitalism, armed with the factory system, organized the work process in a manner which transformed the relation between the worker and nature into a travesty of even its former, very limited self. Because the worker was reduced to a "thing," so the worker became alienated from his or her product, from the manner of producing it, and, ultimately, from nature itself.[38]

That there was something degrading and "unnatural" about such a work process was apparent even to bourgeois consciousness. Indeed, the organization of the factory system appeared just as "unnatural" to the bourgeoisie as it did to those who had to live out their daily lives under its regimen. This understanding, as Raymond Williams points out, was achieved by landed capital well before the industrial revolution:

> The clearing of parks as "Arcadian" prospects depended on the completed system of exploitation of the agricultural and genuinely pastoral lands beyond the park boundaries ... [These] are related parts of the same process—superficially opposed in taste but only because in the one case the land is being organized for production, where tenants and laborers will work, while in the other case it is being organized for consumption. . . . Indeed, it can be said of these eighteenth-century, arranged landscapes not only, as is just, that this was the high point of agrarian bourgeois art, but that they succeeded in creating in the land below their windows and terraces .... a rural landscape ... from which the facts of production had been banished.[39]

With the advent of industrial capitalism, the penchant for actively countering, in their own consumption sphere, what they were organizing for others in the production sphere became even more emphatic for the bourgeoisie. The Romantic poets in Britain—led by Wordsworth and Coleridge—and writers like Emerson and Thoreau in the United States epitomized this reaction to the new industrial order. And the reaction did not remain confined to the realms of the ideologists. It was put into practice in the building of rural estates by the bourgeoisie, the establishment of the country mansion, the flight from the industrial city, and, ultimately, in the design of what Walker calls "the suburban solution."[40] The attempt to "bring nature back into the city" by writers and designers like Olmsted and Ebenezer Howard in the nineteenth century and Ian McHarg and Lewis Mumford in the twentieth, attests to the continuity of this theme in bourgeois thought and practice.[41]

But if the bourgeoisie felt it, the artisan and displaced peasant experienced the alienation from nature very concretely, and they reacted no less vigorously whenever they could. William Blake, the spokesman for the artisan class, complained bitterly of those "dark, satanic mills" and swore with his usual revolutionary fervor that we would "build Jerusalem in England's green and pleasant land." Faced with the brutalizing and degrading routine of the work process in the factory, the workers themselves sought ways to ameliorate it. In part, they did so by resorting to the same mystifications as the bourgeoisie and, thus, came to share a common Romantic image of nature. When asked why the Lowell mill girls wrote so much about the beauties of nature, for example, the editor of their paper responded: "Why is it that the desert-traveller looks forward upon the burning, boundless waste and sees pictured, before his aching eyes, some verdant oasis?"[42]

But merely to dream of some Romantic, idealized nature in the midst of the desert of the factory was scarcely enough, no matter how much it did to help the laborer through the long and tedious day. Consequently, as Bender reports:

> Residents of Lowell made their periodic and apprecia-
> tive contact with the natural landscape in a variety of ways.
> Besides using the cemetery and the public park, they
> sought nature through flights of fancy, through views from
> their windows, by walking out of the city (despite the "no
> trespassing" signs . . .), and through summer visits to the
> country.[43]

The response rested on a mystification, of course, for it reduced "nature" to a leisure-time concept, as something to be "consumed" in the course of restful recuperation from what was, in fact, a degrading relation to nature in the most fundamental of all human activities: work. But the mystification has bitten deeply into the consciousness of all elements in society. To talk of the relation to nature is to conjure up images of mountains and streams, seas and lakes, trees and green grass far from the coal face, the assembly line, and the factory, where the real transformation of nature is continually being wrought.

But there is a sense in which this is a necessary and unavoidable mystification under capitalism. Without it, life scarcely would be bearable. And progressive elements within the bourgeoisie knew this to be as true for

their workers as for themselves. Not surprisingly, therefore, the bourgeois reformers, often under the guise of moral universals and a Romantic
imagery, frequently seek to procure for their workers reasonable access
to "nature." Olmsted, perhaps the most spectacular of these reformers in
nineteenth-century America, saw that "The spontaneous interest of the
worker was a more effective stimulus to work than any artificially imposed
regimen," and it was a short step from this to proposing parks and sylvan
suburbs as an antidote to the usual, daily harassments of urban industrial
life.[44] Turned into practice, in Olmsted's day primarily for the middle
classes but in modern times increasingly for the "respectable" working
class, this solution to the problems of urban-industrial life has had a
powerful effect upon the physical landscapes of our cities. The counter-
point between "nature"—represented by pastoral images of the country—
and a work process—represented by the urban and the industrial—is
central to the history of the capitalist mode of production. And the coun-
terpoint contains a tension between what Raymond Williams calls "a
necessary materialism and a necessary humanity," adding:

> Often we try to resolve it by dividing work and leisure, or
> society and the individual, or city and country, not only in
> our minds but in suburbs and garden cities, town houses
> and country cottages, the week and the weekend. But we
> then usually find that the ... captains of the change have
> arrived earlier and settled deeper; have made, in fact, a
> more successful self-division. The country house ... was
> one of the first forms of this temporary resolution, and in
> the nineteenth century as many were built by the new lords
> of capitalist production as survived, improved, from the
> old lords.... It remains remarkable that so much of this
> settlement has been physically imitated, down to details of
> semi-detached villas and styles of leisure and weekends. An
> immensely productive capitalism, in all its stages, has ex-
> tended both the resources and the modes which, however
> unevenly, provide and contain forms of response to its
> effects.[45]

These "forms of response" serve to define, in part, the meaning for
labor of use values in the built environment. The residents of the contemporary suburbs, whether workers or bourgeois, are no less anxious for
example to banish "the facts of production" from their purview than were
the eighteenth-century landlords because those facts are, for the most
part, unbearable. And insofar as workers, in conjunction with the capitalists, have found ways to do just this, they have created an urban landscape
and a way of life that is founded on what Williams calls "an effective and
imposing mystification"—but a mystification which combines elements of
necessity and cruel hoax. Hanging on to some sense of an unalienated

relation to nature makes life bearable for the worker, if only because it leads to a realistic appraisal of what has been lost and what potentially can be gained. But the Romantic mystification of nature conceals, rather than reveals, the actual source of the sense of loss and alienation that pervades capitalist society. Bourgeois art, literature, urban design, and "designs for urban living" offer certain conditions in the living place as compensation for what can never truly be compensated for in the work place. Capital, in short, seeks to draw labor into a Faustian bargain: Accept a packaged relation to nature in the living place as just and adequate compensation for an alienating and degrading relation to nature in the work place. And, if labor refuses to be drawn in spite of seduction, blandishment, and dominant ideology mobilized by the bourgeoisie, then capital must impose it because the landscape of capitalist society must, in the final analysis, respond to the accumulation needs of capital, rather than to the real, human requirements of labor.

The Interventions of Capital: A Conclusion

Capital seeks to discipline labor as much in the home as in the factory because it is only in terms of an all-embracing domination of labor, in every facet of its life, that the "work ethic" and the "bourgeois values" necessarily demanded by the capitalist work process can be created and secured. The promotion of homeownership for workers establishes the workers' allegiance to the principle of private property and, therefore, fits with this general strategem. Sometimes conflicting with this drive, we see that capital also needs to organize the consumption of the workers to ensure that it is cheap and rational from the standpoint of accumulation. The collectivization of consumption tends to take away the sense of individual responsibility and thereby undercuts the notion of bourgeois individualism if pushed too far. And, running as a counter-thread in all of this, we see capital's need to promote, amid the work force, a sense of satisfaction and contentment which would lead to spontaneous cooperation and efficiency in the work place. This condition cannot be cultivated without giving the worker at least the illusion of freedom of choice in the living place, and of a healthy and satisfying relation to "nature" in the consumption sphere. These illusions are pervasive but not always easy to sustain in the face of the realities enforced by the necessities of accumulation for accumulation's sake, production for production's sake. And the conditions in the work place can never be that easily concealed, no matter how mountainous the mystifications.

Nevertheless, the response of labor to its own condition is constantly subjected to the interventions and mediations of capital. As labor seeks to reorganize its mode of living to compensate for the degradations and disciplines of factory work, so capital seeks to colonize and pervert these efforts for its own purposes, sometimes to be turned cruelly against labor in the course of class struggle. Labor strives to raise its living standards by reducing the cost of living and increasing the use values it can command. But capital constantly seeks to subvert this drive, often through the agency of the state, into a reduction in the value of labor power and into "rational" modes of consumption understood from the standpoint of accumulation. As labor seeks relief from a degrading relation to nature in the work place, so capital seeks to parlay that into a mystified relation to nature in the consumption sphere. As labor seeks more control over the collective conditions of its existence, so capital seeks to establish collectivized forms of consumption and individual homeownership. The power of capital is omnipresent in the very definition of "a use value in the built environment for labor."

Conflicts in the living place are, we can conclude, mere reflections of the underlying tension between capital and labor. Appropriators and the construction faction mediate the forms of conflict; they stand between capital and labor and thereby shield from view the real source of tension. The surface appearance of conflicts around the built environment—the struggles against the landlord or against urban renewal—conceals a hidden essence which is nothing more than the struggle between capital and labor.

Capital may be omnipresent in these struggles, but it is neither omniscient nor omnipotent. The dynamics of accumulation require periodic rationalizations through crises which affect the working class in the form of bouts of widespread unemployment. At such moments the plans to coopt labor by the provision of "healthful and satisfying" living environments, by a contented relation to nature in the living place, go awry. In using the built environment as a coercive tool over consumption, capital ultimately coerces itself because it sets the conditions for the realization of values, quite literally, in a sea of concrete. And, once committed, capital cannot go back. Pullman discovered this elemental fact in his ill-fated model town. When conditions of overaccumulation became apparent in the economy at large, it became necessary to lay off workers; but Pullman could not do so because the profit to be had from the town was contingent upon full employment in the factory. The solution for the individual capitalist is to withdraw from the production of consumption-fund items for the workers he or she employs. But the problem remains for the capitalist system as a whole. As problems of overaccumulation arise in capitalist societies—and arise they must—so the most well-laid plans of the capitalist fall by the wayside and the mechanisms for mystification, cooptation, discipline of labor, and inculcation of the work ethic and bourgeois virtues begin to crumble. And it is at just these times that labor recognizes most clearly that the bargain which it has struck with capital is no bargain at all, but an agreement founded on an idealized mystification. The promises of capital are seen as just that, incapable of fulfillment. And it also becomes more clearly evident that the needs of labor for use values in the built environment are incapable of being met by the captains of the system who promise so much, but who can deliver so little.

Class Consciousness, Community Consciousness, and Competition

The phrase "the standard of living of labor" plainly cannot be understood outside the context of actual class struggles fought over a long period, in particular places, around the organization of both work and living. This continually shifting standard defines the needs of labor with respect to use values—consumption fund items—in the built environment. Individual workers have different needs, of course, according to their position in the labor force, their familial situation, and their individual requirements. At the same time, the processes of wage-rate determination in the work place yield different quantities of exchange value to workers in different occupational categories. The social power that this money represents can be used to procure control over certain use values in the built environment. The way this money is used affects the appropriation of rent and the functioning of the price signals which induce the flow of capital into the production of new consumption fund items. We can envisage three general situations:

Consider, first, a situation in which each worker seeks independently to command for his or her own private use the best bundle of resources in the best location. We envisage a competitive war of all against all, a society in which the ethic of "possessive individualism" has taken root in the consciousness of workers in a fundamental way. If the use values available in the built environment are limited—which is usually the case—then individuals make use of their market power and bid for scarce resources in the most advantageous locations. At its most elemental level this competition is for survival chances, for each worker knows that the ability to survive is dependent upon the ability to secure access to a particular bundle of resources in a reasonably healthy location. There is also competition to acquire "market capacity," that bundle of attitudes, understandings, and skills which permits the worker to sell his or her labor power at a wage rate higher than the average.[46] Symbols of status, prestige, rank, and importance (even self-respect) may also be acquired by procuring command over particular resources in prestigious locations. These symbols may be useful in that they help a worker gain an easier entry into a particularly privileged stratum within the wage labor force. And, finally, we can note that if the relation to nature in the work place is felt to be as degrading as it truly is, then there is a positive incentive to seek a location far enough away so that the "facts of production" are in no way represented in the landscape. In other words, workers may compete to get as far away as possible from the work place.

The competitive situation which we have outlined here is, in most respects, identical to that assumed in neoclassical models of land-use determination in urban areas.[47] Individual households, these models assume, attempt to maximize their utility by competing with each other for particular bundles of goods in particular locations subject to a budget constraint. If it is assumed that the two most important "goods" being competed for are locations with lower-aggregate transportation costs and housing space, then it can be shown with relative ease that individuals will distribute themselves in space according to: (a) the distribution of employment opportunities (usually assumed to be collected together in one central location); and (b) the relative marginal propensities to consume transportation services and living space in the context of the overall budget constraint. Competitive bidding under these conditions will generate a differential rent surface which, in the case of a single employment center, declines with distance from the center at the same time that it distributes individuals by income in space. In this case, the ability to appropriate differential rent is created entirely by the competitive behavior of the working class. This is a crucial argument which we cannot afford to ignore. Also, if new development is typically distributed in response to the pricing signals set by the differential rents, then it is not hard to show that a spatial structure to the built environment will be created which reflects, to large degree, social and wage stratifications within the labor force.

The second situation which we wish to consider is one in which collective action in space—community action—is important. The pervasive externality effects and the collective use of many items in the built environment mean that it is in the self-interest of individuals to pursue modest levels of collective action.[48] Workers who are homeowners know that the value of the savings tied up in the house depends on the actions of others. It is in their common interest to collectively curb "deviant" behaviors, bar "noxious" facilities, and ensure high standards of public service. This collectivization of action may go well beyond that required for purely individual self-interest. A consciousness of place, "community consciousness," may emerge as a powerful force which spawns competition among communities for scarce public investment funds and the like. Community competition becomes the order of the day.

This process relates, in an interesting way, to the appropriation of rent. Community control enables those in control to erect barriers to investment in the built environment. The barriers may be selective—the exclusion of low-income housing, for example—or more or less across the board: a ban on all forms of future growth. In recent years, actions of this sort have been common in suburban jurisdictions in the United States. The cartel powers of local government are, in effect, being mobilized to control investment through a variety of legal and planning devices. Homeowners may use these controls to maintain or enhance the value of their properties. Developers may seek to use these controls for rather different purposes. But "community consciousness" typically creates small, legal "islands" within which monopoly rents are appropriable, often by one faction of labor at the expense of another. This latter situation gives rise to internecine conflicts within the working class along parochialist, community-based lines.

The third kind of situation we can envisage is that of a fully class-conscious proletariat struggling against all forms of exploitation, whether they be in the work place or in the living place. Workers do not use their social power as individuals to seek individual solutions; they do not compete with each other for survival chances, for ability to acquire market capacity, for symbols of status and prestige. They fight collectively to improve the lot of all workers everywhere and eschew those parochialist forms of community action which typically lead one faction of labor to benefit at the expense of another (usually the poor and underprivileged).

Under these conditions the appropriation of rent cannot be attributed to the competitive behavior of individual workers or of whole communities. It has to be interpreted, rather, as something forced upon labor in the course of class struggle. A differential rent surface may arise in an urban area, but it does so not because labor automatically engages in competitive bidding, but because the class power of the appropriators is used to extract a rent to the maximum possible, given that resources are scarce and that they exist in a relative space. Because we witness a consequent social stratification (according to income) in space and a development process which exacerbates this social ordering, we cannot infer that this is simply a reflection of individual workers expressing their "subjective utilities" through the market. Indeed, it may express the exact opposite: the power of the appropriators to force certain choices on workers, no matter what the individual worker may think or believe. The power to appropriate rent is a class relation, and we have to understand it that way if we are to understand how residential differentiation emerges within cities and the degree to which this phenomenon is the outcome of free or forced choices.[49]

The three situations we have examined—competitive individualism, community action, and class struggle—are points on a continuum of possibilities. We cannot automatically assume labor to be at any particular point on this continuum. This is something to be discovered by concrete investigations of particular situations. The United States, for example, appears to be more strongly dominated by competitive individualism and community consciousness when compared to the more class-conscious working class in Europe. From the standpoint of capital, individual and community competition is advantageous because it then seems as if the appropriation of rent results from labor's own actions, rather than from the actions of the appropriators themselves, while the privileged groups of workers can, indeed, gain access to a portion of the surplus. The overt forms of conflict around the built environment depend, therefore, upon the outcome of a deeper, and often hidden, ideological struggle for the consciousness of those doing the struggling. This deeper struggle between consciousness and individual, community, and class alignments provides the context in which daily struggles over everyday issues occur.

A Conclusion

The capitalist mode of production forces a separation between working and living at the same time that it reintegrates them in complex ways. The surficial appearance of conflict in contemporary urban-industrial society suggests that there is, indeed, a dichotomy between struggles in the work place and in the living place and that each kind of struggle is fought according to different principles and rules. Struggles around the consumption fund for labor, the focus of this paper, seemingly arise from the inevitable tensions between appropriators seeking rent builders seeking profit, financiers seeking interest, and labor seeking to counter the secondary forms of exploitation which occur in the living place. All of this seems self-evident enough.

But the manner and form of these everyday, overt conflicts are a reflection of a much deeper tension with less easily identifiable manifestations: a struggle over the definition and meaning of use values; the standard of living of labor; the quality of life; consciousness; and even human nature itself. From this standpoint, the overt struggles (which we began by examining) between landlord-appropriators, builders, and labor are to be seen as mediated manifestations of the deeply underlying conflict between capital and labor. Capital seeks definitions, seeks to impose meanings conducive to the productivity of labor and to the consumption of commodities which capitalists can profitably produce. Like Dickens' *Dombey and Son,* capital deals "in hides but never in hearts." But labor seeks its own meanings, partly derived from a rapidly fading memory of artisan and peasant life, but also from the ineluctable imperative to learn what it is to be human. "Human nature" has, then, no universal meaning but is being perpetually recast in the fires of restless struggle. And, even though capital may dominate and impose upon us a predominantly *capitalist* sense of human nature, the resistances are always there, and the internal tensions within the capitalist order—between private appropriation and socialized production, between individualism and social interdependency—are so dramatic that each of us internalizes a veritable maelstrom of hopes and fears into our present conduct. The human nature which results, with all of its complex ambiguities of desire, need, creativity, estrangement, self-ishness, and sheer human concern, forms the very stuff out of which the overt struggles of daily life are woven. The manner in which these struggles are fought likewise depends upon a deeper determination of consciousness—individual, community, or class based, as the case may be—of those who do the struggling. From this standpoint it must surely be plain that the separation between working and living is at best a surficial estrangement, an apparent tearing asunder of what can never be kept apart. And it is at this deeper level, too, that we can more clearly see the underlying unity between *work-based* and *community-based* conflicts. They are not clearly mirrored images of one another, but distorted representations, mediated by many intervening forces and circumstances, which mystify and render opaque the fundamental, underlying class antagonism upon which the capitalist mode of production is founded. And it is, of course, the task of science to render clear, through analysis, what is mystified and opaque in daily life.

Notes

1. This distinction derives from Marx. See Karl Marx, *Capital,* vol. 2 (New York, 1967), p. 210; and idem, *The Grundrisse* (Harmondsworth, Middlesex: Penguin Books, 1973), pp. 681–87.
2. See Marx, *Capital,* 1:171.
3. This condition can be derived directly from Marxian theory by bringing together the analyses presented in ibid., 1:591–640; and 2:437–48, 515–16.
4. Ibid., 3:773.
5. Ibid., chap. 37.
6. See David Harvey, *Social Justice and the City* (London: Edward Arnold, 1973), chaps. 2, 5.
7. For a more detailed argument, see David Harvey, "Class-Monopoly Rent, Finance Capital, and the Urban Revolution," *Regional Studies* 8 (1974): 239–55.
8. J. R. Kellett, *The Impact of Railways on Victorian Cities* (London: Routledge and Kegan Paul, 1969), chap. 11.
9. G. R. Taylor, "The Beginnings of Mass Transportation in Urban America," *The Smithsonian Journal of History* 1, no. 2 (1966): 35–50; Joel Tarr, "From City to Suburb: The 'Moral' Influence of Transportation Technology," in *American Urban History,* ed. A. B. Callow (New York: Oxford University Press, 1973); David Ward, *Cities and Immigrants* (New York: Oxford University Press, 1971).
10. The McCone Commission Report on the Watts rebellion in Los Angeles in 1964 attributed much of the discontent to the sense of entrapment generated by a lack of access to transportation.
11. Marx, *Grundrisse,* intro.
12. Quoted in *The Recurrent Crisis of London* (London: Counter Information Services, 1973).
13. C. B. McPherson, *The Political Theory of Possessive Individualism* (London: Oxford University Press, 1962); John Rex and Robert Moore, *Race, Community, and Conflict* (London: Oxford University Press, 1967).
14. Michael Stone, "Housing and Class Struggle," *Antipode* 7, no. 2 (1975): 22–37; David Harvey, "The Political Economy of Urbanization in Advanced Capitalist Societies: The Case of the United States," in *The Social Economy of Cities,* ed. Gary Gappert and Harold Rose (Beverly Hills, Calif.: Sage Publications, 1975).
15. The relation between value and prices in Marxian theory is highly problematic and involves us in the celebrated "transformation problem." To avoid making silly mistakes, it is important to bear in mind that the value of labor power is not automatically represented by the wage rate.
16. Thomas R. Malthus, *Principles of Political Economy* (New York: A. M. Kelly, 1968), p. 321.
17. Marx, *Grundrisse,* intro.
18. Thomas Bender, *Toward an Urban Vision: Ideas and Institutions in Nineteenth-Century America* (Lexington: University Press of Kentucky, 1975), pp. 28–29; R. M. Tryon, *Household Manufactures in the United States, 1640–1860* (Chicago: University of Chicago Press, 1917).
19. Edward P. Thompson, *The Making of the English Working Class* (Harmondsworth, Middlesex: Penguin Books, 1968), p. 455.
20. Ibid., chap. 10; Eric J. Hobsbawm, *Labouring Men* (New York: Basic Books, 1965), chap. 7.
21. Marx, *Capital,* 2:516. Dickens satirizes the role of bourgeois philanthropy in relation to workers' consumption in *Hard Times.*
22. Marx, *Grundrisse,* p. 408.
23. The theme of collective consumption has been examined in some detail by the French urbanists. See Edmond Preteceille, *Equipments collectifs, structures urbaines, et consommation sociale* (Paris: Centre de Sociologie Urbaine, 1975); and Manuel Castells, "Collective Consumption and Urban Contradictions in Advanced Capitalist Societies," in *Stress and Contradiction in Modern Capitalism,* ed. L. Lindberg (Lexington, Mass.: Lexington Books, 1975).
24. Simon Kuznets, *Capital in the American Economy: Its Formation and Financing* (Princeton: Princeton University Press, 1961).
25. See the accounts by James Flink, *The Car Culture* (Cambridge, Mass.: M.I.T. Press, 1975); and Helen Leavitt, *Superhighway—Super Hoax* (Garden City, N.Y.: Doubleday Anchor, 1970).
26. An interesting attempt to look at this is J. E. Vance, "Housing the Worker: The Employment Linkage as a Force in Urban Structure," *Economic Geography* 42 (1966): 294–325.
27. Sidney Pollard, *The Genesis of Modern Management* (Cambridge: Harvard University Press, 1965), pp. 161, 207.
28. Harry Braverman, *Labor and Monopoly Capital* (New York: Monthly Review Press, 1974), p. 139.
29. Ibid., p. 151.
30. Pollard, *Genesis,* p. 115.
31. Flink, *Car Culture,* p. 89.
32. All of the quotes that follow are to be found in Antonio Gramsci, *Selections from the Prison Notebooks* (New York: International Publishers, 1971), pp. 285–318.
33. Bender, *Urban Vision,* p. 197.
34. Ibid., p. 151.
35. See Michel Foucault, *Madness and Civilization* (New York: Pantheon Books, 1965); Pollard, *Genesis,* p. 162; David Rothman, *The Discovery of the Asylum* (Boston: Little, Brown, & Co., 1971); and Samuel Bowles

and Herbert Gintis, *Schooling in Capitalist America* (New York: Basic Books, 1975). The relation between school and factory is portrayed with extraordinary insight in Charles Dickens, *Hard Times.*

36. Stanley Buder, *Pullman* (New York: Oxford University Press, 1967), p. 44.

37. Much of this material, as well as the argument, is drawn from Richard A. Walker, "The Suburban Solution" (Ph.D. diss., The Johns Hopkins University, 1976).

38. Karl Marx, "Economic and Philosophic Manuscripts," in *Early Writings* (Harmondsworth, Middlesex: Penguin Books, 1975). See also Alfred Schmidt, *Marx's Concept of Nature* (London: New Left Books, 1971).

39. Raymond Williams, *The Country and the City* (London: Chatto and Windus, 1973), p. 124.

40. Walker, "Suburban Solution."

41. Ebenezer Howard wrote, for example, of ". . . so laying out a Garden City that, as it grows, the free gifts of Nature—fresh air, sunlight, breathing room and playing room—shall be retained in all needed abundance, and so employing the resources of modern science that Art may supplement Nature, and life may become an abiding joy and delight." Ebenezer Howard, *Garden Cities of Tomorrow* (London: Faber and Faber, 1955), p. 127.

42. Bender, *Urban Vision,* p. 90.

43. Ibid.

44. Bender discusses this aspect of Olmsted's thought in detail. Ibid.

45. Williams, *Country and City,* p. 294.

46. See Anthony Giddens, *The Class Structure of the Advanced Societies* (London: Hutchinson University Library, 1973).

47. See, for example, William Alonso, *Location and Land Use* (Cambridge: Harvard University Press, 1964); and Edward S. Mills, *Studies in the Structure of the Urban Economy* (Baltimore: The Johns Hopkins University Press, 1972).

48. The theory of self-interested collective action is laid out in Mancur Olson, *The Logic of Collective Action* (Cambridge: Harvard University Press, 1965); but the theory of community is a mess which will require a good deal of sorting out.

49. I have attempted a preliminary analysis on this theme in David Harvey, "Class Structure in a Capitalist Society and the Theory of Residential Differentiation," in *Processes in Physical and Human Geography,* ed. M. Chisholm, P. Haggett, and R. F. Peel (London: Heinemann, 1975).

Chapter 2

THE URBAN LAND QUESTION

SHOUKRY T. ROWEIS

ALLEN J. SCOTT

Introduction

1. Our objective in this paper is to discuss the phenomenon of contemporary urban land development and the characteristic problems with which it is associated. We situate this phenomenon between two polarities: the process of spontaneous urbanization and the process of deliberate urban intervention.

Our discussion opens with a purely descriptive account of contemporary urban land problems and policies, and we then summarize, and subsequently criticize, the theoretical/analytical underpinnings which seem to sustain those policies. Later, we attempt to lay the foundations of a formal and critical alternative theory of urban land. On the basis of this theory, we present some assertions and hypotheses about the urban land development process as it exists today. Lastly, we identify a number of policy questions that emerge, we hope, not from a gratuitous attitudinizing on our part, but from the fundamental logic of our analysis.

Current Urban Land Problems and Policies

2. In order to initiate our main discussion we now attempt, in a very general way, to survey the main problems and policies that have seemed to dominate the North American urban scene in recent decades. We undertake, first, to construct a general catalog of problems; and, second, to characterize generally the kinds of policies that have developed in response to these problems. In the conclusion to our paper, we shall build upon and extend the basic notions developed in this initial elementary survey. Observe, at the outset, that our survey is restricted to those prob-

This paper is a considerably revised version of a paper originally commissioned by the Canadian Council on Urban and Regional Research and presented to the Ontario Forum on Land Management (Toronto: October, 1976).

lems that have their specific origins in the process of urban land development. This is ultimately the same as saying that, out of the range of problems that occur *in* urban areas, we restrict our attention to problems *of* urban areas.

Urban Land Problems

3. In the twentieth century, the urban problem in North America has been, par excellence, the problem of urban expansion consequent upon general economic growth. This growth confronts society with grave difficulties concerning the collective production and utilization of urban land. Already, by the end of the nineteenth century, these difficulties had made themselves known. They were, thus, not new difficulties, although they were taking on new forms, just as the economic system itself was taking on new forms. The old methods of treating these difficulties were, hence, becoming increasingly inoperative, while effective new methods had not yet been developed.

By the 1920s a prototypical response to the overall problem of urban growth and expansion had evolved in most North American cities. It was a doubly faceted policy involving both aggressive, peripheral urban expansion and the rationalization of land uses by zoning. An early wave of peripheral expansion at the end of the nineteenth century had taken the form of streetcar suburbs; that is, compact, dense, and geographically distinct clusters of suburban settlements. By the 1920s, however, the automobile had become a pervasive and dominating mode of personal transport. Thus, the early pattern of suburban expansion gave way to a new pattern of interminably sprawling, low-density housing. This was associated with the general widening and paving of county roads and the outward extension of utilities, particularly sewers, frequently well in advance of actual housing construction. Annexation as a typical nineteenth-century administrative procedure was gradually abandoned in favor of a system of independent municipal governments in the growing suburbs. At the same time, there were the beginnings of the suburbanization of industrial activities. All of this occurred within a regime of land-use zoning (or restrictive covenants) which encouraged the formation of geographically homogeneous land-use districts, at least in the new suburban areas.

Contrary to much received opinion, this double policy of peripheral expansion and land-use zoning was, by and large, effective in dealing with the urban problem. It allowed for the provision of ample space for industrial expansion; it partly succeeded in rationalizing the geographical configuration of urban infrastructure; it encouraged expansion of the supply of housing, whether directly to high- and middle-income families or indirectly (by filtering) to low-income families; and it expedited the takeover of highly accessible downtown locations by the burgeoning terti-

ary—and especially quaternary—sectors of economic activity. Furthermore, throughout the period stretching from the beginning of the 1920s
to the end of the 1950s, the phenomenal expansion in the supply of
serviced land staved off excessive land hoarding, speculation, and the
formation of oligopolies in the land development industry. Land-use zoning gave rise to significant improvements and economies in the provision
of basic urban infrastructure, and it eliminated many of the uncertainties
that property owners and developers had hitherto faced. Ironically, this
very success became the prime source of most manifest urban land problems in the 1960s and the 1970s.

   4. By the 1950s, the aggressive policy of facilitating urban expansion
was taking the form of massive intraurban highway construction, thereby
encouraging further suburbanization and further utilization of the private
automobile. This same process gave rise to formidable traffic and parking
problems, particularly in the central city. It also provoked significant economic difficulties for intraurban public transport companies. A syndrome
was thus created whereby expressways gave rise to the need for yet more
urban expressways. Suburban expansion itself began to appear increasingly inefficient. Low densities of development meant relatively wasteful
expenditures on basic infrastructure. Thus, the social costs of each incre-
mental development on the urban periphery were significantly higher than
those of previous increments. As commuting distances increased, so the
need for faster (and yet safer) highway travel made itself felt. With these
demands for improved levels of service, highway construction costs began
to mount. Low population densities in the suburbs further meant that the
provision of social and community services involved a considerable degree of waste. Under the pressures of ever-mounting fiscal obligations,
municipalities resorted to discriminatory land-use controls designed to
maximize property tax revenues and to minimize fiscal obligations. These
practices resulted in intermunicipal rivalries and confrontations, and they
tended to impose disproportionate fiscal burdens on the central cities.
These burdens were all the more onerous in the circumstances of a
progressive flight of middle-class families, as well as industrial activities,
from the central cities to the suburbs. A further syndrome was, therefore,
created. The erosion of the tax base of central cities inevitably produced
a deterioration in their levels of social and community services, and this
produced yet further rounds of out-migration. In this process, central
business districts, nevertheless, typically retained, and even added to,
their quaternary office functions (administration and finance). In this way,
the central business districts continued to exist as important white-collar
employment centers. Hence a typical, and economically wasteful, pattern
of daily intraurban travel began to make its appearance. On the one hand,

white-collar workers commuted from the suburbs to the central city. On the other hand, low-income, blue-collar workers commuted from the central city outward to the peripheral industrial districts. Yet more highway links and parking facilities had to be added in the central cities in order to accommodate this wasteful transport pattern. As a consequence, portions of the already scarce stock of central low-income housing were destroyed, a phenomenon exacerbated by the expansion of office activities. Overcrowding and an acute shortage of low-income housing were the result.

5. Although fairly typical, the scenario described above was neither invariable nor universal among North American cities. In some cities, urban land development tended, in certain respects, to follow rather different lines. In particular, in Canada and in some parts of the United States, intraurban expressway construction did not occur on anything like the massive scale that it did elsewhere. In these cases, there tended to be a relative lag in the supply of peripheral, developable land, and this situation led in turn to an overall inflation of land and housing prices. In these circumstances, urban land hoarding became attractive, if not inevitable, and a significant group of professional hoarders made its appearance in the form of large, vertically integrated land development firms. The unusually high land prices, combined with a general land shortage, made highrise residential developments feasible, if not economically necessary, especially in the central city. However, in the process of assembling land units for the purpose of constructing highrise apartment blocks, land developers typically triggered a series of escalating confrontations with neighborhood organizations. Members of these organizations correctly recognized the difficulty of finding viable substitutes for their inner-city homes, and thus tended to hold on tenaciously to them. By contrast, under conditions of increasing demand pressures on the housing market combined with rising land prices, it was economically logical for the development companies (which, in addition, had the necessary financial and organizational capability) to redevelop urban land at maximum feasible densities. The confrontations of developers and neighborhood groups have frequently implicated a variety of government agencies in difficult and costly political and administrative dilemmas.

Under these conditions of a general land shortage due to restricted urban expansion, central business districts retain their hegemony over retail and office activities. The price of land at central locations escalates continually. This escalation of land prices results in two apparently contradictory outcomes: on the one hand, an insistent intensification of land uses; and, on the other hand, land hoarding (typified by the pervasive parking lot in the case of Toronto). By diminishing effective supply, land hoarding drives land prices still higher, producing yet more intensification of land uses. Given that central business district firms tend to be highly labor intensive, land-use intensification soon results in some serious transport problems, such as overloaded transit systems, congested central streets, a scarcity of parking facilities, and the like. Political pressures thus mount over the issue of inadequate downtown transport facilities, and this produces planning intervention in the form of improvements in service and capacity. These improvements augment the locational advantages of the central business district, and this leads to further increases in land prices and in land-use intensification.

In the old residential neighborhoods surrounding the business core, two sorts of pressures characteristically come into play: First, as land prices escalate in the core, pressure mounts to redevelop surrounding low-income residential properties into office and commercial space. Second, as the ratio of white-collar to blue-collar employment in the core rises, so more and more middle-income families are prompted to purchase and renovate properties in old, low-income neighborhoods in close proximity to the core. Both types of pressure threaten to dispossess low-income families of their housing, a situation that is made all the more urgent, given the low rate of expansion of substitute low-income housing on the urban periphery. These pressures then result in political confrontations, the disruption of neighborhoods with a high degree of social cohesion, and further rises of land and housing prices.

6. In the long run, the complex unfolding of these various forces and outcomes diminishes both the political and economic prospects of more rational urban development programs in the future. This assertion is based on two general observations: First, piecemeal increments to existing infrastructure and social overhead capital to cope with bottlenecks as they arise (reactive planning) preempts more general and far-reaching policy options in the future; second, massive, but premature, private investment in localized renovation and redevelopment in conformity with a purely private economic calculus further blocks future possibilities of more socially progressive collective redevelopment schemes.

7. The descriptions presented above are meant to outline only the most general tendencies in the evolution of urban land problems in North American cities in this century. Of course, particular cities will exhibit particular and idiosyncratic deviations from these tendencies. Nevertheless, the tendencies are, in one form or another, virtually everywhere observable in North America. In the face of the pervasive and serious problems raised in this discussion, the question immediately arises: What policies, programs, and modes of intervention have been developed to counter them?

Urban Land Policies

8. In general, urban governments in North America have seemed to intervene in urban affairs in three rather different, yet interrelated, ways: (a) by the application of a variety of fiscal devices; (b) by legally restricting private rights to use urban land in certain ways; (c) by direct physical undertaking of urban development (and/or redevelopment) programs.

9. The first type of urban intervention, the application of various sorts of fiscal devices, includes policy instruments such as the property tax, controls on the pricing of urban goods and services, and direct governmental subsidies and grants. Let us deal with each of these instruments in turn.

The property tax seems to be ubiquitous in North America. Further, in recent years, various mutations of the simple property tax as such have appeared: these include a variety of development levies, speculation taxes, and site value taxes. But, for all their differences, these taxes all have one fundamental characteristic in common: namely, the fact that they have left largely intact the operation of those macroforces (whether economic or social) that determine the structure of the land market as a whole. For this reason, property tax policies have had remarkably little palliative effect on the general urban land problems outlined earlier.

Controls on the pricing of urban goods and services include matters such as rent control, road pricing, legislated limits on mortgage rates, and so on. These policies have definite effects on urban land prices and land uses. However, they tend to be eclectic "plugging" devices, applied in a purely piecemeal way and independently of any global urban planning strategy. At the same time, they tend to overlook the fundamental structural roots of the problems they seek to counter and to treat only their superficial symptoms; rent control is a perfect example of this tendency. In this sense, depending on their conjunctural relationships, they often, in the end, only complicate the problems that they seek to resolve.

Direct governmental subsidies and grants involve a whole gamut of policy instruments, including, for instance, the subsidization of mass transit, the allocation of funds to low-income housing programs, the provision of grants to community services, and so on. Many kinds of urban activities would have been impossible in the absence of this public financial support. Moreover, so long as public revenues were forthcoming in a quantity sufficient to cope with reformist demands, very few individuals, with the exception of a small minority of conservatives could question this type of intervention.[1] However, urban intervention via subsidies and grants tends to have a two-fold drawback. In the first place, as in the case of controls on the pricing of urban goods and services, it has tended to deal with the symptoms, rather than with the fundamental causes, of urban land problems. For example, a fiscal policy (such as the subsidization of nonprofit housing schemes) that seeks to counter the endemic shortage of low-income housing in modern capitalist cities may, indeed, help to alleviate the problem in the short run; but it can never attack the persistent root causes of that shortage: a permanent imbalance in the distribution of the economic surplus. In the second place, urban reform via subsidies and grants tends to be ultimately self-negating. The continued feasibility of these measures requires that, in the long run, aggregate expenditures keep pace with aggregate public revenues. This in turn requires that the demands of revenue-absorbing sectors keep pace with revenue-producing sectors. However, recent empirical experience in North American cities has amply demonstrated that this equilibrium is far from being satisfied. On the contrary, public expenditures tend persistently to outrun public revenues, as the state is called upon, to an ever-increasing degree, to fulfill its role as guarantor of last resort in an unending escalation of urban land problems. Not only do fiscal reforms fail to deal with these problems in any fundamental sense; but, again, in some instances, they actually exacerbate them. Thus, continued subsidization of certain inefficient urban services may very well contribute only to these same services being offered at yet higher levels of inefficiency. Fiscal reforms tend to be both merely palliative and, finally, self-paralyzing.

10. The second type of urban intervention, legal restrictions on land uses, includes planning devices such as official plan provisions, zoning ordinances, subdivision controls, building codes, etc. It also includes certain recent experiments with legal transfers of development rights. These various types of restrictions all possess the *technical potential* of significantly modifying the operation of the urban land market; that is, the determination of the spatial configuration of urban land prices and uses. However, in practice, and for *political* reasons, they have tended to be formulated in a way such that their impacts on the land market have been deliberately restrained. It is clear that if tight and durable controls were imposed, for example, on office building heights at downtown locations, then this would eventually depress land prices at these locations. But the controls must, indeed, be tight and durable. If landowners and developers sense that the controls are liable, sooner or later, to be modified and diluted, then they will continue, more or less, to exchange and develop land as if the controls did not exist. Admittedly, there are innumerable cases in which such legal controls have been quite definite, and they have accordingly had an influence on the urban land market. In other cases, they have not been able to withstand the political pressures to change them. We may ask, What accounts for the observed tightness and durability of controls in certain cases and their ephemeral existence in others?

Cases where legal restrictions on land uses have been significantly durable tend to share a common characteristic: They are typically cases where land prices are *raised* (or at least stabilized), rather than lowered, by the restrictions. The example of land zoned for suburban residential activity is outstanding in this respect. On the other hand, cases where legal restrictions on land uses have been continually relaxed are typically cases where these restrictions would otherwise threaten to depress land prices. Either they threaten to depress land prices, generally, or at least they threaten the interests of a politically significant group of owners. The mutations of planning regulations in the business cores of large metropolitan centers represent an object lesson in this process.

11. The third, and last, type of public urban intervention, direct physical land development (or redevelopment), has probably been of more widespread significance to the urban land question than has any of the other two. It includes activities such as the provision of various types of urban infrastructure and social overhead facilities, public housing construction, urban renewal, the laying out of industrial estates, land banking, and so on. Through this type of intervention, government plays a key role in producing privately developable urban land and in shaping the spatial configuration of urban land prices and uses. Yet, ironically, and despite its crucial role, this type of intervention remains virtually incapable of dealing with *real* urban land problems. Publicly serviced land is left to be exchanged and utilized by innumerable private owners and users, all of them following specific private interests and oblivious to the collective consequences of their actions. This anarchical process leads to uncontrolled, unexpected, and unintended spatial configurations of differential locational advantages; and, hence, of urban land prices, uses, and problems. Despite the definite potential effectiveness government might have through this type of intervention, it, in fact, finds itself participating in the creation of the very problems it seeks to combat.

12. From this very sketchy review of contemporary urban land policies, four fundamental conclusions emerge: First, whereas a wide variety of policies is employed to guide and regulate private rights to the use of urban land, none has seemed to have had very great and unambiguous, long-run effectiveness. Second, whereas governments have assumed a major (and rapidly expanding) responsibility for, and control over, the production of developable land, the spontaneous utilization of this land in the private realm is largely left to follow its own momentum. Third, there are no effective policies seeking to control the *exchange* of urban land. Fourth, and as a consequence of the preceding three points, there remains a large and intractable body of concrete social, political, and economic problems around the issue of the urban land nexus.

In the succeeding section of this paper we consider some of the current theoretical formulations underpinning this lamentable state of affairs.

Current Theoretical Underpinnings of Urban Analysis and Their Policy Implications

13. Current urban land theory in North America seems to fall largely into two opposing approaches: On the one hand, there is a clearly dominant approach that is rooted in conventional North American social science, and especially in marginalist neoclassical economics. On the other hand, there is a minor approach, highly critical of the former, and growing out of it by a sort of mechanical negation. This approach is, self-professedly, radical and reformist, but we prefer (for reasons that will become apparent) to identify it by its central sophism: the manipulated city hypothesis. Much of our purpose in the present account is to describe these two conflicting approaches, to demonstrate their policy consequences, to criticize them, and then to propose what we feel is a more adequate theoretical foundation for thinking about the urban land question.

The Land Market as a Social Harmonizer

14. As we have already indicated, urban economics is currently dominated by a marginalist, neoclassical epistemology.[2] The point of departure of this epistemology is the assertion that individuals construct, for themselves, internalized sets of ordered consumption preferences. Each individual has a fixed and given budget. Then, each individual, in conformity with his specific set of preferences, will select an actual consumption program that maximizes his level of total satisfaction, subject to the constraining influence of his budget.

This general point of departure has the following implications for an analysis of the urban land development process: The level of satisfaction of any individual residing in the urban system is a function of three different components: (a) the quantity of residential space consumed by that individual; (b) the total distance traveled from the individual's residence to various destinations in the urban area; and (c) the aggregate of all other goods and services consumed. In terms of expenses, the individual's budget is allocated to three different items: (a) residential land rent; (b) transport costs; and (c) all other goods and services. In conformity with this global characterization of the nature of economic being in urban space, each individual then seeks a residential location that maximizes his total satisfaction. This involves finding an equilibrium location that fully exhausts the individual's budget, so that any further reallocation of the budget among the three expenditure items listed above results only in a lowering of the individual's total level of satisfaction. Under appropriate assumptions about the structure of tastes and preferences, the residential mobility of urban population, and the fluidity of built urban structures, these processes can be shown to simulate a pattern of urban settlement to the extent that both population density and land prices decline steadily from the city center outwards. An elementary generalization permits extension of this schema from the case of individuals to the case of firms. In brief firms will seek a location such that profits are maximized, where profits are identified as total revenues minus total costs (including land rent).

15. Of particular interest, for our purposes, is the role that land rent plays in this general neoclassical model. Land in this model is a "good," much like any other good. Any plot of land (or, alternatively, any location in urban space) commands a rent or price that is essentially a function of two forces. In the first place, the price is a function of the relative scarcity of similar plots or locations. In the second place, the price is a function of the buyer's willingness to bid for land and the seller's willingness to sell. What this amounts to, then, is a conventional market or supply and demand model, despite the curious geographical heterogeneity of the urban land base. As a corollary, the model covertly insinuates itself as representative of the best of all possible worlds. Thus, urban land in this model is a scarce resource, and the market perfectly harmonizes and coordinates its allocation among competing users. Bidding for land *secures an agreement* between buyers and sellers about mutually satisfactory prices which also guarantee that the quantity of land offered for sale will be identical to the quantity actually bought. In addition, this market equilibrium must be socially optimal (in the context of the model) in the sense that realized land uses (i.e., final resource allocation) will be Pareto efficient.

These properties of the neoclassical model do, indeed, seem to be convincing (overwhelmingly so), and they emerge directly from a logic that is perfectly consistent within its own terms of reference. Unfortunately, as we hope to demonstrate in due course, those same terms of reference are hopelessly inadequate and misleading.

The Manipulated City Hypothesis

16. In recent years a certain body of critical writings has accumulated in opposition to the dominant neoclassical, or liberal, ideology. We might classify these writings as variously contributing to the *manipulated city hypothesis*.[3] In this view, urban land development is not the outcome of the myriad decisions of atomized individuals, each seeking to secure only his own satisfaction. Rather, urban society is seen as an amalgam of special interests, various social formations, neighborhood communities, and the like. Members of these interest groups act in concert. Moreover, social relations are generally dichotomized into relations between *exploiters* and *exploited.* These relations are underpinned by the degree of *social power* that each group possesses.

In the urban context, the main power group is seen as emerging from a coalition between finance capital (banks, trust companies, etc.) and the real estate interest (developers, construction companies, landlords, etc.).[4] This coalition acts as a "class monopoly." By reason of its control over the whole urban land development process, and especially the housing market, it is able to manipulate both the spatial form of the city and (concomitantly) to extract enormous super-profits (or, in Harvey's terms "class-monopoly rents"[5]) from the mass of powerless users of urban land. The instruments whereby the coalition effects this state of affairs are diverse means such as red-lining; blockbusting; fixed mortgage rates; excessive profit markups; political influence; and, from time to time, simple corruption and swindling. In this process, the coalition, with equal indifference, destroys old neighborhoods, ghettoizes ethnic groups, and herds an unwilling populace into sterile highrise apartments. In short, it rapes and then dehumanizes the city, all in a merely pecuniary interest.

Policy Implications

17. Theory is neither neutral nor passive. It embodies *human interests* and, hence, possesses *policy consequences*. Thus, both of the theoretical paradigms outlined above have their characteristic political flavors and, accordingly, their characteristic impacts upon government interventions and policy decisions.

The neoclassical paradigm is associated with a single, dominating norm that emanates from its doctrinaire belief in the naturalness and effectiveness of the market mechanism. That norm is: *Let the market work as long as possible; assist the market, or simulate it, through public intervention, if, and only if, it fails.* Over a century ago, John Stuart Mill advocated this imperative (with the explicit recommendation that it represents the "normal" state of human affairs) in the following terms: " . . . throw, in every instance, the burden of making out a strong case, not on those who resist, but on those who recommend government interference. Laissez-faire, in short, should be the general practice: every departure from it, unless required by some great good, is a certain evil. . . ."[6]

This market norm is, in fact, still widely promulgated, despite the persistent and ever-increasing evidence of "market failure" in the urban system. Consider, for example, the pervasiveness of state-controlled activities such as subsidized housing, municipal transport systems, public utilities, and the rest. Given the phenomenon of market failure, the neoclassical ideology suggests two further operating principles in the matter of urban public policy: In the first place, whenever possible, administratively induce some form of competitive pricing process (e.g., road pricing).[7] In the second place, if direct administrative control is inevitable, then attempt to arrange the outcome as a simulacrum of a free market operation (cf. the public housing model suggested by Herbert and Stevens[8]). This latter principle is, of course, the basis of all modern welfare economics. In any case, the market norm is sustained by an abstract standard of performance that is in one sense totally convincing: the Pareto, or Pareto-Kaldor, criterion. At least it is convincing as a criterion of judgment in a world of perfectly atomized, independent, and ahistorical human beings. The only problem remains: Does it have any relevance to practical policy decisions in the real universe of concrete social and economic processes? We shall argue that it does not because it abstracts away from the historically specific property relations of capitalist society. In the end, the neoclassical paradigm seems to lead only to a general, ameliorative philosophy ultimately eclectic, shortsighted, and self-restricting.[9]

18. By contrast, the theorists of the manipulated city see (no doubt correctly) the neoclassical doctrine of universal harmonies as only an ideological smoke screen masking the exploitative social relations of modern technological society. Of all these relations, those of particular concern to these theorists are the ones that emanate from the nexus of real estate interests. Such interests are seen as being guided in their actions uniquely by an implicitly unscrupulous and mysteriously subjective profit motive. Thus, having rejected market rationality as a norm, these theorists (and their activist colleagues) seem to deny its empirical existence as well. To them, there is no immanent structural logic (to be revealed by analysis) that will account for urban land problems as a general social phenomenon. Rather, it is all simply a matter of a greedy, powerful, and unprincipled clique of *individuals* who have chosen, out of a purely idiosyncratic ethical *lapsus,* to pursue a set of private interests which are, by faith and definition, opposed to those of "the people."

The policy consequences of this position are, of course, evident: Stop urban growth; stop large-scale developments; preserve what exists; control rents and impose taxes on speculation; substitute the moral principle of "equity" for the economic principle of efficiency (as if the two were mutually exclusive). The positions taken in recent years by many ratepayers' associations and by the so-called reform aldermen of the city of Toronto and their theoretical spokesmen represent a perfect example of this philosophy in action.

A Critique and Evaluation

19. Of course, there is something of value and interest in current theories of the land development process, both in the neoclassical mainstream and in the reformist critique. However, both approaches seem to us inadequate, mystified, and, in various respects, misleading. The following evaluation, therefore, deals with current theoretical underpinnings of urban analysis from the point of view of their inadequacies as statements of social theory and their failures as guidelines for policy making.

In recent years much has been made of the rather artificial, and often unrealistic, assumptions that are so pervasive in neoclassical analysis: perfect competition and perfect knowledge; the absence of externalities and of legal and social restraints; ubiquitous transport facilities and monocentric cities; instantaneous and costless residential relocation; and so on. In fact, to criticize the theory from this formalistic perspective is to miss the whole point: namely, *the fundamental epistemological inadequacy of the neoclassical problematique.* In this paper we consider and criticize three especially crucial aspects of the general neoclassical approach as it is applied to the analysis of urban land. These are: (a) the question of consumers' tastes and preferences and the formation of residential space; (b) the social and property relations that govern the production, exchange, and utilization of urban land; and (c) the nature of the state and the logic of public policy formulation.

20. First, then, "tastes and preferences," as such, are purely epiphenomenal. They are part of a larger cultural momentum that is itself embedded in, and grows out of, a global, social/historical process. This is the evolutionary development of a *mode of production,* by which phrase we mean not only a set of production techniques, but, more importantly, a web of social, political, and legal relations governing human interactions in the processes of production and exchange. It is in the context of a specific mode of production, and a derivatively specific social formation, that humans acquire and develop their tastes and preferences. The latter emerge, not from a capricious and abstract subjectivity, but from a series of collective human intentions, aspirations, and life projects made realistically realizable within a specific social formation. In a word, the system of production, in the sense given above, both historically and epistemologically precedes the system of consumption. Concomitantly, any attempt to establish a general theory of demand as an *exogenous* determinant of the processes of production and exchange is to engage in a *petitio principii* in the classical sense of taking what is to be proved as part of the would-be proof.[10] Neoclassical urban theory à la Alonso, Muth, and Solow, engages in the same kind of logical error.[11] It takes the spatial pattern of land prices and uses as a direct outcome of exogenously given consumers' tastes and preferences, whereas both are certainly part of a single explicandum. This scientific nullity is made finally evident by the fact that neoclassical urban models *can never in practice refute the alleged relationship* between land prices and uses, on the one hand, and tastes and preferences, on the other, for in these models "tastes and preferences" are always themselves taken to be revealed in the realized pattern of land prices and uses. This is a process of explaining the thing by itself with a vengeance. But, more importantly, all such analyses are profoundly quietistic. For, if current urban patterns are nothing more than the expression of consumers' preferences, then on what grounds (in a democratic society) can public intervention ever be justified?

21. Second, it is certainly true that a private land market is *one* way of allocating land to competing users, and in certain senses an administratively efficient way. However, to leave matters there, with the self-serving addendum that competitive market allocation is Pareto efficient (if not also eminently "fair," according to certain enthusiasts) is to lose sight of a whole underlying level of analysis. The neoclassical paradigm abstracts away from the social and property relations of production and exchange. Thus, the so-called "factors of production"—capital, labor, and land— lose their socio-historical specificity as articulations of human relations and interests. They are simply reduced to neutral and mutually substitutable *technical inputs* to an abstract economic process that rewards them according to their marginal productivity. In particular, this mystified conception conceals the peculiar nature of urban land and, hence, fails to grasp its two-fold contradictory status, namely: (a) as a human product that is collectively produced, yet whose specific use values depend upon the uncontrollable ways in which it is privately utilized; and (b) as a human product that is collectively produced, yet whose benefits are privately appropriated in the form of land rent.

We shall return to this important issue in due course. For now, it is necessary to point out that this failure to grasp the peculiar nature of urban land has grave policy implications. Neoclassical analysis suggests that there are *no* fundamental irrationalities in the ways in which urban land is produced, exchanged, and utilized, and that those problems that do exist are the consequence of simple market imperfections that can be corrected in a series of simple, *ad hoc,* "fine tuning" operations.

22. Third, we see no reason whatever to accept, either as a statement of fact or as a *desideratum,* that liberal notion of the state (hence, public policy and intervention) that is implicit in the neoclassical paradigm: namely, the state as a disinterested referee above and outside of society, intervening in the affairs of society only when some abstract, formalistic criterion of social optimality requires it. On the contrary, *the rationality of the state derives from the rationality of the civil society within which the state is historically embedded.* By ignoring this entirely self-evident premise, and by seeking to construct a series of abstract and disembodied criteria of social optimality and state intervention, the neoclassical paradigm (particularly as it is applied to urban land analysis) has thrown itself into something approaching a crisis of credibility; palpably, its policy prescriptions become ever more irrelevant.

23. The reformist critique has the merit of suggesting an analysis whose purely descriptive accuracy is frequently all too painfully evident.

But what it gains at the level of surface appearances, it loses at the level of essence. From an epistemological point of view, the singling out of the property development (and finance capital) interests as the villain of the piece seems to us strained and artificial. It is the role and raison d'être of capital as a whole that are at issue here. In particular, the property development industry generally is a capitalist branch of production like any other capitalist branch and is *subject to the same general, overarching capitalist structure and logic*. From the observation that the activities of the property development industry generate uniquely problematical outcomes, the manipulated city theorists have been lured into the belief that the fundamental logic leading to these outcomes must itself be unique. This is precisely where the manipulated city theorists are in error. For the uniqueness—real as it is—of the outcomes is not due to some unique logic governing the activities of the property development industry, but rather to the application of a perfectly general capitalistic logic to a unique object of production and exchange: urban land. For this reason, the repeated attempts on the part of the manipulated city theorists to attack the property development industry *as such* have always failed fundamentally. This proposition is reinforced by consideration of the evident fact that landlords (and their cohorts) no longer in North America form a distinctive and identifiable social *class* apart. Along with land-holding and land-development activities themselves, landlords have been generally assimilated into the life and momentum of capital at large. Thus, any analysis of urban land and property processes must begin with an analysis of late capitalism as a general structure. And assertions of theft and conspiracy (to call things by their names) scarcely offer a very promising foundation from which to undertake such an analysis. Long ago Engels, in his attack on Proudonhist philosophy, showed, in *The Housing Question*, that the rhetorical banner of that philosophy—"Property is theft"—is scientifically and politically null: scientifically because owners of production units extract surplus value in the form of unpaid labor *not* by theft, but in the perfectly normal course of events; politically because, to the degree that property owners are indeed swindlers, then to the same degree can they be dealt with by *existing* juridical arrangements.[12] The fundamental core and the central question of capitalism is not the pervasiveness of theft and conspiracy, but the process of the extraction and appropriation of surplus value. This process is hidden in the deep structure that lies below the commonly accepted social relations of capitalist society, and it is not peculiar—as the reformists seem to suggest—to the real estate interests but is spread out over all spheres of productive activity.[13] In spite of these castigations, the spirit of Proudhon lives on, and, for example, in the form of the recent antideveloper movement in Toronto, it has succeeded only in exacerbating an already severe housing shortage. More recently, overtaken by a fit of moral indignation at the alleged cupidity of landlords, it has given us a policy of rent control that is surely destined ultimately to produce many more problems than it solves.[14]

The theory that we propose below is, we suggest, more far reaching than current theoretical formulations of whatever tendency. It paints a view of the world that is more real (hence progressive) than the view of the neoclassical theorists but, at the same time, infinitely more intractable (hence historically meaningful) than the world of the New Proudonhists.

The Urban Land Nexus

24. We now attempt to set up a general theoretical framework for the elucidation of the urban land question as we see it. The inextricability of human knowledge and human interests makes it imperative, indeed inescapable, that we adopt a specific "point of view" on this question. In any case, limits on human time, knowledge, and the ability to conceptualize problems impose this imperative.

Our dominant interest in the urban land question is in policy and its action consequences. The issue to us is not only what *can* be done about urban land problems, but also what *must* be done. At the same time, this point of view is not merely capricious or idiosyncratic; it is given to us historically. We do not live in a peasant society or in a science fiction utopia. We live within a capitalist, socio-economic system that is markedly and specifically *urban* in character, and, as we have shown above, that is beset by a number of difficult congenital problems. Our consciousness of these problems is less a matter of personal choice than it is a matter of a controlled response to a given historical circumstance. Further, consciousness of these urban problems is not contingent upon the prior formulation of some abstract, speculative, ideal image of urban life. On the contrary, it is contingent upon the concrete structure and development of capitalist society itself. North American society has not engaged in frequently bitter urban controversies and disputes over property rights, institutionalized zoning, urban renewal, highway construction, and the rest simply because existing urban realities did not measure up to certain abstract urban visions. It was only when urban growth and development began to produce real problems that society started to act consciously to counteract them. It is precisely in this way that the sense and purpose of urban analysis are historically given. By the same token, a historically concrete urban analysis that is self-conscious about the course of policy and urban intervention will automatically withhold itself from posing intellectual puzzles that are purely abstract, formal, and pretendedly universal (such as, for example, the notion of a general urban equilibrium under perfect market assumptions). It will, rather, actively seek out those specific

and concrete questions that appear in the context of socially and historically given modes of the organization of production (i.e., the necessities
of social being) and of the conditions of reproduction (i.e., of human
attitudes, job skills, and simple physical existence). To abstract away from
these historically determinate parameters, relations, and problems is to
rob analysis of its real social power and meaning. For this reason we
initiate our discussion of the urban land nexus by mapping out the fundamental structure of the global socio-economic order within which urbanization processes and urban land problems are embedded.

Commodity Production: A Brief Statement

25. Capitalist society is organized around the general social relations of
commodity production and exchange. This presupposes—historically and
analytically—the presence of three conditions: first, that humans have
achieved a stage of technological productivity in a way such that they can
produce an economic surplus over and above what is needed for immediate consumption; second, that production has become sufficiently articulated and advanced to allow for the emergence of specialized
commodity producers; and third, that wage labor, involving the exchange
of labor power for wages determined on a labor market, has become the
customary mode of organizing work relations. Given these conditions,
commodity production emerges in the manifest form of entrepreneurial
organization, where capitalist firms hire labor to work on materials and
means of production (capital). In this way *commodities* are produced and
sold for money prices. The revenues thus received are then spent partly
to pay for labor, materials, and depreciated capital. Whatever is left after
these payments are made is profit. Payments made to labor in the form
of wages are spent on consumption commodities, and this consumption
process ensures that commodity production as a whole is sustained. Profits are reinvested to enlarge the sphere of production. Thus proceeds
commodity production and with it, the accumulation of capital.[15] These
various, interlocking relations are demonstrated graphically and enlarged
upon in figure 2-1.

Commodity production, however, does not occur in a "wonderland of
no dimensions," to borrow a phrase from Isard.[16] It is articulated in
geographical space. It takes place *on land.* Concomitantly, the overall production process is mediated by a transport system. Nucleated clusters of
firms and households come into being in order to minimize the friction
of distance. More specifically, within each urban nucleation a configuration of relative spaces and locations emerges, and with it, a definite pattern
of land uses. In particular, we can distinguish three principal kinds of
urban land uses: namely, land used for commodity production and exchange (production space); land used for residential activity (reproduction space); and land used for transport (circulation space). The first two

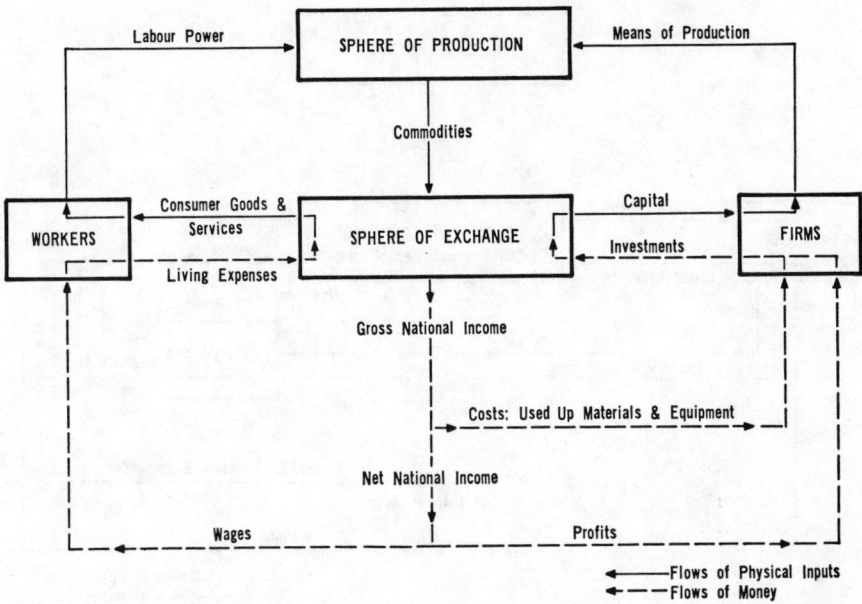

Figure 2-1. Commodity Production: A Simple Schema of the Interrelations of Capital and Labor

kinds of uses generally appear on privately owned land, while the last generally appears on publicly owned land. Depending on its relative location, any plot of land will be more or less valuable in exchange. A pattern of urban land rents (hence, prices) then emerges as a reflection of these differential locational advantages. Privately owned urban land is exchanged accordingly. On commodity-producing land, rent is paid out of profits, and it thus represents to firms an explicit reduction of profits. On residential land, rent is paid out of wages, and it represents to workers a reduction in their standard of living. In both cases, however, rent is ultimately, in aggregate, a simple proportion of net national income, specifically appropriated by owners' land. These various propositions are clarified by figure 2-2, which also shows, by comparison to figure 2-1, how land inserts itself into the process of commodity production, generally.

26. Underlying these evident market relations there exists a deep structure of social and property relations. This structure underpins market exchanges, though it is not itself always clearly visible through them. At its core is an ongoing socio-political conflict (hence an ongoing, theoretical-*cum*-ideological controversy) over the distribution of the total social surplus (the net national income in figures 2-1 and 2-2) into profits, wages, and land rents. For a given surplus, the higher the share of any one of these claims upon that surplus, the lower the shares of the other two. The socio-political conflict over income shares is thus structural, intrinsic,

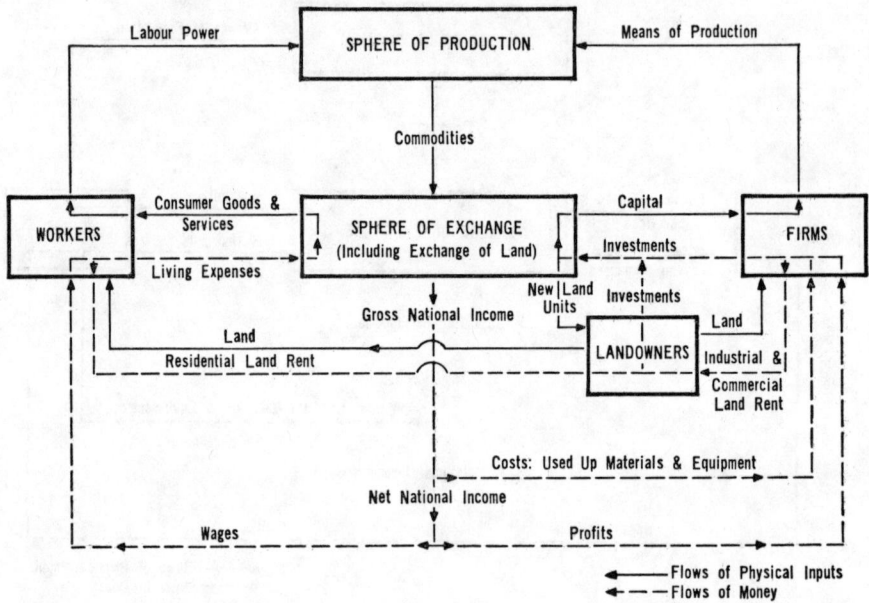

Figure 2-2. Commodity Production: A Simple Schema of the Interrelations of Capital, Labor, and Land

and ineluctable within the capitalist system of production. Furthermore, *the market does not eliminate (i.e., dissolve) this conflict*; quite the contrary, for continued market exchange is possible only in the circumstance where there exists a political power capable of maintaining the tense social balance between the three antagonistic claimants to the social surplus: capital, labor, and land. Observe that for the present we do not suggest, a priori, that these claimants inevitably constitute distinct, concrete social classes, though they do represent definite and distinguishable economic interests. We will return to this question in the final section of this paper.

Now, the neoclassical doctrine that free market exchange leads to an efficient (if not just) distribution of the social surplus by rewarding each production factor according to its marginal productivity is essentially a theoretical and ideological diversion. In fact, market prices (the sine qua non of exchange) are themselves nothing but the observable *results* of that central socio-political conflict over the distribution of the social surplus. For, as the work of the so-called Cambridge School has shown, commodities cannot be priced *before* the distribution of the social surplus is known.[17] In short, prices are empirically and analytically subsequent to profits, wages, and rents, with these economic categories in turn dependent upon the deep structure of capitalist property relations. Clearly, a scientific and, hence, useful political economy (and urban analysis) must start out on the basis of those historically given social and property relations which underlie and shape observable exchange relationships. In relation to urbanization processes and urban land problems, then, *the essential point of departure for us is not the phenomenon of competitive bidding for land, but the deep structure of urban property relations in relation to which the competitive bidding for land is only the faintest and most superficial pulsation.* However, in order to pursue this matter of urban property relations, we must first elucidate certain essential characteristics of urban land. We must distinguish urban land as an object of exchange from commodities in the strict sense and, thereby, clarify those peculiar social relations that govern the production, exchange, and utilization of urban land.

The Nature of Urban Land

27. Unlike raw land, urban land is only partly a primeval natural endowment. It is, in addition, *serviced* land. It is land on which humans have expended labor materialized in the form of infrastructural and structural artifacts. In this sense, urban land is a product of human labor. But is it similar to other human products such as wheat, typewriters, or haircuts? To answer this question we need to consider a crucial, analytical distinction between goods and services which *are* producible in the commodity form, and goods and services which are not.

Producibility in the commodity form is taken here to mean *the possibility of continued (unshackled) production of use values by individual capitalist firms as products capable of realizing their exchange values in the market, and hence capable of yielding at least the ongoing rate of profit to their producers.* The stability and viability of capitalist commodity production, as such, require the absence of external, that is, nonmarket barriers to private production. For the system to work, supply must be responsive to price signals. There are two complementary dimensions to this condition: First, it must be institutionally feasible for private producers to produce commodities on a continuing basis by the application of labor and materials. Second, private producers must have *no option* but to produce in the commodity form, and this limitation is enforced by competition among firms. In brief, commodity production requires that supply be responsive to price signals; that same responsiveness requires that goods and services be producible *in the commodity form.* It is important to point out that the notion of producibility in the commodity form does not signify producibility in the simple, physical, technical sense, but rather the possibility of production within the system of historically specific social relations of capitalism.

In capitalist society, however, certain goods and services may well be socially and economically useful, or even essential, and may be readily producible in the simple technical sense, yet are not producible in the commodity form. This may occur for one or more of the following reasons: First, whenever production in the strict commodity form entails the necessity of output levels at scales so massive as to lead to the emergence of monopolies or oligopolies (e.g., mass transport and communications), the state will frequently intervene and banish the commodity form, either by regulating or taking over production. This, of course, will occur only if the monopolistic or oligopolistic practices begin to have serious and deleterious effects on other key sectors of the economy. Second, goods and services which are essential to the survival of capitalist society, and yet which cannot be sold in such quantities or at such prices as will yield their producers at least the ongoing rate of profit, will not be produced in the commodity form, but in some other form (e.g., low-income housing). Third, the state will take over, or severely regulate, the production of any goods and services whenever the social stability of capitalist society requires that those goods and services be supplied in conformity with delicate political or ideological criteria (e.g., education, police, alcoholic beverages). This, we may point out, will occur even if such goods and services *can* be produced in the commodity form. Fourth, some economically useful by-products of human activity (i.e., externalities, such as concentrations of shoppers in central business districts) emerge in the form of purely spontaneous and nonmarketable benefits. Goods and services that are characterized by any possible combination of these circumstances are not commodities. For brevity we refer to them as *noncommodities*.

28. This distinction between commodities and noncommodities has far-reaching analytical and, more importantly, policy-related implications. Noncommodities confront capitalist society with significant social, political, and administrative problems; for the production, exchange, and utilization of these noncommodities require modalities and norms of decision making that are quite alien to, and frequently irreconcilable with, the logic of capitalist society at large. Urban land is clearly a noncommodity in the sense that its intrinsic use value—differential locational advantage—is produced not by individual capitalists, but through the agency of the state and the *collective effects* of innumerable individual social and economic activities. Specifically, urban land is produced in a complex collective dynamic where the state provides major infrastructural services as well as various public goods which cannot be adequately produced in the commodity form; in addition, land finally becomes urban only when its private utilization consummates the "useful effects of urban agglomeration."[18] Like wheat, typewriters, or haircuts, urban land is essentially a human product; but, unlike them, it is a noncommodity. Admittedly, it is possible here and there (particularly in past historical periods) to find examples of the production of urban land in the commodity form (e.g., the development of new towns by private companies), though the total quantity of land produced in this way is evidently negligible and certainly destined to

diminish even further, given the growing complexity and indivisibility of urban equipment. At the same time, while urban *land* is definitely a noncommodity, urban *floor space* is a true commodity in the strict sense, produced whenever private owners intensify the use of their land. The possibility of intensification, however, presupposes the *prior* existence of urban land. Intensification only gives access to an existing and socially given use value represented by urban land in the noncommodity form (i.e., a set of differential locational advantages). At the same time, and paradoxically, any increment in urban floor space in the commodity form inadvertently produces as an externality an increment in urban land in the noncommodity form. That is, any increase in the quantity of floor space generates for all *other* urban activities an increase in the supply of differential locational advantages.

29. Now, in contemporary North American society, the process of production of urban land occurs in two different phases involving two distinct and ultimately incompatible sets of social and property relations of production and exchange. The first phase is one in which the state provides (either directly or by subsidization) major infrastructural and other public facilities. The output of this phase consists of serviced, developable, but not yet developed land. So far as the use characteristics of urban land are concerned, this product is, as it were, unfinished; for the final spatial configuration of differential locational advantages is as yet undetermined. In the second phase, this serviced land is exchanged through a series of private market transactions which determine the geographical pattern and intensity of urban land uses. Only then does urban land, qua a system of differential locational advantages, acquire its final use characteristics. Of course, in reality, urban land is not then frozen in stasis, but is in a continual process of change and redevelopment.

The two phases of urban land development described above differ significantly. Whereas the first phase involves various forms of collective decision making concerning the quality, location, and timing of public facilities, the second phase is a purely anarchical process whose outcomes —despite a variety of land-use controls—are unplanned and undecidable at the outset. The first phase can, in principle, be undertaken according to the criteria of social costs and benefits. But the second phase can be undertaken only according to the criteria of purely private costs and benefits. In short, *while the outcomes of the first phase are objects of collective decisions, the outcomes of the second phase are not.* Consequently, since the second phase is a decisive element (both as cause and effect) in the production of urban land, it follows that the production process *as a whole* (as currently realized) is inevitably anarchical. Thus, under current social and property relations, the spatial configuration of differential locational advantages (and, hence, of land uses and land rents) is *not* an object of collective decisions. Nor can it ever be rationally planned in the absence of significant changes in existing social and property relations.

30. There is a further and equally important phenomenon that determines the nature of urban land. This is the slow convertibility of the built urban environment. This phenomenon is fairly obvious at the level of simple physical appearance. However, its analytical and policy-related implications are rather more subtle, requiring amplification.

In and of itself, slow convertibility has no special consequence in terms of the social and property relations that govern the production, exchange, and utilization of urban land. Its analytical and policy consequences derive from the relationship of slow convertibility to the non-producibility of urban land in the commodity form and to the collective undecidability of its use characteristics. In the first place, had it been possible to accommodate urban activities within nondurable, instantly convertible structures, the non-producibility of urban land in the commodity form would have resulted in markedly fewer urban problems than is currently the case. In these circumstances, any increase in the demand for urban land would have always called forth, and been met by, an immediate response on the part of private developers in the form of land-use intensifications giving increased accessibility to existing urban land. Had this been the case, we would have undoubtedly witnessed a vastly denser development of urban activities than is now the rule. Similarly, had urban infrastructural facilities been sufficiently easy to implant and renew, then the process of private land-use intensification would have resulted in few infrastructural shortages and bottlenecks. Under conditions such as these, urban land would have resembled one of those theoretical agricultural landscapes à Von Thünen, whose productivity, use characteristics, and geographical articulation can be instantly adjusted to meet every possible contingency. In the second place, had urban structure and infrastructure been swiftly convertible, the undecidability of the use characteristics of urban land would have posed only negligible difficulties. Collective irrationalities and negative external effects due to this undecidability would have been purely ephemeral. Moreover, every perturbation in the existing spatial configuration of differential locational advantages would have instantly produced a counterresponse in the form of an overall conversion of preexisting structures to correspond to the changed configuration of differential locational advantages. Under these hypothetical conditions, the vast majority of the urban land problems that we discussed above would have remained only temporary and self-correcting, minor inconveniences.

In spite of the patent unreality of those analytical assaults on the urban land question that suppose, as a point of departure, that urban land uses are indeed perfectly fluid, such analyses seem to be the rule rather than the exception. Small wonder, then, that mainstream urban theory so frequently ends up producing comforting fictions about the processes of urban growth and development, together with mystified policy prescriptions built around the notion of the market as universal panacea. Hence, the land market is seen as: an auto-regulating phenomenon; an efficient allocator of scarce land units among competing users; a maximizer of collective benefits; a rational sorter and arranger of land uses; an operationalization of consumers' tastes and preferences; and so on. Quite apart from our earlier criticisms of mainstream urban theory, the evident fact of the slow convertibility of urban land itself poses a central dilemma for that theory. This is not, it should be noted, a dilemma that can be solved by simply rewriting the equations of spatial equilibrium to take account of certain inertial properties of the urban environment. It is, rather, a case of a fundamental, perennial, and intrinsic dissonance in capitalist cities: *the permanent mismatch of urban form, as the inert outcome of a private decisional calculus, and the functional imperatives of a transcendent social rationality.*

The Urban Land Nexus and the Genesis of Urban Land Problems

31. In a society where urban land is produced, exchanged, and utilized in conformity with the social and property relations outlined above, certain immanent structural contradictions inevitably arise. These contradictions represent the mutual and dynamic opposition of antithetical component elements of the whole land development process; they are concretely manifested in the kinds of urban land problems discussed earlier. Attempts to deal with these manifest problems are likely to continue to fail unless the fundamental structural contradictions that underlie them are resolved. This can only occur when existing social and property relations are themselves fundamentally reformed.

32. In a capitalist system of production, the compelling force of competition turns every entrepreneur's technical *potential* for improved productivity into an *actuality.* Under the threat of ruin, individual firms are constantly forced to seek out their best possible (profit-maximizing) set of production relations. The consequence is a tendency to ever-increasing social productive capacity and, in theory at least, efficiency in resource allocation. By the term *efficiency,* we mean here exactly what the neoclassical economists mean: A given allocation is efficient if it is not possible to increase the output of some desired goods and services (urban accommodation, transport services, etc., in our case) except by decreasing the output of some other desired goods and services. It is our object here to show that the logic of land ownership and utilization in capitalist society can never lead to efficiency in this sense. That is, the allocation of urban land to competing uses under capitalism must persistently and inherently undermine whatever general tendencies may otherwise exist in the direction of efficiency.

33. At the outset, note that potential sporadic movements *away* from efficiency are endemic within contemporary cities. These movements will occur whenever there is a change in the spatial pattern of differential locational advantages (e.g., as a result of the servicing of peripheral urban land, the modification of existing infrastructure, or the private redevelopment of any plot of land, etc.). These events provoke derivative readjustments in land-use patterns. The question now remains: Can a competitive land market, over time, restore equilibrium, given disturbances of this nature?

Neoclassical theory has a ready answer to this question: The private urban land market can indeed restore efficiency, *but only under circumstances of perfect constancy in all conditions exogenous to this land market.* [19] Let us throw the best light that we can on this assertion and see what it implies. Thus, all (exogenously given) changes in the geography of differential locational advantages must take place in an episodic temporal pattern, in a way such that any initial set of changes is followed by a prolonged period of quiescence (in exogenous conditions). This period of quiescence must be *at least* as long as the longest economic life of all preexisting urban structures whose location is made problematical by the initial change. Such structures will be those where land rent and the marginal productivity of the land are no longer equal, thus necessitating land-use conversions if efficiency is to be restored. Clearly, however, such quiescence is the exception, rather than the rule, in contemporary North American cities; indeed, the spatial configuration of differential locational advantages is in a state of constant flux. Thus, even assuming that there is a convergent process of readjustment as the urban system seeks to accommodate itself to some specific exogenous impulse, long before even a first round of readjustments has been accomplished a further exogenous impulse will have pushed the urban system once more away from equilibrium. [20] And even if a first round of readjustments *were* possible, this in and of itself would change the existing pattern of differential locational advantages, which in turn would require yet further rounds of readjustments in order to restore efficiency, and so on. We have shown, then, that on two counts the time period theoretically necessary for a free land market to restore efficiency once it has been lost is unrealistically long. At the same time, not only are land-use readjustments to *past events* rarely socially efficient, they are also rarely efficient with respect to potential *future events.* As Teitz has very convincingly demonstrated, locational decisions that are made in conformity with purely private costs and benefits tend to be intrinsically "myopic" in the sense that they tend to preempt collectively rational options in the future. [21] In these various circumstances, only an administrative arrangement that transcends the market could harmonize and synchronize all decisions, inducing a condition of social efficiency, both spatially and temporally.

34. It is obvious that the state of affairs described above imposes various sorts of *collective* penalties on urban society. In addition, this inherent market inefficiency has deleterious effects on *individual* commodity producers and workers. Thus, a firm may make what initially appears to be an optimal (profit-maximizing) locational decision from its own point of view. Then, in the course of time, it is faced with unforeseen changes in the configuration of differential locational advantages that either vastly truncate or vastly augment its production possibilities. In either case, the firm's original decision is now revealed to be suboptimal in its own purely private terms. Moreover, the firm's committed fixed capital costs prevent it from readjusting to a fully optimal level, at least in the short run (though, of course, the firm will still seek to optimize whatever choice variables remain within its command in the interim). The more dramatic the changes in the configuration of differential locational advantages (e.g., the massive shift from rail to road transport some time around the 1940s), the more pervasive such dysfunctionalities. For similar reasons, urban residents and workers have frequently incurred heavy penalties as a consequence of urban change, especially as a consequence of the rapidly shifting location of work places relative to residential areas. This has led to many cases of social conflict and unrest, to frequent and recurrent demands for higher wages.

From all of this, it follows that capitalist social and property relations create two major contradictory tendencies around the issue of urban land. On the one hand, the logic of commodity production and the private appropriation of profit call for functionally efficient urban land-use patterns. On the other hand, the private ownership and control of urban land lead to a tendency away from such efficiency.

35. If this is true (that is, if market allocation of urban land gives rise to a tendency away from efficiency), then what prevents cities from falling progressively into massive disarray? In fact, land-use allocations in contemporary cities are not determined purely by a market, but are the outcome of a peculiar partnership: a *market* allocation process that leads away from efficiency and a *political* allocation process that unceasingly attempts to rectify this inefficiency (while simultaneously producing yet other inefficiencies by altering the fundamental distribution of differential locational advantages). It is not pure, idle speculation to suggest that widespread urban disarray would probably have been the rule in the absence of ever-increasing political intervention. The history of cities under early laissez-faire capitalism lends some credence to this assertion. A cursory recollection of the empirical circumstances preceding the enactment of urban hygiene laws in the nineteenth century, the municipalization of urban

utilities, the application of zoning and subdivision controls, the introduction of the various planning enabling acts, etc., provides further strong support in favor of this notion.[22]

More generally, it seems evident that state intervention in commodity production is a historical necessity imposed by the developmental logic of commodity production itself and made irrevocable by the innate self-destructive tendencies of commodity production. As a consequence, the logic of this intervention derives directly from the structural conditions of commodity production, and it changes historically as these structural conditions change. In the domain of urban land development, and given the basic contradiction outlined immediately above, *state intervention derives its basic character from the necessity to mediate this contradiction as and when the socio-economic outcomes of the contradiction begin to undermine the viability of commodity production.* Given this historically specific task, and given that urban land problems tend to emerge slowly and gradually, rather than suddenly and cataclysmically, the state understandably tends to search for policies which promise maximal effectiveness, yet which require minimal changes in existing social and property relations. This double-edged strategy contributes to the emergence of a number of dilemmas and predicaments, whereby in seeking to resolve urban problems, the state finds itself participating in the creation of new problems. To complete our argument, we deal here briefly with four illustrative dilemmas.

36. **Dilemma 1.** In their perennial search for profits, firms seek out ever more technically efficient production processes. In short, over time they tend to intensify their use of capital. One manifestation of this process is the continual intensification of land uses at certain locations. In an earlier paper it was shown that a profit-maximizing logic induces a pronounced process of land-use intensification at locations where land rents are already high; i.e., at accessible, centralized, and polarized locations.[23] However, as intensification proceeds, so these locations became progressively more congested and overloaded, and their transport access, progressively less adequate. This calls forth a response (i.e., reactive planning) on the part of the state, which intervenes to correct these problems through new investments in basic infrastructure. This immediately increases the differential locational advantages of any set of locations thus treated and sets in train a new round of land-use intensifications. The state is obliged once more to intervene, and so on.

Dilemma 2. Individual locators actively seek out beneficial urban agglomeration effects. Because these effects cannot be produced as commodities, locators are thus impelled to drift towards urban districts, where such beneficial effects have *already* emerged in definite and irreversible form. Conversely, locators tend to shun those districts where agglomeration effects are negative. This, however, leads to a self-perpetuating, vicious circle: Where agglomeration effects exist (due to historical circumstances), they grow; where they do not exist, they have little chance of appearing spontaneously. This process is further accentuated by the very same phenomenon of reactive planning and land-use intensification that we noted in the last paragraph. In this way, then, the capitalist logic of urban land development is self-constricting, for it discourages the very social outcomes (the emergence of new poles of aggregate urban activity with beneficial agglomeration effects) which might further its ends.

Dilemma 3. Rapid peripheral urban expansion has been a characteristic feature of urban growth for many decades. It is at once a solution to certain problems, and yet itself creates new problems. Because of the distortions and disequilibria induced by past economic growth, the state has tended to encourage peripheral expansion as a way of relieving pressures in central cities. This encourages out-migration of urban activities. And where peripheral expansion has been especially aggressive (as in certain U.S. cities), this leads in the course of time to moribundity of the central core. The state typically responds by treating only the symptoms of this process; i.e., by urban renewal. Urban renewal itself then produces a typical sequence of problems, especially the destruction of low-income housing.

Dilemma 4. Throughout much of North America, large metropolitan regions are characteristically split up among semi-independent municipalities. Each municipality competes with other municipalities in seeking to maximize its own tax revenues. In this process, municipalities adopt zoning laws and fiscal arrangements that compromise the global efficiency of the whole metropolitan region. This leads typically to central city decay (and fiscal crisis), while the surburban communities enjoy an affluence that is bought at the expense of this decay.

In these four illustrative dilemmas we have tried to show that, given the fundamental social and property relations of commodity-producing society, the state becomes a part of the urban problem in the very process of seeking solutions.

In the light of the entire preceding argument, we shall now attempt to embed the urban land question more thoroughly in a map of contemporary social and political relations.

The Historical Process Today

Current Developments in State Strategies

37. From the time of its inception, capital has never been able to provide for itself the social preconditions of its own existence. That is to say, the social underpinnings of the processes of the production and appropria-

tion of surplus value have never been producible by capitalist means. For this purpose, capitalism has always required a *state* which confronts individual units of capital and labor as an agent of general collective capitalist imperatives.

Even so, the extent of state intervention in capitalist society has never been constant but has displayed a very pronounced historical tendency to grow. Under early capitalism, the state adopted the simple, yet effective, strategy of laissez-faire, while guaranteeing the specific social and property relations necessary in a regime of free competitive enterprise. However, the historical trajectory of this system revealed its tendency to self-paralysis, a paralysis that culminated in the Great Depression of 1873 and the later collapse of 1929. These events ushered in the end of a laissez-faire strategy. This strategy was supplanted in the 1930s by a form of interventionism (justified theoretically by Keynes) that blossomed in due course into a full-blown Welfare-Statism. The state found itself compelled now to intervene directly in the processes themselves of production and reproduction. It had to create conditions for the more effective deployment of underutilized capital and labor, to underwrite the social costs of capitalist production, to regulate the economic cycle, and so on. Moreover, this new interventionism was visibly reflected in, and indeed largely effectuated through, *urban* policies and programs. In particular, throughout the 1950s and the 1960s, the state committed massive and ever-increasing quantities of public funds to interurban and intraurban transport systems, to urban renewal, to the provision of public housing, to new towns program, and the rest. This aggressive interventionism had two major effects: First, by making elaborate networks of *collective* goods available for *private* use, the state helped raise labor productivity and, hence, the general profitability of capital. Second, while dealing fairly effectively with the urban question in the short run, this interventionism set in motion certain secondary circuits of appropriation that have contributed significantly to the growing problems of the welfare state. This latter point will be taken up again below.

38. Welfare-Statism was predicated upon the Keynesian faith that an aggressive state effort to underpin a system of propulsive economic activities (that is, to influence microeconomic decisions by the manipulation of macroeconomic variables) could secure continued smooth economic growth and social stability. The problem was that, for a time at least, the faith worked only too well. By the end of the 1960s, Welfare-Statism itself (and that structure of commodity production that it had helped to engender) began to evince signs of self-paralysis. The propulsive branches of economic activity were rapidly monopolized by a small number of firms, and this had deleterious effects on weaker and less technically advanced branches of production. Unable to withstand the growing economic power of the monopolies, the nonmonopolized branches of production have required increasing state support. Backward regions, heavily subsidized, failed to "take-off," continuing to absorb growing streams of public funds. Welfare programs turned more and more unemployedinto permanent welfare recipients. Large metropolitan regions began to develop the first signs of a mounting fiscal crisis, and so on. Most severe of all, the state has been caught in a predicament where it cannot stimulate new growth without producing severe inflation; yet, if it does not stimulate new growth, high unemployment continues unabated. The result is an endemic condition of "stagflation." In brief, it is because Welfare-Statism was so successful in the 1950s and 1960s that it began to encounter growing difficulties by the beginning of the 1970s. Welfare-Statism has gradually eliminated precisely those structural conditions which made it workable at one time.

39. State strategy is now at a crossroads, and some new strategic directions are clearly imperative if major economic dislocations and concomitant social unrest are to be averted. In an case, a simple return to a full-blown welfare-state strategy seems scarcely to be practicable. Much less, of course, is there any possibility of a return to anything even approaching laissez-faire. In a definite sense it is apparent that yet *more* collective action is called for. At the same time, given the failures, inadequacies, and dangers of Keynesian strategies, future policy formulations in this domain are likely to be cautious and highly selective. There remains, however, a further domain of interventionist possibilities that has hitherto been explored, in practice, in only the most superficial and tangential ways, and yet would appear to offer some significant solutions to current policy dilemmas. This is the domain of *collective management,* in the sense of bureaucratic control, planning, and harmonization over wide areas of economic and social activity. Recent experiences with wage and price controls in many of the advanced capitalist countries would seem to represent an incipient phase of this new strategy that is quite evidently emerging.[24]

What these observations imply for the urban land question is that the palpable geometric increase in urban planning activities in recent decades is almost certain to continue unabated, but with some altered modulations. On the one hand, the state will undoubtedly continue to provide massive injections of public funds into physical urban infrastructure, though in a more highly discriminating and rationalized manner than has been the case in the recent past. On the other hand, the state will, to an increasing degree, impose administrative rules whereby the urban game is played. Zoning regulations and urban general plans, for example, are only the mildest apprehensions of this development. Thus we might expect yet more control of the housing market, yet more collective decision making about the development and redevelopment of urban land, yet more government direction of industrial locational decisions, yet more attempts to rationalize municipal finance, and so on. The compelling motivation of this activity, of course, is that it responds to urgent social and economic problems with little risk of triggering new rounds of inflation and/or unemployment. But it also means that urban life, in general, must become increasingly mediated by the state and, hence, directly politicized. We pursue this question further in the succeeding argument.

Current Developments in Class Relationships

40. As we have shown in figure 2-2, the total net national income generated by capitalist commodity production divides without residue into profits, wages, and rents. These abstract *claims* on net national income are appropriated by specific concrete *claimants*, so that they represent not simply analytical economic categories but, more importantly, real human interests. These interests, in fact, are the outward manifestation of a set of class relationships that are themselves determined by an underlying pattern of social and property relations. Moreover, because profits, wages, and rents are mutually exclusive quantities, the human interests that attach to them collide in various ways and thus have a definite political dimension.

In the course of the evolution of capitalist society, the abstract analytical categories—profits, wages, and rents—have remained as perennially unchanging and unambiguous claims on net national income. The claimants to profits, wages, and rents, however, have been markedly more mutable, and the class relations of late capitalist society are quite definitely different from those that characterized early capitalist society. This change has been made all the more complex by the fact that the primary distribution of net national income into profits, wages, and rents via the development of competitive markets is now complemented by (among other things) a complex series of secondary circuits of appropriation. Of all these circuits, those that emanate from the process of urbanization and urban planning are of particular significance and interest.

Let us now ponder the detailed relevance of these general matters for an extended analysis of the urban land question.

41. The structure of early capitalist society was fairly straightforward. It consisted of: capitalists who owned the means of production and appropriated a profit; workers who owned labor power that they sold for a wage; and landlords who owned land and appropriated a rent. These social groups, of course, were not perfectly internally homogeneous, nor were other kinds of social fractions absent. Even so, this tripartite social structure was the dominant historical (and classical) situation in England towards the end of the eighteenth century and the beginning of the nine-

teenth century. As a corollary, conflicts over income shares were visibly expressed in the form of an ongoing series of social and political struggles among these three different groups. These conflicts were, however, uneven. In the early stages of the development of capitalist production, capitalists fought a long and ultimately successful battle against the entrenched power and privileges of landed property (the hereditary aristocracy). Once this battle was won, decisively with the repeal of the Corn Laws in the early nineteenth century, capitalists and landlords tended to form an uneasy alliance against labor as an emerging social force on the basis of their shared material interest in the institution and ideology of private property.

42. Late capitalist society represents a significant departure from this early social map. In particular, the progressive nineteenth-century trend to a deliquescence of a specific landlord *class* has been definitely resolved, and this class has now more or less disappeared as a distinctive element of capitalist society. This is not to say that land as a factor of production has ceased to have significance or that land rent has ceased to exist as a specific share of net national income. On the contrary, they remain as significant and as real as ever. However, the class identity of owners of land (hence claimants to rent) has become quite diffuse. This diffuseness itself results from the fact that land in late capitalist society has been totally converted into an alienable and commercial value on a par with stocks, bonds, productive equipment, and the like. In this manner, land ownership has lost its former social specificity. Land is now owned severally (by commodity producers, financial institutions, a handful of professional *rentiers*, and by workers themselves) and variously applied to the purposes of production, residential activity, and simple speculative investment. However, whereas *ownership* of land has become diffuse, *private control* over land development has become gradually more concentrated. For one thing, the tendency towards technical amelioration that is a persistent element of all capitalist branches of production has led to the emergence of a progressively rationalized and vertically integrated property development branch. For another, the increasing lumpiness of infrastructural artifacts has induced large-scale operations in this branch by permitting the internalization of significant external economies. The end result has been that this specific branch of capital generally, in pursuing a perfectly normal capitalistic logic, has come to be in dominant control of the whole land development process.

43. If the theses advanced above are correct, then the ways in which urban land problems translate themselves into specific social and political issues must have become markedly different from what was formerly the case. We shall take up this matter again briefly in the concluding paragraphs of this paper. For the moment, two points must be stressed:

First, with the general diffusion of land ownership, the prediction (frequently made by many Marxian theorists) of an irrevocable and impending confrontation between capitalists and landlords is quite certainly without foundation. No doubt this prediction had a certain validity in the context of the kind of social conditions that existed in England at the end of the eighteenth century. But in the context of modern capitalist society, the socio-economic function of land rent has been transformed, just as a landlord class has been largely dissolved. More particularly, land rent is no longer a kind of exogenously imposed tax on economic progress, a tax that is then dissipated by the extravagances of a parasitic landowning class. Rather, *as soon as it is appropriated, rent enters into the stream of new investment capital at large.*

Second, with the concentration of control over private land development into a functionally specific branch of production, conflicts over the urban land question have been absorbed (though with some ambiguity) into the conflict between capital and labor, generally. But, in addition, this same concentration has meant that some of these conflicts have taken on the form of specific conflicts among different branches of capital. As we have stressed in an earlier section, there is nothing unique about the general structure and rationality of the property development branch that causes it to be different in kind from other capitalist branches of production. What is unique, as our analysis suggests, is the final product: urban land itself. Moreover, precisely because this uniqueness resides, at least in large part, in the character of urban land as a rather curious phenomenon that is collectively produced but privately appropriated, exchanged, and utilized, conflicts over land issues have resulted in the ever-escalating intermediation of the state.

44. The state itself, then, has become intimately bound up with the urban land question. Furthermore, the state, through its planning apparatus, has become the nexus of a series of secondary circuits of appropriation of net national income. More particularly, profits, wages, and rents are now in part a direct function of state planning and control.

Thus, on the one hand, the state levies differential taxes on profits, wages, and rents, thus diminishing these quantities. The revenues raised in this way are then in part devoted to the multifarious material and immaterial infrastructures that are typically supplied by the state in modern urban centers: the construction and coordination of transport linkages, public housing projects, the establishment of recreational facilities, the administration of construction and zoning regulations, the subsidization of industrial enterprises, and so on. These benefits are then recaptured in the form of various increments to profits, wages, and rents. In the first place, these benefits increase *profits* by providing a variety of subsidized inputs to commodity production. In the second place, they increase *wages* (in the sense of total final consumption) both by direct subsidization and by augmenting the total range of social consumption and amenities. In the third place, they increase *land rents*, since all spatially differential improvements in the quality of the urban environment are ultimately capitalized in the price of land. Indeed, it appears more than likely that the predominant share of net national income that is redistributed via urbanization is finally captured in land rent.

Whatever its exact quantitative realization, this process of redistribution of net national income via state intervention in urban development has become the focus of an important secondary manifestation of the primary conflict described above over the distribution of net income shares to capital, labor, and land. This conflict is made politically tangible in the efforts and aspirations of various social groups, including those that have a purely territorial identification to ensure that public decisions on matters of urban development and control are dominantly favorable to them. But, more importantly, the emergence of these new circuits of appropriation has, to some degree, repoliticized and sharpened social and political conflicts. What was once left, for better or for worse, to the agency of a "naturalistic" and, hence, depoliticized market is now the consequence (and is *seen* to be the consequence) of political and administrative decisions. In view of this development, we can now understand how it is that urban planning, which (at least in its institutionalized versions) began its history as a rather innocent and negligible undertaking, has in recent years been moving inexorably into a focal position of controversy and social significance. Concomitantly, it seems that urban planning is also deeply implicated in the "legitimation crisis" of the modern state that Habermas has recently so cogently described.[25]

Prospects for the Urban Land Question

45. If our assessment of the historical process today has any validity, then certain major developments (of far-reaching importance for the urban land question) are likely to become increasingly evident.

Thus, to the extent that the state itself becomes predominantly instrumental in controlling the distribution of the economic surplus, then to the same extent is the locus of socio-economic conflicts likely to shift from direct confrontations between workers and firms to indirect confrontations between workers and firms *via* clashes with the state apparatus. For example, in Canada today, much of the conflict over wage and price controls takes the form of unions and management independently pressuring and lobbying government agencies. In addition, recent events in many of the advanced capitalist countries suggest that the state is more and more likely to mediate subsidiary conflicts among various fractions of the citizenry at large. As it matures, this structural shift in the nature of social conflicts (causing the state to move ever-increasingly into a pivotal situation with respect to those conflicts) is likely to have a decisive impact on political consciousness and, hence, on political practice. It means that all social relations must now become more and more openly politicized. At the very least, this phenomenon is likely to repoliticize the workers' movement, encouraging it to go far beyond simplistic forms of trade unionism to rediscover its own origins in the search for human emancipation and self-determination.

As a corollary, that search, in all probability, will be nowhere more visible than in the general domain of urban life. Hitherto, this domain has tended to be splintered in a way such that workers' movements as such have focussed on wage demands, while citizens' movements as such have focussed on attempts at improving various aspects of the quality of the urban environment. Yet, for all the reasons adduced above, it is especially in the matter of urban development that we would expect the hand of the state to be evident in the near future. This emerging tendency may well finally reveal the structural connections (rooted as they are in a single, global process of appropriation of net income) between exploitation in the work place and disparities and dislocations in the community. In this way, there would seem to be real possibilities for progressive and mutually beneficial coalitions between workers' and citizens' organizations. Paradoxically, the great danger is that this same increased politicization of urban issues will have precisely an opposite effect, and that augmented doses of "planning" will merely intensify intergroup and intercommunity antagonisms. This is surely an area in which meaningful political education is a real possibility and, indeed in part, a decisive element in the future that we choose for ourselves.

46. Clearly, prospective developments in state strategies, class relations, and political practices are likely both to undergo significant transformations in the future and to open up definite possibilities for political action around the urban land question.

In conclusion, it needs to be stressed that while we have predicted a number of future developments, we by no means assert the inevitability of those developments; they seem to us to be implicit in the current conjuncture, though they are definitely not certainties. Nevertheless, our analysis has revealed what is surely an irreversible historical process at the core of the urban land question; namely, the social momentum that emanates from the contradiction between the socialized production of urban land in its totality, on the one hand, and the privatization of concomitant benefits, on the other. For structural reasons, this momentum evolves progressively in the direction of yet more socialization but less privatization of the urban land nexus. Given this trend, conflicts surrounding the issue of urban land will likely (but not necessarily) lead to the gradual maturation of a specifically socialist political praxis. In the end, the fact that we refrain from any easy and rhetorical conclusions is only a recognition of the evident condition that the extent to which human beings *act* is contingent upon the degree of their political organization, education, and determination. These are matters that in part depend upon an adequate prior theoretical clarity, but they also crucially depend upon a real engagement in ongoing political practice.

Notes

1. Cf. Edward C. Banfield, *The Unheavenly City* (Boston: Little, Brown, & Co., 1973).
2. For a very thorough review (from within) of this epistemology, see Harry W. Richardson, *The New Urban Economics: And Alternatives* (London: Pion, 1977).
3. Cf. Stephen Gale and Eric G. Moore, eds., *The Manipulated City* (Chicago: Maaroufa Press, 1975).
4. Consider, for example, Graham Barker, Jennifer Penny, and Wallace Seccombe, *High-Rise and Super-profits* (Kitchener, Ontario: Dumont Press Graphix, 1973); also, James Lorimer and E. Ross, eds., *The City Book* (Toronto: James Lorimer & Co., 1976).
5. David Harvey, "Class-Monopoly Rent, Finance Capital, and the Urban Revolution," University of Toronto Department of Urban and Regional Planning, Papers on Planning and Design no. 4 (Toronto, 1974). While the notion of class-monopoly rents is evidently Harvey's, it would, nevertheless, be unfair to treat Harvey as a simple manipulated city theorist. His work, in fact, has been consistently of a rigorousness and sophistication that sets it far above the easy assertions of those theorists.
6. J. S. Mill, *Principles of Political Economy* (New York: Kelley, 1965).
7. Note, however, that these prices are not determined through the interplay of market forces, but through managerial control.
8. J. D. Herbert and Benjamin H. Stevens, "A Model for the Distribution of Residential Activity in Urban Areas," *Journal of Regional Science* 2 (1960): 21–36.
9. A philosophy that is criticized from within, as it were, on two fronts: the Romantic (cf. Jane Jacobs, *The Death and Life of Great American Cities* (New York: Random House, 1961); and the reactionary (cf. Banfield, *Unheavenly City*).
10. To dramatize the point: If we could somehow return to the Middle Ages and take a sample of consumer preferences, is it even remotely conceivable that we might discover hidden, however deeply, in the psyche of some serf, a primeval dream of a suburban bungalow neatly set within a rectangle of lawn? Ultimately, the doctrine of consumer sovereignty bears a disconcerting resemblance to Hegel's World Spirit. In this regard, Preteceille calls the doctrine "*idealist*" in the sense that it presupposes that objective socio-historical conditions are simple matters of subjective decidability; whereas, in fact, human subjectivity acquires a real (as opposed to a metaphysical) existence only in the context of a *given*, concrete historical reality. Cf. Edmond Preteceille, "Besoins sociaux et socialisation de la consommation," *La Pensée*, no. 180 (1975): 22–60.
11. William Alonso, *Location and Land Use* (Cambridge: Harvard University Press, 1965); Richard F. Muth, *Cities and Housing* (Chicago: University of Chicago Press, 1969); Robert M. Solow, "On Equilibrium Models of Urban Location," in *Essays in Modern Economics*, ed. Michael Parkin (London: Longmans, 1973), pp. 2–16.
12. Friedrich Engels, *The Housing Question* (Moscow: Progress Publishers, 1970).
13. The credulity of the reformist position is succinctly typified in a recent statement by Lorimer:

> ... city governments in Canada are strongly and directly tied to the property investment and land development industry, with the strongest links being the arrangement which puts a hard core of small-time property industry people like contractors, real estate agents, architects, developers, and real estate lawyers on city councils. These politicians with property industry connections form the centre of a majority voting bloc which implements policies protecting and promoting the interests of developers, property investors, and other industry members. (Cf. James Lorimer, "Canada's Urban Experts: Smoking Out the Liberals," in Lorimer and Ross, *City Book*, p. 98.)

Lorimer goes on with the well-meaning, but finally vapid, suggestion that "The alternative to property industry domination of city hall is a radical alliance ... [which could] ... end the exploitation of city residents and the city itself by the property industry."
14. Cf. the recent symposium *Rent Control: A Popular Paradox* (Vancouver: The Fraser Institute, 1975). Admittedly, this is a conservative organization and one less than adequate in its prescriptions, though devastatingly accurate in its analysis of the deficiencies of rent control policies.
15. No statement as to the general nature of commodity production can be complete without a concomitant theory of value (hence, a theory of profit). However, this is a complex, subtle, and controversial question. Since we cannot do justice to the question in present context, we reluctantly adopt the *pis aller* of neglecting it.
16. Walter Isard, *Location and Space-Economy* (Cambridge, Mass.: M.I.T. Press, 1956).
17. See, in particular, Piero Sraffa, *Production of Commodities by Means of Commodities* (Cambridge: Cambridge University Press, 1960).
18. C. Topalov, *Capital et propriété foncière* (Paris: Centre de Sociologie Urbaine, 1973).
19. Note, however, that the early work of Koopmans and Beckmann has seemed to show that, even under these circumstances, competitive locational systems are intrinsically unstable and divergent from equilibrium. This work has always had something of a maverick position in mainstream urban and spatial economic theory. We suggest that it may well prove to be of central importance in the light of our own discussion. Cf. Tjalling C. Koopmans and Martin Beckmann, "Assignment Problems and the Location of Economic Activity," *Econometrica* 25 (1957): 53–76.

20. In seeking to maximize their private gains, individuals will, of course, undertake land-use conversions only when the private opportunity costs of conversion exceed the actual private costs of conversion; that is, these conversions are always delayed by a factor that is a function of the privately incurred fixed costs sunk into existing structures. In practice, these fixed costs are invariably heavy. The conversion process will, therefore, be far from instantaneous.

21. Michael B. Teitz, "Toward a Theory of Urban Public Facility Location," *Papers of the Regional Science Association* 21 (1968): 35–51.

22. See, for example, the two outstanding historical studies: Leonardo Benevolo, *The Origins of Modern Town Planning* (Cambridge, Mass.: M.I.T. Press, 1967); and Karl Polanyi, *The Great Transformation* (Boston: Beacon Press, 1944). A theoretical overview is presented in Shoukry T. Roweis, *Urban Planning in Early and Late Capitalist Societies,* University of Toronto Department of Urban and Regional Planning, Papers on Planning and Design no. 7 (Toronto, 1975).

23. Allen J. Scott, "Land Use and Commodity Production," *Regional Science and Urban Economics* 6 (1976): 147–60.

24. A strategy that Offe and Ronge have also recently identified as a strategy of so-called "administrative recommodification." See Claus Offe and V. Ronge, "Theses on the Theory of the State," *New German Critique* 6 (1975): 137–45.

25. Jurgen Habermas, *Legitimation Crisis* (Boston: Beacon Press, 1973).

Chapter 3

CONFLICT AVOIDANCE AND CONFLICT SUPPRESSION: THE CASE OF URBAN POLITICS IN THE UNITED STATES

KENNETH NEWTON

Much of the writing on political conflict deals with actual or manifest conflict; that is, with conflict as it actually breaks out in an observable form. Not infrequently this work is based on a consensus model of society which assumes that conflict is something which interrupts the "normal" conditions of a stable equilibrium. And, not unusually, the approach is a conservative one which views conflict as "a bad thing" (even if it does have its positive functions) and one which is more concerned with explaining how the status quo is maintained than how it is changed.

There is another approach: Instead of treating conflict as an aberration, society can be seen as a web of tensions and incompatible interests which make conflict a ubiquitous part of the social order.[1] From this perspective it is not the presence, but the absence, of conflict which needs explanation. In other words, while the concensus model leads to the questions: "Why is there so much conflict in society? and What are the situations typically generating it?" the conflict model stands these questions on their heads and asks, "Why is there little overt conflict in society? and What are the circumstances typically suppressing it?"

The purpose of this paper is to examine the conflict-avoiding and conflict-suppressing consequences of the institutions of urban government as they have developed in the United States over the past two hundred years. A major theme of the paper is that there has been an institutionalization of bias against overt political conflict, especially class conflict. To explain this approach it may be helpful to say briefly what is meant by "the institutionalization of bias." E. E. Schattschneider's famous statement that "organization means the mobilization of bias" has generally been used to refer to the capacity of individuals to suppress issues and to make nondecisions.[2] It refers to the more or less conscious intentions of people.[3] The institutionalization of bias, however, refers to a capacity of social institutions and structures to affect the course of events irrespective of the conscious intentions of individuals or groups. In this sense it has the same sort of structural connotations as the term "institutionalized racism" and, thus, one claim of the paper is that political institutions have exercised an effect on whether conflict emerges in American urban politics or not, and that this effect has sometimes operated independently of the behavior and motivations of groups or individuals.

Underlying the central theme of the paper is the problem of "American exceptionalism."[4] In contrast to most western, industrialized societies, especially those in northern Europe, urban politics in the United States displays some notable characteristics, including: relatively poorly developed party systems; an absence of socialist parties; relatively low levels of political participation; low levels of structured political conflict, especially class conflict; and the provision of a narrow range of public services.[5] It will be argued that part of the explanation for American uniqueness lies in the success with which the institutions of urban government have managed to suppress, defuse, deflect, and avoid overt political conflict, particularly class conflict.[6]

Any discussion of the absence of conflict, however, raises important questions about dealing with things that do not happen. In the same way that some have claimed that nondecisions are nonevents which cannot be empirically studied,[7] so the absence of conflict may be something which cannot be studied. Yet many areas of the social sciences try to account for things which have not happened: the absence of a strong revolutionary movement in contemporary Britain, for example. In addition, there are empirical studies and theoretical arguments which show that nondecisions can be examined in much the same way as are actual decisions.[8] Besides, explanations of both conflict and its absence are ultimately dependent upon purely conjectural arguments involving counter-factuals: statements about why conflict breaks out are bound up with notions about the conditions in which it does not break out; statements about why it does not break out are bound up with notions about why it does.

The paper has four sections, each of which will discuss the main historical types of urban government which have existed in the United States since the eighteenth century. The first considers the nature of local democracy and political conflict in preindustrial townships, and the second considers the period of transition from small townships to large industrial cities, a period dominated by the machines and their Bosses. The third then considers the consequences of reformed governments, which were set up in reaction to the machine. And the fourth examines some of the effects of the fragmented government of modern metropolitan areas. A final section then argues that the analysis has some implications for general conflict theory and modifies the theory accordingly.

Conflict in Preindustrial Townships

Acute and overt political conflict was not a great problem in most preindustrial townships. Most were small and isolated, ruled by elites who exercised power over jobs, housing, education, land, the church, and charity. Even without this control over physical and spiritual life, small communities often exert powerful pressures for social conformity and conservatism, and they tend to develop clear and rigid social hierarchies.[9] Dissidence of any kind had a high social and economic cost and, consequently, political conflict and change is notable for its absence.[10] In this sense the term "communal" is synonymous with "traditional."[11]

One can get a rough idea of political life in the typical preindustrial community by examining the isolated townships which exist even now, although they are changing under the powerful influences of modern society. A graphic picture of one such community as it existed in the 1950s is drawn in Vidich and Bensman's study of "Springfield," a township of 2,500 in upper New York State. The community shared an ideology of equality and democracy, but this contrasted starkly with the realities of a rather rigid and hierarchical social structure in which social distinctions and exclusiveness were matched by a virtual disenfranchisement of large sections of the community. The factionalism of community life was not expressed overtly or politically; and, in fact, issues were scarcely aired in the formal political arena, for the system was dominated by a small elite of businessmen and wealthy farmers whose main aim was to minimize taxes. Politics consisted of an endless ritual of indecisive talk which led to nondecisions and the avoidance of issues. The result was political paralysis and the maintenance of the status quo.[12]

When set against this, the picture of the New England township as the final resting place of direct democracy turns out to be not merely idealized or romanticized, but also, plain wrong. Government by public meeting is possible only in small places, but small places tend to create claustrophobic political atmospheres which make it difficult to express grievances without turning them into rather explosive, personal matters.[13]

Small towns and villages could not last for ever, of course, for with the growth of industry came cities, with their huge and concentrated urban working class. The breakdown of the old, preindustrial order presented acute problems for all societies, but there were special difficulties in the United States. First, while many European cities were old enough and large enough to have built up social and political systems which could absorb large numbers of migrants,[14] American cities were virtually created out of large waves of migrants who had little or no experience of urban life; early industrial cities in the United States were urban places populated mainly by rural people. Second, these people were drawn from a wide variety of different racial, religious, ethnic, and national groups. This alien, uprooted, disorganized, and tumultuous mass created severe political problems for the United States.[15]

The Machine

The problem was met on a variety of fronts, the machine being the political response. While the industrial cities of northern Europe were developing trade union and working-class movements, American cities were creating machine politics, their own unique form of political organization which used patronage and spoils, bribery and corruption, to buy immigrants' votes and then sell them in the political marketplace. Since it was virtually impossible to appeal to the broad class interests of an enormously diverse urban population, the machine used material and specific inducements in the forms of money, goods, and jobs to appeal to particular social and ethnic groups.

The machine had a profoundly conservative influence upon American politics, for, in the first place, it did nothing to organize the working class into a powerful and coherent political force; to the contrary, it had an interest in maintaining a divided population, for in this way it could manipulate and control the electorate. With its highly developed form of ethnic and community-based politics, the machine reinforced differences within—rather than among—social strata, and thus "it divided the poor against each other."[16] The machine did not create the social fragmentation of American cities, but it thrived upon it, and hence "its preoccupation with ethnic-coalition politics to the virtual exclusion of class politics."[17] By dividing it could rule, provided only that the divisions did not find an organized form of political expression.[18] In addition, the machine was a conservative influence because it offered immediate material inducements rather than long-term economic or political change. It bought votes with bribes, not election promises, and it put corruption and ward heeling before issues and ideology. It emphasized control and manipulation rather than participation or discussion. Whatever else they may have been, Bosses were not rabble rousers; to the contrary, as George Washington Plunkitt made clear, the Bosses rarely made political speeches.[19] Their power lay in an ability to buy votes, and this depended upon the political quiescence of the electorate. The last thing the machine wanted was an active electorate with an interest in city government. As one precinct captain explained: "I never take leaflets or mention issues or conduct rallies in my precinct. After all, this is a question of personal friendship between me and my neighbours."[20] The machine flourished where the only form of political activity was the selling of votes, where people were ignorant of political ideas and issues, and where apathy ruled the day. In brief, the machine was conservative, divisive, and conflict suppressing.

The machine's ability to defuse explosive political issues and control political conflict has been well recognized.[21] Meyerson and Banfield, for example, point out the machine's ability to:

> ... insulate traditional democratic values and institutions from the forces which unscrupulous demagogues using mass communications media can so easily unloose in a society deeply divided by ethnic, economic, and other conflicts. Naively to destroy the political machines ... is to run the risk of deepening the conflicts which already exist, while at the same time discarding a social structure by which conflicts may be confined and managed.[22]

Meyerson and Banfield fail to explain how the machine, of *all* forms of political organization, could possibly insulate *democratic* values, just as they fail to explain how the amorality of the machine differs from the "unscrupulousness" they refer to. They are quite right, however, to emphasize its conflict-confining and conflict-managing function. It performed this role most efficiently in its day and had a lasting impact on American politics at both national and local levels.[23]

But why did the Bosses want to win elections and control city governments? Many studies of the machine are so fascinated by its organization that they forget to ask this question, although contemporary critics of the machine knew the answer well enough. Writing about Boss Butler of St. Louis, Lincoln Steffens makes the point that the business of the machine was not politics at all, but business itself. Moreover, this business involved influential citizens, capitalists, and great corporations to whom the Bosses sold the privileges, franchises, and real estate of their cities.[24] The source of machine corruption was, in Steffens' view, not the bottom of society, but the top; it was not the ordinary citizen who sold his vote, but leading businessmen who bought contracts.[25]

Even if businessmen did not actually create machines, they certainly worked closely with them and profited from them. Machines helped to build a political order in which business could operate, and they were able to consolidate the popular vote and deliver it into the hands of those who would "be considerate of business interests."[26] The Boss served, as Merton writes, as "the business community's ambassador in the otherwise alien (and sometimes unfriendly) realm of government ... the Boss and his machine were an integral part of the organization of the economy."[27] In a marvelous piece of understatement in his famous study of the functions of the machine, Merton argues that with the Bosses on their side, businessmen could "avoid the chaos of uncontrolled competition" and so "meet their objectives of maximizing profits."[28] In other words, Bosses and businessmen created monopolies and they realized the profits which followed.

But the machine was a transitory phenomenon which bridged an awkward period between rural and urban society. It served well while people of peasant stock adjusted to a new environment, but by the second and third generation, and with increasing affluence, it was no longer so effective. It disintegrated not because its goals were challenged, but because its means became inappropriate in a more modern and developed economic system. There is evidence to show that as the economy of the nineteenth century changed, so also did the kinds of businessmen who took an interest in the machine, and that as the century drew to a close, so businessmen came to prefer a new political system altogether.[29] First, the machine became too expensive and took too large a share of profits.[30] Second, the largest corporations were trying to break down local monopolies in order to create national markets. Third, there emerged a new generation of young businessmen who had inherited, not earned, their fortunes and who criticized their elders for supporting the crude corruption and amorality of the machine.[31] The new wave wanted to replace the machine with a new set of political institutions which would serve its own interests.

Reformed Government

These institutions took the shape of reformed government, the ostensible aim of which was the elimination of corruption, the promotion of efficiency and democracy, and the representation of the public interest.[32] While some reformers were sincere in wanting these things, the rhetoric of others has to be decoded in order to get at its real meaning. For them, efficiency means minimizing government activity and cutting taxes on the grounds that no government is good government; the public interest meant the interest of those who knew that what was good for business was good for America; and democracy meant decision making by "the best qualified"; that is, by businessmen and their professional assistants.[33]

At any rate, the reform movement was led by top businessmen and professionals, and their reform almost always favored them.[34] The introduction of nonpartisan elections which made political parties illegal (in theory, if not in practice) took away one of the major assets of the man in the street: his right to combine with others to form a party which could then be used to finance and organize election campaigns. Those who have ample private resources and who do not rely on the collective resources of political parties start the nonpartisan electoral race a full lap in front.

Thus, summarizing a considerable amount of research, Dye writes that nonpartisanship reduces the turnout of low-income, labor, ethnic, and democratic voters, while increasing the influence of well-educated, high-income WASPs. It also increases the influence of civic associations and the press, and both usually endorse high-status candidates.[35]

At-large elections have a similar effect. They generally handicap working-class and minority groups, since they increase the costs of election campaigns. They also put high-status election candidates at an advantage, since their standing in the community gives them high visibility and they can better afford the high costs of election campaigns.[36] In contrast, ward elections favor the less advantaged. Working-class or black wards, for example, stand a good chance of returning working-class or black representatives, no matter how low the election turnout; and, since candidates can fight on their own territory, they do not need to spend a lot of campaign money. In practice, at-large and nonpartisan elections tend to reinforce conservatism, to restrict public officials to the wealthier strata, to reduce the accountability of elected officials, and generally to place obstacles in the path of working-class and minority political involvement.[37]

But the institutions of reformed government should be assessed ultimately by the quality and quantity of their products: the provision of public services and the distribution of costs and benefits. In this respect it is interesting that not only do reformed cities spend less and tax less, but also that they are less responsive to internal community conflicts.[38] Not only are reformed governments less likely than others to respond to social conflict among their citizens, but they are also unlikely to handle any kind of political conflict if they can help it.[39] Thus, a study of Oakland, a fairly typical council-manager city, finds that "If there is one thing that Oakland city councilmen do not like, it is conflict. And they have become adept at conflict avoidance."[40]

While the machine encouraged the working class to use its vote (if in an apolitical way) and gave positions of modest political power to working people, the beauty of reformed government is that it minimizes political participation without actually disenfranchising anyone. It obstructs working-class, and even middle-class, participation, and it raises the costs of putting some sorts of issues on the political agenda. In other words, reformed government helps to secure the political power of the wealthy and helps insulate them from political attack. In a word, reform is a mechanism of conflict avoidance and conflict suppression.

Between the Civil War and the New Deal almost every big city had a machine at one time or another.[41] Now, however, most large cities have one or another of the characteristics of reformed government,[42] while a high proportion of small, middle-class cities have taken on the whole reform program of at-large, nonpartisan elections and either council-manager or commission forms of government.[43] Why were the big cities never wholly captured by the reform movement? The answer lies in the fact that, first, working-class opposition was too strong[44] and, second, that the reformers found a much better solution to their problems. Rather than stay in the city and fight the machine on its own ground, they were able to use the newly available automobile and move to the country. The wealthy simply moved out to the suburbs, drew political boundaries around themselves, gave themselves the trappings of reformed government, used the full panoply of zoning, tax, and building regulations to keep out undesirables, and settled down to a pleasant and peaceful life insulated socially, politically, and economically from most of the nastiness of the big city.

Suburban Autonomy and Metropolitan Fragmentation

It is usually argued that big businessmen withdrew from city politics in the early twentieth century mainly because the growth of national corporations produced socially and geographically mobile managers who had no stake in local politics. While there is much truth in this line of argument, it is, at the same time, not the whole story. Another part of it concerns the flight to the suburbs.

The importance of suburbanization is hinted at in some studies, but it is not fully recognized. Clelland and Form, for example, found differences between the city of "Wheelsburg," where economic dominants still played an active role in community politics and social life, and the city of "Cibola," where they had withdrawn almost entirely from city politics. They attribute these differences to a whole variety of factors, but they also point out—albeit in an incidental footnote—that many of Cibola's economic dominants lived outside the city, whereas this was not the case in Wheelsburg.[45] Similarly, Bradley and Zald explain the withdrawal of social and business leaders from politics in Chicago, and while they also offer all sorts of good reasons, they hit upon suburbanization almost as an afterthought. "Furthermore," they write, "movement to the suburbs removed many of them [social and business leaders] from the political scene."[46] In the case of both Cibola and Chicago, movement to the suburbs seems to have been one factor which caused big business withdrawal from city politics. To this extent, the new suburban elite did not participate because it no longer lived in the city, no longer paid taxes there, and no longer sent children to school there.

The proliferation of politically autonomous suburbs during the first half of this century may have played as important a part in social and political life in the U.S. as the growth of the joint-stock company has played in the development of its economic life. In particular, the incorporation of thousands of new suburbs has contributed to what is probably the dominant characteristic of metropolitan government in the United States: its fragmentation in combination with a large measure of municipal autonomy.[47] In 1967 there were, in the United States, over 38,000 counties, municipalities, and townships, plus another 43,000 school districts and special districts.[48]

The significance of metropolitan fragmentation is increased enormously by the fact that local government boundaries tend to coincide with important socio-economic cleavages in the population. This is no accident, of course, since the economic logic of metropolitan fragmentation entails the wealthier municipalities, using every means at their disposal, to maintain their tax base while minimizing demands on their public services. Since the wealthier communities generally have slightly more powerful weapons with which to protect themselves against the less affluent,[49] the result is a hierarchy of local government units which runs from the small enclaves of the super-rich all the way down to the central cities. The latter are socially quite mixed, and they have their central business districts; but they generally have the most acute social and economic problems and the fewest resources to deal with them. The economic consequences of this system are widely discussed and understood,[50] but the political ones have often been misinterpreted or misunderstood.[51] It would take much more than the space available in the rest of this essay to discuss these consequences fully, but those involving the suppression and avoidance of political conflict can be sketched briefly.

The creation of a large number of political arenas at the local level has a tendency to reduce political conflict and competition. Social groups can confront each other when they are in the same political arena, but this possibility is reduced when they are separated into different arenas. Political differences are easier to express when groups occupy the same political system and share the same political institutions, but this is more difficult when the groups are divided by political boundaries and do not contest the same elections, do not fight for control of the same elected offices, do not contest public policies for the same political units, or do not argue about the same municipal budgets. If different groups in the same municipality disagree about how public money should be spent, then they can, in principle, compete for control of the budget. If they are divided into distinct jurisdictions, they have no legal or political claim on one another. Norton Long has written that "American government has been largely based on placing its fundamental politics out of reach of its formal politics,"[52] and the multiplicity of local governments is a major cause of this disassociation.

The fact that it is difficult to deal with some sorts of issues at the local level does not mean that the issues cannot climb the political system to the state or federal level. Indeed, groups do take their grievances to a higher level of government, or else they move sideways into the courts. However, to conduct a political campaign at a higher level often takes more money, time and organization than does local activity. The whole purpose of grass-roots democracy is to provide ordinary people with a level of government which can be dealt with on a simple, day-to-day basis; all it requires is a few friends and neighbors, a minimum of funds and skill, and a modicum of political determination. To move to a higher level inevitably raises the price of political effort, and this handicaps the less affluent.

The same is true of sideways movement into the courts because legal action usually takes time and money and because, while each individual has the right of access to elected political representatives, not every political grievance has the legal basis which makes it eligible for a court hearing. In short, the move to state or federal levels, or into the courts, helps to exclude some groups from the political arena and makes effective political action relatively expensive for others.

Robert Dahl has argued that the existence of a huge number of territorial units has the merit of denationalizing conflict; that is, of taking strain off the national political arena which is already overpopulated by potentially explosive issues.[53] However, since fragmentation also tends to delocalize conflict as well, the end result is a tendency to remove political conflict from the whole system. Moreover, to delocalize conflict is to reduce the chances of this conflict ever reaching the national level at all because many interests need a local base on which to organize themselves. An effective party system at the national level, for example, is difficult to sustain without thousands and thousands of party branches at the local level. Without them, national party organization is likely to be a puny affair. In other words, to delocalize conflict is to denationalize conflict, and to do both is to depoliticize the system altogether.

The tendency to eliminate politics works at two levels of the local system: politics within communities tends to be a low-key affair, while the politics of whole metropolitan areas is often notable for its absence. Thus, the suburbs are noted for their nonpolitics. In Robert Wood's words, "In the final analysis, the suburban man may become a-political altogether . . . whatever conflict of interest exists in the suburb must express itself informally, secretly, and without the sanction of law."[54] In many ways the wheel has turned full circle, the suburban community creating the claustrophobic, apolitical atmosphere of the preindustrial township.

This is complemented by low levels of political activity in some large cities. For example, Pressman describes how Oakland lacks strong and active groups and parties and, consequently, how public officials lack the means and the incentive to find out about public preferences to create programs. According to Pressman, "It often appears as though politics in

Oakland does not exist."[55] Oakland is not unique, for local election turn-out is low in the U.S.,[56] and local parties, which most contemporary theo-rists insist are cardinal for democracy, are generally weak.[57] Similarly, voluntary organizations are much less active and numerous than some pluralists have assumed. Although there is remarkably little empirical research, one of the few systematic studies found that relatively few volun-tary organizations participated in community affairs and concluded that their role in creating pluralist conditions should be questioned.[58] When pieced together, this general picture of low turnout, weak parties, and relatively sparse and passive voluntary associations strongly supports Pressman's statement about Oakland: it often appears as if politics does not exist.

The politics of whole metropolitan areas is even more difficult to find. The balkanization of the metropolis means that there is no machinery for governing the whole metropolis; and, hence, it is difficult to make, or even think about, areawide decisions for areawide problems. The politics of a large number of political units is unlikely to be much more than the sum of its parts, simply because carefully maintained boundaries make it dif-ficult to put anything larger together. The result is a series of parish-pump and parochial politics in which small issues rule the day for want of a political structure which could handle anything larger. The statement that "there is only one way to lay a sidewalk" epitomizes the system; it assumes that local government should be concerned with laying sidewalks and not with social and economic planning on a grander scale. And, since large-scale solutions to large-scale problems are virtually ruled out, then some lines of political development (with its attendant conflict) are stillborn, if they are ever conceived at all. For this reason Lowi concludes that Ameri-can cities are well run but badly governed.[59]

All this is to say that fragmentation breeds the politics of nondecision making and nongovernment. To quote Luther Gulick: "Once an indivisi-ble problem is divided, nothing effective can be done about it."[60] But if fragmented government is nongovernment, then nongovernment is good government, at least, for those with the resources to solve their own problems.[61] Nongovernment means noninterference with the workings of the economy, low taxes, and low levels of government output. This, in turn, reduces political activity and conflict because there is little sense in becoming involved in a government which does little about public prob-lems. The less a government does, the less is at stake in the political system and the less is one induced to become involved at any stage of the political process; hence, a low election turnout, weak parties, and relatively inactive pressure groups. Where there is not much output, there is not likely to be much input.

Ironically, the subject which generates less controversy than almost any other matter, public or private, is the existence of tens of thousands of local political units. Although the structure of urban government is a public matter, and thus a potential subject for public debate, there is a tendency to take the existence of political boundaries for granted. In fact, political boundaries are often treated as given, citizens seeing them as things which are as much a part of the local topography as rivers or lakes or hills.[62] They are not regularly reviewed, nor are they the subject for annual debate (unlike the municipal budget, for example), so they continue as unquestioned rules of the game.

The issue of metropolitan reform has, of course, been discussed in some circles, especially by academics who see fragmentation as a prime cause of immobilism. However, it has not been very difficult for those who enjoy the status quo to reject reform proposals. In the early years these people were primarily middle-class suburbanites, but more recently it has been the black power and community-control movements. It is difficult to know where these movements will turn when they discover that their political success gives them control mainly over their own poverty. For the most part, however, metropolitan reform is not an issue which arouses great excitement.[63] To this extent fragmentation not only reduces conflict, but the very existence of a fragmented system is unlikely to become the subject of public controversy. Thus, the system contains the seeds of its own preservation.

The system also preserves itself because it is seen primarily as a social and economic artifact, not as a political one. Inequalities in municipal resources and differences in the public services they can buy are viewed as inevitable products of the economic system. Yet, while the economic system is undoubtedly the major cause of individual inequalities, it cannot be held responsible for *municipal* inequalities. While most societies generate economic inequalities, some of them use their political systems to redress the balance by redistributing resources, using relatively centralized and unified local government systems to do so. In the United States, however, political powers such as zoning, building regulations, and taxing are used to perpetuate and even increase municipal inequalities. At first glance, however, it seems that the invisible hand of the pricing system distributes resources among municipalities, and thus the market gets blamed for something the political system has accomplished. The effect of this is a reduction of political conflict and a reinforcement of social and economic divisions.

And, lastly, the system tends to preserve itself because it cannot do anything else. It has already been argued that fragmented government is nondecision-making government, so it comes as no surprise to note that fragmented government is generally incapable of taking the decision to change itself. Past attempts at metropolitan reform have been notoriously unsuccessful, and few people now think of reform as politically feasible. To this extent most actors within the political system seem to accept the structure and work within it, rather than try to change it. Thus, fragmentation not only reduces the amount of conflict over political issues, but it also reduces the amount of conflict over the issue of what sort of government structure is best suited to handling these issues.

Some Implications for Conflict Theory

According to the argument of the last part of this paper, the particular combination of social, economic, and political patterns which one finds in the metropolitan areas of the United States has the effect of reducing the amount of conflict in the political system. These social and economic patterns include the spatial segregation of different class, status, and ethnic groups. The political pattern consists of a fragmented governmental structure in which metropolitan areas are divided and subdivided into many different units of government to form a bewildering mosaic of political units. Furthermore, the social, economic, and political patterns tend to coincide or to overlap, to a large degree, since the boundaries were originally built around and subsequently used to reinforce fundamental social, economic, and ethnic differences. And, finally, the superimposition of political boundaries on top of social cleavages has the effect of markedly reducing the amount of political conflict among different social groups, not only at the local level of the political system, but also at higher levels.

This thesis seems to be basically at odds, however, with the classical theory of conflict as expounded by writers such as Simmel, Coser and Dahrendorf.[64] They argue that conflict is much *more* likely to break out when lines of cleavage are superimposed on one another in a manner such that they reinforce each other. Superimposed cleavages mark out social groups as different from one another on several different fronts—social, economic, linguistic, political, or religious—and with each cumulative difference the chance of open conflict among the groups increases. This would seem to be the situation in urban America where social, economic, and ethnic differences are institutionalized by the boundaries of a fragmented government system. One would have thought, given a general agreement in the literature about the importance of superimposed or reinforced cleavages, that these local government boundaries would have marked out the battle lines for very acute conflict among the different municipalities. How are the claims of classical theory to be reconciled with the approach developed in this paper?

First, there is a point which is itself included under the rubric of classical conflict theory. Although urban political boundaries may divide major social groups, one set of boundaries may well divide the working class internally.[65] To the extent that jurisdictional boundaries crisscross metropolitan areas they may do as much to reinforce divisions within classes as among them. This is well recognized in the conflict literature as a pattern of divisions which tends to integrate society by its inner conflict.

The second point is more important, for it suggests a major modification of orthodox conflict theory: While the superimposition of social, racial, and economic cleavages is likely to increase *social* conflict among groups, the further superimposition of political boundaries on top of these lines of division is likely to reduce *political* conflict. This is for the reason given earlier in this paper: groups divided into different political arenas are likely to find it difficult to fight each other politically for the simple reason that they are in different political arenas, having their separate elections, parties, pressure groups, public services, and budgets. Political boundaries, in other words, tend to have the effect of containing political conflict within them, unless conflict can climb the political system and find its way into a higher government unit embracing the lower ones. Orthodox conflict theory assumes that all social groupings live and work in the same political system (i.e., the nation state), and it overlooks the crucial role that subnational political boundaries can play in splintering conflict generated by superimposed social cleavages. It is not entirely surprising that writers like Simmel, Dahrendorf, and Coser should overlook the effects of political boundaries, for sociologists have not usually been interested in the possible significance of formal constitutional arrangements, disregarding mundane matters such as local government boundaries.

Local government boundaries, however, cannot dissolve political conflict altogether: They cannot make it vanish or disappear. They can, however, deflect it into nonpolitical channels and turn it in on itself. The tendency for conflict to break out *within* individual units of metropolitan government rather than *among* them has already been discussed, but the effect of fragmentation in deflecting conflict into nonpolitical channels has only been hinted at. There is, first, the general tendency for fragmented government to be nondecision-making and ineffective government. This, in turn, encourages citizens to use means other than political ones to change or improve their situation. In other words, it is "exit" via social and geographical mobility that is seen as the solution to problems, not "voice" in the form of political action.[66]

Since those in some of the most powerful offices of urban government have often been unable to do much either to change the political system or to improve its performance,[67] there is even less that the ordinary man in the street can do. As a consequence, it is perfectly rational to try to work for individual, economic improvements, rather than collective, political ones.[68] Thus, energy is directed away from the political system with consequences for low political participation and low levels of political conflict.

Yet the social and economic aspirations of some sections of society are also blocked, and this is due, in part, to the fact that the better-off municipalities are caught up in a system which forces them to defend their boundaries against the less well off. Since neither exit nor voice is a real alternative, these groups resort to economic and political passivity or to illegitimate forms of economic or political action: i.e., to stealing and mugging; to political protests, such as bombing or demonstrations; or to mixtures of both, such as race riots or attacks on police. All these forms of political activity are prevalent in the United States by comparison to many other western industrial societies. In short, since conflict cannot be easily or effectively handled by the formal institutions of urban government, it expresses itself in a different form, and this helps to explain why interpersonal violence is relatively high in the United States, while political conflict is subdued.

Perhaps the most common explanation for the high level of interpersonal violence in the U.S. is Merton's theory of anomie which argues that American culture places a heavy emphasis on the goal of economic success, without an equally heavy emphasis on the legitimate means by which this goal might be achieved.[69] The argument advanced in this paper is a structural one which explains the pattern in terms of the lack of appropriate political institutions by which classes or social groups might improve their economic situation. Merton's theory is essentially an individualistic and cultural one, while this paper propounds a structural explanation of class behavior. Nevertheless, the two kinds of explanations are complementary, not incompatible.

Notes

1. The approach is elaborated by Ralf Dahrendorf, "Out of Utopia: Toward a Re-Orientation of Sociological Analysis," *American Journal of Sociology* 64 (1958): 115–27.
2. E. E. Schattschneider, *The Semi-Sovereign People* (New York: Holt, Rinehart, and Winston, 1960), p. 71.
3. On this point see Steven Lukes, *Power: A Radical View* (London: Macmillan & Co., 1974), pp. 21–25.
4. A recent and useful discussion of American exceptionalism can be found in Ira Katznelson, "The Patterning of Class in the United States: An Approach to American Exceptionalism" (Paper presented to the 1976 Annual Meeting of the American Political Science Association, Chicago, September 2–5, 1976).
5. I have in mind, particularly, the contrasts between urban politics in the U.S. and Britain, for which see L. J. Sharpe, "American Democracy Reconsidered," pts. 1 and 2, *British Journal of Political Science* 3 (1973): 1–28 and 129–67; Kenneth Newton, "City Politics in Britain and America," *Political Studies* 17 (1969): 208–18; idem, "Community Decision Makers and Community Decision Making in England and the United States," in *Comparative Community Politics*, ed. Terry N. Clark (New York: John Wiley, 1974), pp. 55–86.
6. This is not to say that these institutions have not also encouraged political conflict in some ways; only that, among other ways, they may be examined in terms of their capacity to suppress political conflict, and that this capacity is inadequately recognized at present. Nor is it to say that institutional or structural explanations are incompatible with cultural or behavioral ones, to the contrary; but cultural and behavioral explanations have been very widely explored already. I shall return briefly to this theme at the end of the paper.
7. See, for example, Nelson W. Polsby, *Community Power and Political Theory* (New Haven, Conn.: Yale University Press, 1963), p. 97.
8. Matthew A. Crenson, *The Un-Politics of Air Pollution* (Baltimore: The Johns Hopkins University Press, 1971); Lukes, *Power: A Radical View;* Frederick W. Frey, "Comment: On Issues and Non-Issues in the Study of Power," *American Political Science Review* 65 (1971): 1081–101.
9. Some European conservatives advocated extending the franchise in rural areas on the grounds that the voters would support the local notables; see Reinhard Bendix and Stein Rokkan, "The Extension of Citizenship to the Lower Classes," in *European Politics: A Reader,* ed. Mattei Dogan and Richard Rose (London: Macmillan & Co., 1971), p. 19.
10. On this point, see Robert A. Dahl and Edward R. Tufte, *Size and Democracy* (Stanford, Calif.: Stanford University Press, 1973) p. 138.
11. William Kornhauser describes communal society in terms of the inaccessibility of its elites, its traditionally ascribed and fixed social standards, and the difficulty of mobilizing its population in William Kornhauser, *The Politics of Mass Society* (London: Routledge and Kegan Paul, 1960), p. 40.
12. Arthur J. Vidich and Joseph Bensman, *Small Town in Mass Society* (Garden City, N.Y.: Anchor Books, 1960). For an account of how conflict is avoided in small towns and villages in Britain, see Ronald Frankenberg, *Communities in Britain* (Harmondsworth, Middlesex: Penguin Books, 1966), pp. 256–75.
13. Robert A. Dahl, "The City in the Future of Democracy," *American Political Science Review* 61 (1967): 961.
14. Most European cities had already absorbed a large quantity of migrants in the centuries preceding the industrial revolution and had developed a whole set of social, political, and economic institutions to manage the task.
15. For an analysis of the potentially disruptive consequences of migration in the United States, see Oscar Handlin, ed., *Immigration as a Factor in American History* (Englewood Cliffs, N.J.: Prentice-Hall, 1959).
16. Ira Katznelson, *Black Men, White Cities* (Oxford: Oxford University Press, 1973), p. 122.
17. Walter Dean Burnham, "Party Systems and the Political Process," in *The American Party System,* ed. William Nisbet Chambers and Walter Dean Burnham (New York: Oxford University Press, 1975), p. 287.
18. Katznelson, "Patterning of Class," p. 103, argues that the New York machine had a stake in the racial status quo.
19. William L. Riordan, *Plunkitt of Tammany Hall* (New York: Dutton, 1963), p. 8. See also p. 72, where Plunkitt describes political arguments and campaign literature as "rot."
20. Quoted in Martin Meyerson and Edward C. Banfield, *Politics, Planning, and the Public Interest* (Glencoe, Ill.: The Free Press, 1955) p. 72.
21. Good discussions can be found in Ira Katznelson, "The Crisis of Capitalist Society: Urban Politics and Social Control," in *Theoretical Perspectives on Urban Politics*, ed. Willis D. Hawley et al. (Englewood Cliffs, N.J.: Prentice-Hall, 1976), p. 225; and James C. Scott, "Corruption, Machine Politics, and Political Change," *American Political Science Review* 63 (1969): 1144.
22. Meyerson and Banfield, *Public Interest,* pp. 292–93.
23. The longer-term effects on American politics have been discussed by Burnham, "Party Systems."
24. Lincoln Steffens, "The Shamelessness of St. Louis," in Handlin, *Immigration,* p. 97.
25. See Lincoln Steffens, "Who, or What, Started the Evil?"; and Henry Jones Ford, "Separation of Powers Necessitates Corruption," both reprinted in *Urban Government,* ed. Edward C. Banfield (Glencoe, Ill.: The Free Press, 1969), pp. 248–51 and 237–38.
26. Ford, "Corruption," p. 238.
27. Robert K. Merton, *Social Theory and Social Structure* (Glencoe, Ill.: The Free Press, 1957), p. 76.
28. Ibid., p. 75.

29. For an excellent account of how different business interests fought for the control of the New York machine, see Martin Shefter, "The Emergence of the Political Machine: An Alternative View," in Hawley, *Theoretical Perspectives*, pp. 14–44.

30. On the expense of the machine politics, see Scott, "Political Change," pp. 1157–58.

31. Some evidence on this point is presented by Shefter, "Political Machine," p. 39.

32. These features are picked out by Edward C. Banfield and James Q. Wilson, *City Politics* (New York: Vintage Books, 1963), p. 138.

33. The role of "experts" and "the best qualified" in reformed government is discussed by Banfield, *Urban Government*, p. 140.

34. Samuel P. Hays, "The Politics of Reform in Municipal Government in the Progressive Era," reprinted in *Social Change and Urban Politics*, ed. Daniel N. Gordon (Englewood Cliffs, N.J.: Prentice-Hall, 1973), pp. 107–27. James Weinstein has written that ". . . the initiative for commission and manager government came consistently from chambers of commerce and other organized business groups." He also notes that the effect of reform was to place city government firmly in the hands of businessmen. James Weinstein, *The Corporate Ideal in the Liberal State* (Boston: Beacon Press, 1968), p. 99. Reform had exactly the same effect on the control of the educational system—see W. W. Charters, "Social Class Analysis and the Control of Public Education," *Harvard Educational Review* 23 (1953): 268–83.

35. Thomas R. Dye, *Politics in States and Communities* (Englewood Cliffs, N.J.: Prentice-Hall, 1969), pp. 276–78. There is some evidence to show that at-large elections have been introduced as a *conscious* attempt to head off militant political groups, just as some historical research shows that some city governments were reformed in the early part of the century in order to neutralize growing socialist movements. See Kevin R. Cox, *Conflict, Power, and Politics in the City* (New York: McGraw-Hill, 1973), pp. 80–82; and Edward C. Hayes, *Power Structure and Urban Policy: Who Rules in Oakland?* (New York: McGraw-Hill, 1972), pp. 10–14.

36. Oliver P. Williams and Charles R. Adrian, "The Insulation of Politics Under a Non-Partisan Ballot," *American Political Science Review* 53 (1969): 152–63.

37. See, for example, Charles R. Adrian, "Some General Characteristics of Non-Partisan Elections," *American Political Science Review* 46 (1952): 766–76.

38. Robert L. Lineberry and Edmund P. Fowler, "Reformism and Public Policies in American Cities," *American Political Science Review* 61 (1967): 701–16.

39. The political weakness and vulnerability of officials in reformed cities seems to be a major cause of this conflict-avoiding behavior.

40. Jeffrey L. Pressman, "Preconditions of Mayoral Leadership," *American Political Science Review* 66 (1972): 516–17. On the conflict-avoiding tendencies of council-manager cities, see also Charles R. Adrian, "Leadership and Decision Making in Manager Cities," *Public Administration Review* 18 (1958): 208–13; and Oliver P. Williams and Charles R. Adrian, *Four Cities* (Philadelphia: University of Pennsylvania Press, 1963), pp. 292–93. Gilbert's reanalysis of data obtained from 166 cities supports these findings strongly. She finds that conflict is much more prevalent among machine cities than among reformed cities. Claire W. Gilbert, *Community Power Structure* (Gainesville: University of Florida Press, 1972), p. 13.

41. Banfield, *Urban Government*, p. 116.

42. Ibid., p. 148.

43. Raymond Wolfinger and John Osgood Field, "Political Ethos and the Structure of City Government," *American Political Science Review* 40 (1966): 306–26.

44. Meyerson and Banfield, *Public Interest*, p. 290.

45. Donald A. Clelland and William H. Form, "Economic Dominants and Community Power: A Comparative Analysis," *American Journal of Sociology* 69 (1964): 511–21.

46. Donald S. Bradley and Mayer N. Zald, "From Commercial Elite to Political Administrator: The Recruitment of the Mayors of Chicago," *American Journal of Sociology* 71 (1965): 164.

47. Among western societies probably only France, with almost 38,000 communes, is more fragmented; but then France is not a federal state and it is a highly centralized one. It is a high degree of local autonomy combined with fragmentation which gives urban government in the U.S. distinctiveness.

48. The figures are given in Robert A. Dahl, *Democracy in the United States: Promise and Performance* (Chicago: Rand McNally, 1972), p. 212.

49. The point is made by Robert C. Wood, *Suburbia* (Boston: Houghton Mifflin Co., 1958), pp. 212–21; and by Anthony Downs, *Opening Up the Suburbs* (New Haven, Conn.: Yale University Press, 1973).

50. See, for example, the papers in John P. Crecine, ed., *Financing the Metropolis* (Beverly Hills, Calif.: Sage Publications, 1970); Cox, *Politics in the City*; Benjamin Chinitz, ed., *City and Suburb: The Economics of Metropolitan Growth* (Englewood Cliffs, N.J.: Prentice-Hall, 1964); Matthew Edel and Jerome Rothenberg, eds., *Readings in Urban Economics* (New York: Macmillan Co., 1972); Harvey S. Perloff and Lowdon Wingo, eds., *Issues in Urban Economics* (Baltimore: The Johns Hopkins University Press, 1968).

51. Some of the misunderstandings and misinterpretations are discussed in Kenneth Newton, "American Urban Politics: Social Class, Political Structure, and Public Goods," *Urban Affairs Quarterly* 11 (1975): 241–64.

52. Norton E. Long, "Political Science and the City," in *Social Science and the City,* ed. Leo F. Schnore (New York: Praeger, 1967), p. 247.

53. Dahl, "Democracy in the United States," pp. 220–23.

54. Wood, *Suburbia,* pp. 196–97.

55. Jeffrey L. Pressman, *Federal Programs and City Politics* (Berkeley and Los Angeles: University of California Press, 1975), pp. 28, 55, 57.

56. Appropriate comparisons are difficult, but the proportion of adults voting in city elections in the United States appears to be considerably lower than that in France, Italy, the Netherlands, or in England and Wales. For a comparison of local election turnout in the U.S., England, and Wales, see Sharpe, "American Democracy Reconsidered," p. 22.

57. On the importance of party competition for democracy and its weakness in local politics in the U.S., see Dahl, *Democracy in the United States,* pp. 228–31, 241.

58. Robert Presthus, *Men at the Top* (New York: Oxford University Press, 1964), pp. 267–71. See also Betty H. Zisk, *Local Interest Politics* (Indianapolis, Ind.: Bobbs-Merrill, 1973), pp. 21–31, 147–49.

59. Theodore J. Lowi, *The End of Liberalism* (New York: Norton, 1969), p. 193.

60. Luther H. Gulick, "The Rationale for Metropolitan Government," reprinted in *Metropolitan Politics,* ed. Michael N. Danielson (Boston: Little, Brown, & Co., 1966), p. 124.

61. This point is made by Oliver P. Williams, *Metropolitan Political Analysis* (New York: The Free Press, 1971), p. 51; Ross Stephens, "The Power Grid of the Metropolis," in *Future Directions in Community Power Research,* ed. Frederick M. Wirt (Berkeley, Calif.: Institute of Governmental Studies, 1971), p. 135.

62. Stein Rokkan remarks on the tendency to take political boundaries for granted in his foreword to Kevin R. Cox et al., eds., *Locational Approaches to Power and Conflict* (New York: Sage-Halsted, 1974), p. 9.

63. For discussion of reform as a non-issue, see Charles R. Adrian, "Public Attitudes and Metropolitan Decision Making," in *Politics in the Metropolis,* ed. Thomas R. Dye and Brett W. Hawkins (Columbus, Ohio: Charles E. Merrill, 1967), p. 454.

64. Georg Simmel, *Conflict and the Web of Group-Affiliations* (Glencoe, Ill.: The Free Press, 1955); Lewis A. Coser, *The Functions of Social Conflict* (London: Routledge and Kegan Paul, 1956), especially pp. 72–80; Ralf Dahrendorf, *Class and Class Conflict in an Industrial Society* (London: Routledge and Kegan Paul, 1959), pp. 213–15.

65. These divisions may be subtle but they are not negligible—see Bennett M. Berger, *Working-Class Suburb* (Berkeley and Los Angeles: University of California Press, 1968), pp. 80–90.

66. John M. Orbell and Toru Uno, "A Theory of Neighborhood Problem Solving: Political Action vs. Residential Mobility," *American Political Science Review* 66 (1972): 471–89.

67. See, for example, a recent assessment on the rather dismal political record of the mayors of large- to moderate-sized cities—John P. Kotter and Paul R. Lawrence, *Mayors in Action* (New York: Wiley, 1974), pp. 239–43.

68. This is not to say that collective political action is the most rational strategy, only that its likelihood of being used tends to be reduced by the structure of urban government.

69. Merton, *Social Theory,* pp. 131–60.

Chapter 4

LOCAL INTERESTS
AND URBAN POLITICAL PROCESSES
IN MARKET SOCIETIES

KEVIN R. COX

In general terms, this paper is concerned with the relationships between market processes and local political processes in urban areas. In particular, the objective is to specify the conditions under which, in market societies, local interests are likely to be reflected in spatially decentralized, localistic political processes.

More specifically, the paper addresses itself to a curious Anglo-American contrast. American cities are characterized by a vigorous competition between local groups and their political agents solicitous of the future of respective turfs. In British cities this structure of relationships does not emerge with equal clarity.

The paper has two major sections. In the first the contrasting structures of local political processes in American and British cities are identified. In the second major section an attempt is made to arrive at a specification of: first, the general conditions under which these contrasting structures are likely to emerge; and, secondly, of those particular attributes of American and British societies which contribute, to a differential degree, towards the satisfaction of these conditions.

The Structure of Local Political Processes

In American metropolitan areas, distinctively localized political processes can be identified at two geographical scales: that of the jurisdiction and that of the neighborhood. At the jurisdictional level one can document a variety of attempts by respective local governments to manipulate locational relationships to the advantage of their constituents and, presumably, to their own advantage as well. Broadly speaking, a local government attempts, on the one hand, to attract into its jurisdiction that which is utility enhancing; and, on the other hand, to keep out that which is utility detracting. "Utility" at this jurisdictional level is defined largely in fiscal terms.[1] A major policy objective of local governments in American metropolitan areas is to minimize the tax rate. Achievement of this goal depends on maximizing the tax base relative to expenditures and, therefore: (1) attracting into the jurisdiction those individuals and associated land uses which provide positive fiscal externalities; and (2) keeping out those imposing negative fiscal externalities.[2] Somewhat less important goals are behavioral in nature: attracting those residents who will provide positive behavioral externalities in the educational, public safety, and property maintenance areas and keeping out those unable to do so.[3]

The fiscally desirable are attracted by low tax rates which, however, are achieved by keeping out the fiscally undesirable. Achievement of fiscal goals, therefore, depends largely on a variety of exclusionary policies. The most publicized of these are the minimum lot size and single-family residential zoning policies that go under the blanket term "exclusionary zoning."[4] There are other exclusionary policies, however. These include building codes calling for expensive construction, and "gold-plated" subdivision regulations.[5] These can add costs to new homes and, hence, exclude those poorer families likely to generate more in terms of need for public service spending than they would contribute to the local tax base. Failure to implement a program of public housing is an additional exclusionary strategy.[6]

These policies are particularly appropriate for those jurisdictions large areas of which are yet undeveloped. Those inner suburbs and central cities which are entirely built over have focussed on a different set of strategies designed to counter the policies of outer suburbs. It is no exaggeration to state, for example, that one of the attractions of urban renewal and highway construction programs in central cities has been physical removal of the fiscally burdensome poor.[7] Other approaches have included housing code enforcement policies designed to monitor incoming families and attempts to secure rights of extraterritorial taxation.[8]

Policies of this nature, intended primarily to achieve fiscal goals, also facilitate achievement of certain behavioral objectives. Provision of desirable fiscal externalities by households tends to be a concomitant of the behaviorally more desirable. Households consuming relatively large amounts of housing and land and generating little in terms of need for public safety expenditures or other poverty-linked services also tend to be more middle class. Behaviorally, middle-class households are regarded as more desirable by local governments and the constituents they represent: they are publicly safe, their children provide desirable peer groups, and they are more likely to maintain their property.

At the neighborhood level an analogous structuring of the political process is apparent. In this case, however, the counterpart of the local government is the neighborhood organization; and instead of a jurisdictional turf, concern is with geographically more restricted neighborhood turfs. Nevertheless, broad objectives are similar: attract into the neighborhood that which is utility enhancing and keep out that which is utility detracting. More specific expressions of utility, however, do not extend to the fiscal. Rather, major concerns are confined to neighborhood schools, public safety problems, and property values.[9] These three issues, moreover, are clearly interrelated. Public school problems in terms of pupil composition are likely to be reflected in increased delinquency and vandalism in the neighborhood and, possibly, in more mature forms of criminality. Property values represent competitive bids for residential property; these bids, in turn, will be partly based on evaluations of public safety and school problems in the neighborhood.[10]

As at the jurisdictional level, attracting those who provide the positive externalities at issue depends on keeping out those who do not. Exclusion, however, is achieved by policy acts designed to enhance demand for local housing and place it beyond the financial means of families regarded as less desirable. Rezonings, alterations of school pupil composition, alterations in school catchment areas, the location of public housing—all are seen as affecting the demand for neighborhood real estate and, hence, through the price filter, the social composition of the neighborhood. Given the public source of these effects, it is logical to expect neighborhood organizations to attempt to manipulate them in favor of their neighborhood: to lobby, therefore, for those policies thought to enhance the residential quality of the neighborhood and, hence, demand for housing there; and to lobby against those public policies and administrative decisions regarded as having adverse effects on such demand.

In fact, in very general terms, it seems reasonable to characterize these locally based policies, at both neighborhood and jurisdictional levels, as attempts to control housing market processes to local advantage. Housing markets in American cities have welfare impacts of a highly localized character. The view of the metropolitan area held by those directly involved in the production and exchange of housing is as an investment surface. Certain areas are seen as ripe for development, while other areas are regarded as less profitable. Banks regard some neighborhoods as good for mortgage loans, while others are red-lined and starved of credit.[11] Alternatively, banks may merely follow the red-lining activities of insurance companies.[12] Realtors, on the other hand, may regard certain neighborhoods as ripe for social change and attempt to instigate it by blockbusting. The result is a geographical structure of housing opportunities which goes far to explain residential shifts and investment flows among neighborhoods and among jurisdictions.

Residential shifts, however, have important welfare consequences for the residential populations left behind and for those into the midst of whom the newcomers move. Suburban local governments, for example, may find themselves having to raise tax rates in order to cope with an influx of residents moving into properties which detract from, rather than enhance, the jurisdiction's per capita tax base. Older city neighborhoods find themselves having to compete for middle-class residents with newer suburban developments or fashionable prestige rehabilitation projects in the central city. Failure to attract new middle-class residents into existing vacancies results in a deterioration in local school quality, public safety problems, and a general decline in property values.[13]

The function of attempts to manipulate public policy in favor of the neighborhood or to protect the fiscal position of a jurisdiction is to alter the geography of housing investment opportunity. Neighborhood-based action, for instance, serves to maintain the attractiveness of the neighborhood for middle-class buyers and, hence, to preserve a flow of mortgage money into the area. Exclusionary policies on the part of suburban local governments serve to enhance the attractiveness of the jurisdiction for investment in properties, the ultimate owners of which will provide positive, rather than negative, fiscal externalities.

In brief, in American cities households are increasingly forced to participate in the operations of the residential property market. This they do either indirectly, by attempting to make the neighborhood attractive to the housing investor, or directly, by participation in the real estate market itself. With respect to the latter, the degree to which neighborhood organizations form their own real estate operations to bypass private realtors is impressive.[14]

This structuring of urban political processes in America is in substantial contrast to that existing in Britain. Fiscal mercantilism of the sort engaged in by American local governments is—with a few exceptions—virtually unknown.[15] Neighborhood activity is also less apparent. On those occasions when it does emerge, the issues are quite different. Issues of public safety and local schools are notable for their absence. Much more common are, for example: concerns over traffic resulting from road widenings, bridge construction, or the implementation of one-way street systems; concerns over obnoxious land uses, such as polluting activities, taverns, or nightclubs; and concerns over the destruction of historically meritorious physical fabric. Symptomatic is the contrast in disputes over the location of public housing: these seem endemic to the American urban scene, while in Britain dispute is much more exceptional.[16]

In addition, it seems fair to claim that in the British case the interest of local groups and local governments in manipulating housing market flows to local advantage is considerably less apparent.[17] Moreover, in the view of this writer, the housing market focus of local political processes in the U.S. is critical for understanding the conditions under which they emerge. In brief, it has been argued that the competitive involvements of local groups in the urban political process are a response to the localized welfare impacts of urban housing markets. By structuring flows of funds and of residents between jurisdictions and neighborhoods, the welfare of local groups may be placed at risk. Local political involvement is an attempt to manage these housing market flows to local advantage.

This, however, begs two critical questions: First, under what conditions does the housing market have localized welfare impacts? If it is true that local political processes are a response to welfare impacts, then additional clarification should be provided by an understanding of the forces underlying their emergence. Moreover, if this is a correct viewpoint, conditions promoting localized welfare impacts should be more apparent in the American case and less evident in the British one.

The second question focusses on the form taken by the response to local welfare impacts. While it frequently assumes a political form, there has been no obvious reason why this should be so. Given localized welfare impacts, some areas are likely to gain and some to lose, so that the welfare of those in areas which have tended to be adversely impacted could be maintained by relocating to areas favorably affected. In fact, this second question can be handled rather more briefly than the first and is addressed initially in the following section.

Understanding Local Political Processes

Political Response

Critical significance attaches to the role of homeownership. For many households in advanced market societies, the house they own and occupy represents their biggest investment, far exceeding in value other assets, such as savings deposits, securities, and durable consumer goods. Like other investments, moreover, it is one from which they expect a rate of return in the form of a capital gain. Relatively favorable tax treatment of capital gains increases the attractions of the house as an investment so that, for example, a dollar invested in housing is worth considerably more than a dollar invested in a savings account.[18]

Capital gains in the housing market, however, are very dependent on what goes on in the vicinity. The nature of the neighborhood and, in particular, the social character of residents, exercise a serious effect on demand for residential property there and, hence, upon housing values. Housing, moreover, has the important quality of immobility. Relocation of the housing unit and the lot on which it stands to a neighborhood where values are appreciating is precluded by the nature of things.

Protection and enhancement of the value of the house as an investment, therefore, shifts the balance from solutions to localized welfare impacts of a relocational character to in situ political solutions. Consequently, where there are threats to the residential desirability of a neighborhood, one should expect the homeowners to be the ones to become most involved in local political activity. Renters, on the other hand, would be more likely to relocate. There is, in fact, some empirical evidence consistent with this interpretation. Homeowners are substantially more likely to belong to neighborhood-based voluntary organizations, even when holding household income constant.[19] In addition, the fact that renters are almost twice as likely to move as homeowners is well known.[20]

Localized Welfare Impacts

Nevertheless, homeownership only assumes this significance for local political action where there is some stimulus in the form of a threat to the value of housing: i.e., a localized welfare impact. In explaining these localized welfare impacts, moreover, substantial significance is attached to the nature of residential preferences.

Localized welfare impacts presuppose some locational structuring of the housing market which, in turn, sets in motion flows of housing market money and residents having welfare impacts on local populations. Basic to both this locational structuring and resultant welfare impacts are residential preferences. In market societies, three aspects of residential preferences are regarded as important to the argument presented here: In the first place, it is suggested that residential preferences converge more and more on preferences for co-residents; alternative residential locations are increasingly evaluated in terms of the social composition of existing residents.[21] This may be related, for example, to the desirable behavioral externalities provided by middle-class families—desirable peer groups for children, low crime rates, etc.—and to the fiscal externalities provided via their substantially greater per capita consumption of real property.

Second, preferences for co-residents are of a remarkably homogeneous character. In particular, it is assumed that both lower-class and middle-class households prefer to live in middle-class neighborhoods.[22] This is not to say that the preferences of lower-class households are of the same intensity as those of middle-class households[23] or that middle-class neighbors are attractive to lower-class households for the same reasons that they are attractive to middle-class households.[24] Rather, it is to argue that there is some basis, rooted in preference functions, for the attempts of developers, for example, to introduce lower-income housing developments into more middle-class ambiences.

Third, and finally, preferences for co-residents have an asymmetric character about them. While all prefer to live in middle-class neighbor-hoods, not all are able to contribute to the maintenance and enhancement of that "middle classness." While a lower-class household may satisfy its desire to live in a middle-class neighborhood, its presence there reduces the "middle classness" of the neighborhood for existing residents. This is in contrast to a situation in which preferences for co-residents are symmetric, so that those desiring certain co-residents are able to contrib-ute mutually the social attributes regarded as desirable.[25]

While these statements are applicable to residential preferences in market societies everywhere, the *intensity* of preferences for co-residents could conceivably exhibit considerable variability: it is perfectly possible, for example, that households would be more indifferent about co-resi-dents in some national contexts than in others. This has important conse-quences for the emergence of localized welfare impacts.

Consider, for example, the implications of the following set of circum-stances: A town is divided into two areas, one of which is more middle class in its residential composition than the other; preferences for middle-class co-residents are especially intense. Two results follow: On the one hand, there will be a demand to relocate residentially from the more lower-class area to the more middle-class area. This demand will be exhib-ited by both middle-class and lower-class households. To the extent that money can be made from facilitating the relocation of lower-class households into the middle-class area, one can anticipate that this will take place. The real world phenomena of blockbusting, partition into apart-ments for lower-class use of large houses in erstwhile middle-class areas, and the like suggest that this is not an unreasonable expectation. As a general consequence, the housing market will exhibit considerable order of a locational character, investment occurring in the more middle-class area and disinvestment occurring in the more lower-class area.[26]

The result of this locational structuring of the housing market, how-ever, will be serious welfare impacts for some residents of the more middle-class area. As some neighborhoods become socially more mixed, so schools will be seen to deteriorate and problems of public safety, to be aggravated.[27] If the initial partition into middle-class and lower-class areas happens to coincide with a jurisdictional division, then fiscal concerns will be added to these behavioral ones.

On the other hand, consider the consequences of a situation where preferences for co-residents are characterized by a greater degree of indifference. The housing market will exhibit less geographic structuring in terms of social class as other facets of residential desirability become relatively more significant. At the same time the welfare impacts of lower-class residents in middle-class neighborhoods will be substantially re-duced. Residential preferences, therefore, provide the nexus linking up the geographic structuring of the housing market on the one side and its localized welfare impacts on the other.

To clothe these speculations with some predictive power, however, it is necessary to ask why, in some societies, preferences for co-residents might be more intense than in others. Critical in this respect, it is suggested, are the interactions between the social differentiations induced by market processes on the one hand, and nation-specific aspects of culture and jurisdictional organization on the other.

Socially, for example, market relationships tend to differentiate people in manners critical for their acceptability as co-residents. The income inequality typical of market societies, therefore, has implications for variations in the consumption of real property and, hence, for differences in fiscal desirability. It may also be apparent in variations in those public behaviors which distinguish the residentially less desirable from the more desirable. As Smolensky and Gomery have written:

> Reductions in income inequality are good in our view because within obvious limits, it is desirable to get individuals in an urban setting to restrict the range of differences in their consumption bundles. For those activities which we assign to the private sector, some chosen consumption bundles lead to significant negative externalities for everyone, but particularly (at least over significant time intervals) middle-income groups.[28]

How residentially undesirable lower-class people are seen to be, however, depends on the specific nature of the national cultural legacy. The interaction of market processes with aspects of history and culture in the U.S., for example, serves to make the lower class considerably more crime-prone than, say, the lower class in Japan.[29]

Similar interactions can be observed between the socially differentiating effects of market societies and jurisdictional organization. A variety of jurisdictional organizations, for example, appear compatible with market societies. As an important consequence, the degree of local home rule in funding and public provision can vary considerably from one national context to another. This has implications for the desirability of socially differentiated co-residents; the poor, evidently, are seen as considerably more undesirable fiscally where home rule applies than in those cases where local governments receive the bulk of their revenue from the central government.

The U.S.-British Contrast

Consider, in review, the argument thus far: In the first section of the paper the locationally decentralized character of political processes in American metropolitan areas was contrasted to urban political processes in Britain; it was then related to attempts to manage, to local advantage, the localized welfare impacts of the housing market. Subsequent arguments presented an abstract explanation for emergence of localized welfare impacts. These were related to particularly intense preferences for co-residents which result in a locational structuring of the housing market and serious welfare impacts for residents in the areas regarded as desirable. The intensity of preferences for co-residents was, in turn, related to interactions between the socially differentiating effects of the market on the one hand, and aspects of national culture and jurisdictional organization on the other.

Consider now the relevance of this argument for the U.S.-British contrast. Since this has been related to variations in the localized welfare impact of the housing market, it should be indirectly traceable to variations in the intensity of preferences for co-residents; i.e., these preferences should be substantially more intense in the U.S. than in Britain. Unfortunately, there is no direct, cross-national evidence bearing on this question.[30] Intensity of preferences for co-residents, however, was also related to variations in national culture and jurisdictional organization. On these variations there *is* evidence, and it is to this that attention now turns.

To the extent that these differences can be documented, one can make out a case for preferences for co-residents being considerably more intense in the U.S.; this should allow one to make contact with those localized welfare impacts held to be basic to the emergence of decentralized political processes in urban areas.

In terms of jurisdictional organization, a major contrast is the extent of local government home rule. Where central government grants account for large proportions of local revenue and, furthermore, where those grants are redistributional in character, then fiscal externalities will be markedly attenuated. Consider in this context sources of money in the U.S. and Britain, respectively, for the critical local function of education. Local spending on education amounts to fifty-five percent of total spending in American cities[31] and to fifty-two percent of total spending in the British case.[32] In the American case, over half (fifty-five percent) of the money for education must be found locally.[33] In the British case, the appropriate figure is closer to twenty percent.[34]

In fact, local spending, as a whole, is much more subsidized by central government grants in the United Kingdom. Approximately two-thirds of local spending comes ultimately from central government taxation.[35] In the U.S., state and federal financing of local government amounts to about forty-five percent of total revenue needs.[36] In addition, British government grants to local government have a strong redistributive element: for those local governments with an assessed valuation of property per capita less than the national average, the central government intervenes with a grant to provide the per capita revenue that would have been derived locally if assessed valuation per capita had been the same as the national average. There is in the United Kingdom, therefore, an institutionally mandated lower limit below which negative fiscal externalities will not be experienced. This is a considerable deterrent to the local government fiscal mercantilism common in the U.S.

Indeed, interstate variations in funding arrangements in the U.S. lend additional credence to this viewpoint. A recent study suggests that local government exclusionary policies are of substantially reduced significance where state grants make up a large proportion of local government spending. Further, where state grants are redistributional in character, the exclusionary incentive is even further attenuated.[37]

A second pertinent aspect of jurisdictional organization concerns arrangements for education. A crucial, historical difference between the U.S. and Britain has been the role of the neighborhood school. As a result of the structure of the British educational system up until the late 1960s, residential location had limited significance for school peer group. This was the result of a two-tier educational system which, at the age of eleven, segregated the brighter, usually more middle-class, pupils from the less bright. Those passing the "eleven-plus" examination went on to the so-called grammar schools, while those failing proceeded to quite separate secondary modern schools. In the mid-1960s the proportion proceeding to grammar school was about twenty-nine percent.[38] This stream, moreover, was evidently more middle class than the secondary modern stream. In London in the early 1950s the middle-class/lower-class ratio was 20:80 in secondary modern schools and 48:52 in grammar schools.[39] And the lower-class children attending grammar schools were the brighter representatives of their class, anyway, and therefore more acceptable to middle-class parents. In addition, a vigorous private school system segregated large numbers of middle-class children from the lower class.[40]

As a consequence, in the British case it has historically been possible for middle-class and lower-class households to live in the same neighborhood and for the children to attend different schools. This is in sharp contrast to the American situation, where application of the neighborhood school concept in the absence of academic segregation among schools has served to increase the intensity of preferences for co-residents.

In Britain the two-tier educational system is now being phased out and replaced with a system of comprehensive schools akin to the American high school. As a consequence parents have become more dependent on those living around them for the type of peer groups their children have in school. On the basis of American experience, one would expect this to generate residential shifts between school catchment areas based on the reputation of different schools and the social class composition of their pupils. It will be important to see if this change in institutional arrangements is also reflected in an increased local involvement in the political process aimed at enhancing neighborhood social class composition.

A third, and final, contrast significant for the intensity of preferences for co-residents resides in aspects of culture. More specifically, this involves the public safety problem. This has been well publicized and requires little additional comment here. Suffice it to say that in Britain, public safety is rarely a basis either for residential choice or for locally based political action. This contrast to the U.S. would appear, however, to be of major importance, for in addition to its additive effects on intensity of preference, it also interacts with aspects of jurisdictional organization. In particular, the neighborhood school concept intensifies the impact of school vandalism and delinquency on resident welfare in predominantly middle-class areas.[41]

There are good reasons, of a broadly cultural and institutional character, therefore, for expecting preferences for co-residents in the U.S. to be markedly more intense than in the British case. These preferences provide the precondition, first, for a housing market structured by considerations of social class geography; and, second, for the localized welfare impacts resulting from investment flows and residential relocations set in motion by this housing market. In their turn these localized welfare impacts create the conditions necessary for the emergence of locationally decentralized political processes. The absence of those same conditions in the British case, where local interests are substantially less apparent in urban political processes, lends support to this view.

Concluding Comments

Broadly speaking, this analysis has attempted to explain the differential form assumed by urban political processes in different countries in terms of the conditioning of the housing market by aspects of cultural and jurisdictional organization peculiar to those countries. One might summarize our findings regarding that conditioning by postulating that the housing market in American cities has historically been much more sensitive to social class geography than has the housing market in British cities.

This is pertinent to certain other observations one might make about housing markets in American and British cities. In general, major American cities have been characterized by rapid rates of suburbanization and by a general deterioration in the viability of inner-city housing markets: in the extreme case, of course, this loss of viability is expressed in the abandonment of whole neighborhoods.[42] In British cities, on the other hand, not only has suburbanization been less rapid, but inner-city abandonment in the American style is virtually unknown.[43] Rather, rehabilitation of deteriorating neighborhoods for middle-class use is much more common. This also appears to be the pattern in Canadian cities.[44]

Of course, the link between suburbanization and decline in the viability of inner-city housing markets could be forged in a number of ways. According to one theory, for example, it could be related to the filtering down of older, less fashionable housing to lower-income families in a city in which the desirability of housing stock increases with increasing distance from the city center. More recently, however, attacks on conventional filtering theory have underlined the significance of neighborhood desirability, particularly in terms of neighborhood social class composition; change in neighborhood occupancy, it is hypothesized, stimulates the demand for suburban housing and distance from "them."[45] The image conveyed, therefore, is one in which pressure to live in socially more desirable neighborhoods results in a continual outward pressure on the spatial form of the city, resulting in the collapse of inner-city housing markets.

The desirability of middle-class neighborhoods, it could be argued, is due precisely to those considerations of public safety and public schools which loom so large in American urban consciousness—and which seem to play so small a role in British residential preferences. Of course, this line of reasoning does raise difficulties of its own. Recent work in Britain and the U.S., for example, has drawn attention to the effects of urban containment policies in Britain: reduced rates of suburbanization and low vacancy rates in inner-city housing markets.[46] To what extent, however, could one justify the view that these institutional considerations are exogenous to the system? In the American context it may well be that the payoffs to suburban development are such as to preclude the type of rigid land-use control characteristic of the British rural fringe and appropriate to a less buoyant suburban housing and land market.

Notes

1. Discussion and documentation of this viewpoint is provided by Mason Gaffney, "Tax Reform to Release Land," in *Modernizing Urban Land Policy*, ed. Marion Clawson (Washington, D.C.: Resources for the Future, 1973) pp. 115–51.
2. The concept of fiscal externality refers to the fiscal implications of a land use or individual for a local government. If the individual or land use generates a greater demand (in dollar terms) for public services than its contribution to local revenue, then negative fiscal externalities are said to be imposed. Those individuals or land uses contributing more to local revenue than the value of the public services provided as a result of their presence are said to provide positive fiscal externalities.
3. The significance of these concerns at the neighborhood level in American cities is discussed in Anthony Downs, *Opening Up the Suburbs* (New Haven, Conn.: Yale University Press, 1973), chap. 7.
4. For an exhaustive discussion of exclusionary zoning and its welfare implications, see Lynne B. Sagalyn and George Sternlieb, *Zoning and Housing Costs* (New Brunswick, N.J.: Rutgers University Center for Urban Policy Research, 1972).
5. See Gaffney, "Tax Reform to Release Land," pp. 126–27.
6. Municipalities are under no obligation to provide federally subsidized public housing; they merely have the right to if they so desire. See Kevin R. Cox and John A. Agnew, "The Location of Public Housing: Towards a Comparative Analysis," Ohio State University Department of Geography Discussion Paper no. 45 (Columbus, 1974), p. 12.
7. This has been documented in U.S., Commission on Civil Rights, *Above Property Rights* (Washington, D.C.: Government Printing Office, 1972), pp. 21–22.
8. An excellent example of a code-enforcement strategy was implemented by University City in the St. Louis metropolitan area. See U.S., Commission on Civil Rights, *Hearing Before the United States Commission on Civil Rights: St. Louis, Missouri, January 14–17, 1970* (Washington, D.C.: Government Printing Office, 1971), pp. 314–21.
9. The salience of local school and public safety issues is clearly apparent in a recent study of the St. Louis housing market: James Little et al., *The Contemporary Neighborhood Succession Process*, (St. Louis, Mo.: Washington University Institute for Urban and Regional Studies, 1975), p. 133. The same emphases are apparent in a recent survey of changing neighborhoods in Chicago. See Brian J. L. Berry et al., "Attitudes Towards Integration: The Role of Status in Community Response to Racial Change," in *The Changing Face of the Suburbs*, ed. Barry Schwartz (Chicago: University of Chicago Press, 1976), chap. 9.
10. There is a wide variety of studies of the determinants of residential property values. A useful review of these studies can be found in Michael Ball, "Recent Empirical Work on the Determinants of Relative House Prices," *Urban Studies* 10, no. 2 (June 1973): 213–33.
11. U.S., National Commission on Urban Problems (The Douglas Commission), *Building the American City* (Washington, D.C.: Government Printing Office, 1968), p. 101. See also: Calvin P. Bradford and Leonard S. Rubinowitz, "The Urban-Suburban, Investment-Disinvestment Process: Consequences for Older Neighborhoods," *Annals of the American Academy of Political and Social Science* 422 (1975): 77–86; and Arthur J. Naparstek and Gale Cincotta, *Urban Disinvestment: New Implications for Community Organization, Research, and Public Policy* (Washington, D.C.: National Center for Urban Ethnic Affairs, 1976).
12. On the spatial choices of insurance companies, see Richard F. Syron, "The Hard Economics of Ghetto Fire Insurance," *New England Economic Review* (March/April 1972), pp. 2–11.
13. See, for instance, Eleanor P. Wolf and Charles N. Lebeaux, eds., *Change and Renewal in an Urban Community* (New York: Praeger, 1969), pt. 1.
14. For instances, see Harvey Molotch's study of the South Shore area of Chicago: Harvey Molotch, *Managed Integration: Dilemmas of Doing Good in the City* (Berkeley and Los Angeles: University of California Press, 1972); see also a study of the Bagley neighborhood in Detroit: Wolf and Lebeaux, *Urban Community*.
15. Some of the few instances include: David E. C. Eversley, "Rising Costs and Static Incomes: Some Economic Consequences of Regional Planning in London," *Urban Studies* 9, no. 3 (October 1972): 347–68; and G. McDonald, "Metropolitan Policy and the Stress Areas," *Urban Studies* 11, no. 1 (February 1974): 27–37.
16. Cox and Agnew, "Location and Public Housing," pp. 42–43.
17. For example, there are no instances, to the author's knowledge, of attempts by neighborhood groups to intervene directly in the real estate market such as those referred to in note 14 (above).
18. In particular, taxation of capital gains in the U.S. is deferred if a new house is bought for more than the old house was sold. In Britain there is no capital gains tax on the sale of first homes.
19. According to one study carried out in the late 1960s, membership of renters in community organizations was about 10 percent, irrespective of income; for homeowners, membership rates increased from 11 percent (for those with annual incomes below $5,000) to 25 percent (for those with incomes over $10,000). See Irving A. Spergel, ed., *Community Organization* (Beverly Hills, Calif.: Sage Publications, 1972).
20. Peter A. Morrison, "Population Movements and the Shape of Urban Growth: Implications for Public Policy," in *Population Distribution and Policy*, ed. Sara Mills Maizie (Washington, D.C.: Government Printing Office, 1972), p. 301.
21. There is no firm empirical evidence on this point, though providing such evidence would not seem beyond

the ingenuity of historical property value studies. Moreover, there are good reasons for expecting such a shift in emphasis. With improved mobility, for example, access to the work place should decline in significance and permit greater discretion in residential choice. The closing words of Williams and Eklund's paper (chapter 9 of this volume) are pertinent in this regard:

> ... the very technology that allows people to be less dependent, in general, on location for structuring their interactions produces some urbanites who are now freer than ever before to use location with exquisite precision to achieve their lifestyle values.

22. On the basis of the findings of numerous studies of residential choice and neighborhood change, this proposition seems obvious. Studies of neighborhood deterioration, for example, have shown how incoming lower-income populations are attracted by the good schools and low crime rates of middle-class neighborhoods; since incoming populations, of course, tend to detract from these qualities, the existing middle-class populations move out in search of more homogeneous middle-class neighborhoods. See, in particular: Molotch, *Managed Integration;* Wolf and Lebeaux, *Urban Community;* and Gary A. Tobin, "An Analysis of Attitudinal Responses of Movers in Transition Neighborhoods," Washington University Institute for Urban and Regional Studies Working Paper HMS 7 (St. Louis, Mo., n.d.).

Despite its obviousness, however, there is little direct evidence on residential preferences themselves. The most direct evidence I have been able to identify comes from my sample survey of 110 households in Columbus, Ohio, in 1973. Respondents were asked to rank three neighborhoods in terms of their desirability as places in which to live (assuming no budgetary obstacles): a relatively upper-class suburb, a lower middle-class, older neighborhood, and a respectable working-class neighborhood. Irrespective of respondent social class, the rankings were of a highly repetitive character: Almost invariably the upper-class suburb was preferred to the lower middle-class neighborhood, and the lower middle-class neighborhood was preferred to the respectable working-class district. In addition, respondents were asked to rate their own neighborhood as a place in which to live; this showed a reasonably strong and significant relationship (Pearsonian $r = .53$) with a measure of census tract social class.

23. A number of existing statements, for example, tend to support the idea that lower-class households have less intense preferences for middle-class neighborhoods than do middle-class households. Martin Bailey, for example, has written: "It is generally true that people consider it unpleasant to live near groups of people with lower incomes and with tastes and habits 'inferior' to their own, while the reverse is sometimes and perhaps generally not the case." See Martin Bailey, "Note on the Economics of Residential Zoning and Urban Renewal," *Land Economics* 35, no. 3 (August 1959): 288. More recently, Alan Evans has suggested that both high-income and low-income households are prepared to pay more to live in upper-income neighborhoods; the intensity of the preferences of lower-income households, however, is considered less than that of upper-income households. See Alan Evans, "Economic Influences on Social Mix," *Urban Studies* 13, no. 3 (October 1976): 257.

24. Recent evidence from St. Louis, for example, suggests that public safety considerations are of major significance in the attractions of middle-income neighborhoods for those of lower income. For those of higher income, on the other hand, the major attractions of the middle-class neighborhood derive from the quality of local schools. See Gary Tobin, "Moves in Transition Neighborhoods," pp. 13–20.

25. A clear instance of this symmetry is that which relates Protestants and Roman Catholics to their coreligionists in the Belfast context. See F. W. Boal, "Territoriality on the Shankill-Falls Divide, Belfast," *Irish Geography* 6, no. 1 (1969): 30–50.

26. If we carry this logic a little further, it is clear that ultimately the housing market will result in convergence in the social composition of the two areas and consequent elimination of differentials in residential desirability.

27. Wolf and Lebeaux, *Urban Community;* and Molotch, *Managed Integration.*

28. Eugene Smolensky and J. Douglas Gomery, "The Urban Problem as an Exercise in the Theory of Efficient Transfers," University of Wisconsin Institute for Research on Poverty Discussion Papers 100–171 (Madison, n.d.), p. 8.

29. David H. Bayley, "Learning About Crime—The Japanese Experience," *Public Interest,* no. 44 (Summer 1976): 55–68.

30. Inter-nation comparison of levels of residential segregation, though difficult, might provide some indirect evidence on this point.

31. Dick Netzer, *Economics and Urban Problems* (New York: Basic Books, 1970), p. 172.

32. John Pratt et al., *Your Local Education* (Harmondsworth, Middlesex: Penguin Books, 1973), p. 82.

33. Netzer, *Economics and Urban Problems,* p. 173.

34. Pratt, *Your Local Education.*

35. Sir Harry Page, "Local Government—The Final Phase?" *Three Banks Review,* no. 106 (June 1975): 13.

36. Netzer, *Economics and Urban Problems,* p. 172.

37. Bruce Hamilton, Edwin Mills, and David Puryear, "Benefits and Costs of Metropolitan Area-wide Govern-

ment," in *Fiscal Zoning and Land Use Controls,* ed. Edwin S. Mills and Wallace E. Oates (Lexington, Mass.: Lexington Books, 1975).

38. John Vaizey and John Sheehan, *Resources for Education* (London: Allen and Unwin, 1968), p. 60.

39. H. T. Himmelweit, "Social Status and Secondary Education Since the 1944 Act: Some Data for London," in *Equal Opportunity in Education,* ed. Harold Silver (London, Methuen, 1973), p. 123.

40. In 1965, somewhere between seven and eight percent of all pupils aged eleven and over were in private schools: this estimate is based on information supplied in Vaizey and Sheehan, *Resources for Education*: a figure of 2,921,713 for all school pupils aged eleven and over (p. 61); and a figure of 217,823 for all pupils aged eleven and over in private schools (p. 109).

41. For instance, see Wolf and Lebeaux, *Urban Community,* p. 80

42. A good survey of this problem is provided in U.S., Department of Housing and Urban Development, *Abandoned Housing Research: A Compendium* (Washington, D.C.: Government Printing Office, 1973).

43. Marion Clawson and Peter Hall, *Planning and Urban Growth* (Baltimore: The Johns Hopkins University Press, 1973), chap. 4.

44. S. T. Roweis and A. J. Scott, "The Urban Land Question," chapter 2 of this volume.

45. Little, *Neighborhood Succession Process.*

46. Clawson and Hall, *Planning and Urban Growth.*

PART 2

Locational Conflict

Overview

Three papers are presented in this section. Those by Michael J. Dear and Jonathan Long, David R. Reynolds and Rex Honey are more theoretic in content, attempting to identify the circumstances under which locational conflict may or may not occur; John A. Agnew's paper, however, also tests some hypotheses and is perhaps indicative of the tremendous scope for work existing in this area.

By locational conflict we refer to conflicts over the location of facilities, land uses, etc., having implications for good or ill for those in the immediate area. These include public housing, highways, incinerators, municipal parks, and the like. As Dear points out, what is at issue is the arrangement of the spatial externality fields of these facilities. Externalities are, by definition, uncompensated welfare impacts, and it is precisely this lack of compensation which provides the sense of injustice that fuels controversy.[1] The externalities, moreover, may be manifest not only in the immeasurables of noise, physical threat, parking problems, and the like, but also in the pecuniary form of property values.[2]

Not that the externalities are necessarily negative in character. As Reynolds and Honey indicate, controversy may surround the location not only of *noxious* land uses, such as airports or sports stadia, but also of *salutary* facilities, such as public parks or schools. Locational outcomes in the two cases, of course, are likely to be quite different. As Reynolds and Honey go on to point out, in the case of salutary facilities there will be pressure to multiply facilities so as to maximize the numbers benefiting; opposition in this case will come from those located near existing facilities who would like to retain the scarcity value in the housing market of their accessibility advantage. In the case of obnoxious facilities, on the other hand, the pressures will be of a different character, the attempts of neighborhood groups to keep facilities out resulting in their concentration somewhere, presumably in neighborhoods lacking bargaining power.[3] Indeed, in his paper Agnew uses opposition to mixing of public with private housing as a measure of hostility to the location of public housing in the vicinity.

The precise geographical scope of the conflict depends, of course, upon the configuration of the spatial externality field. While distance-decay patterns are common, as in the noise from an airport or smoke from a chimney, there are also jurisdictional effects. Jurisdictional effects can be of a fiscal character and, as such, may be capitalized into property values: while a shopping center, therefore, may impose certain inconveniences of traffic congestion, glaring lights, etc., on those in the immediate vicinity, the property and sales taxes it provides for the jurisdiction may be fiscally welcome while also increasing the demand for real estate in the jurisdiction. To complicate the field of effects still further, the shopping center may provide certain benefits of access to those living just far enough away to avoid traffic nuisance, hazard, and the like. In the papers presented here, Agnew's discussion of public housing location controversies exemplifies the classic case of an obnoxious land use with a spatial externality field of the distance-decay form. Reynolds and Honey, on the other hand, consider the more complex case where there are both distance-biased effects and areal effects of a jurisdictional character.

Already there is a considerable literature dealing with locational conflict.[4] Nevertheless, as Dear and Long point out, much of this is of a descriptive character and a theory of locational conflict has been slow to emerge. The papers presented here, therefore, suggest a number of approaches—both inductive and deductive—by which this theory might be fashioned. As Dear and Long go on to point out in their paper, for instance, theory must address itself to the fact that there is no necessary link between some locational event with local welfare implications and the emergence of controversy. While opposition may be expressed in the form of "voice," exit may also be apparent as people vacate the neighborhood for more satisfactory residential conditions elsewhere. Alternatively, residents may simply resign themselves to the threat: In many cases there may be no apparent opposition at all.

Agnew's points of departure, on the other hand, are of a cross-national character: controversy over the location of public housing has been more apparent in the U.S. than in Britain, and homeowners in the U.S. are more likely to see the home in exchange-value, investment terms than are homeowners in Britain. He is then able to show that the two facts are related: that those most concerned about the exchange value of the home are also the most likely to be concerned about the location of public housing. Explaining the cross-national difference in controversy over public housing is, then, reduced to the problem of explaining cross-national attitudes towards the home.[5]

In this regard the paper by Reynolds and Honey is suggestive. Working in a deductive framework they criticize the demand theory extant in standard public choice theory. This argues that individual households seek to adjust their preferences to local public provision—of either a salutary or obnoxious character—by relocating. This, however, ignores the fact that these households will also be concerned with the effects of salutary and obnoxious facilities on the pecuniary terms on which they can leave the community. Households, therefore, become concerned with the property value implications of such land uses. This is consistent with Agnew's suggestion that concern for the home as an investment might have something to do with levels of residential mobility: levels which are considerably higher in the U.S. than in Britain.

NOTES
1. This is the viewpoint adopted in Kevin R. Cox and Michael J. Dear, "Jurisdictional Organization and Urban Welfare," Ohio State University Department of Geography Discussion Paper no. 47 (Columbus, 1975), pp. 59–74.
2. The impact on property values, of course, is contingent upon zoning designations. For a revealing study

of the importance of this, see R. W. Crowley, "The Effects of an Airport on Land Values," Ministry of State for Urban Affairs Working Paper A. 72.4 (Ottawa, 1972).

3. See, for instance, Eileen Wolpert and Julian Wolpert, "From Asylum to Ghetto," *Antipode,* 6, no. 3 (1974): 63–76.

4. For example, the studies edited by Julian Wolpert, "Research on Conflict in Locational Decisions," University of Pennsylvania Department of Regional Science Discussion Paper Series (Philadelphia, n.d.). Though many of these studies were concerned with documenting the specifics of particular cases, there was also a concern with developing an understanding of locational controversy so as to facilitate conflict resolution. Instances include C. Murray Austin, Tony Smith, and Julian Wolpert, "The Implementation of Controversial Facility-Complex Programs," *Geographical Analysis* 2 (1970): 315–29; and Anthony Mumphrey and Julian Wolpert, "Equity Considerations and Concessions in the Siting of Public Facilities," *Economic Geography* 49, no. 2 (April 1973): 109–21.

5. The homeowner's concern with the value of his asset and with the neighborhood events which affect that value is also discussed in David Harvey, "Labor, Capital, and Class Struggle Around the Built Environment in Advanced Capitalist Societies," chapter 1 of this volume

Chapter 5

COMMUNITY STRATEGIES IN LOCATIONAL CONFLICT

MICHAEL J. DEAR

JONATHAN LONG

The Victoria Park area is one of Hamilton's inner-city neighborhoods and has been a center of controversy for several years. Dissatisfaction with actions of the local government has been displayed at two levels: first, as a result of a feeling that the area is not getting a "fair deal" over the provision of public services; and, secondly, due to an attempt long under way to widen York Street, a major thoroughfare transecting the neighborhood. Planning proposals for the area have been numerous, and in 1966 the whole area was earmarked for urban renewal, but this proposal was eventually cut back until it became no more than a large road-widening scheme. Almost without exception, the residents feel the area is in need of some kind of improvement, but not all of them feel that this end would be best served by the proposal to widen York Street.

Victoria Park is a public park in the neighborhood. It has a baseball diamond and stand in one corner and is used by a fastball team playing in a provincial league. This team is sponsored by a Hamilton businessman who wanted to put a wooden fence around the diamond to ensure that those wishing to see the game would have to pay an admission charge, thus guaranteeing improved finances for the fastball team. However, the opinions of local residents differed; they held that a public park should remain public. They voiced their opinions at city meetings and warned that "accidents can happen to fences." Shortly afterwards, the part of the fence that had already been erected was found lying on the ground. On re-erection, it was again torn down. . . .

In attempting to explain urban spatial processes, geographers are increasingly turning to a paradigm based in conflict theory.[1] In these studies, the social geography of the city is seen as an outcome of a power struggle among various groups. It is important to emphasize, moreover, that power is an endogenous factor in conflict analysis, in contrast to the more traditional approaches in geography and spatial economic theory, where power per se is an exogenous variable.

In this essay, we focus attention upon community power at the neighborhood level. We wish to explain why the Victoria Park residents failed to prevent a road-widening scheme, while successfully blocking the proposed enclosure of part of their local park. Community power, and its effect on urban outcomes, is conceived as a set of strategies available to a group facing changes in environmental quality. In what follows, we have not attempted any formalism in our presentation. But hopefully the model outlined here can be used heuristically in the systematic comparison of widely differing conflict studies. Specifically, this paper has three purposes: (a) to outline our approach to the theory of locational conflict; (b) to examine community power, as manifest in the range of strategic options available to a group engaged in conflict; and (c) to consider the effect of time on strategic choice.

Theory of Locational Conflict

It seems unlikely that it is possible to construct a "general theory of conflict." Rapoport, inter alios, has argued that conflict ". . . may be no more than a word that expresses our interpretation of (and attitude toward) a multitude of widely disparate phenomena, governed by entirely different principles."[2] Locational conflict has been described as overt public debate over some actual or proposed land-use development.[3] It is concerned, therefore, with those conflicts which arise from the geographical or spatial dimensions of decision making, especially in the public sector. The focus of research in locational conflict has been on both a micro- and a macroscale. The former is concerned with the precise cause or source of any given conflict (e.g., an urban renewal proposal), while the latter concentrates on the role of the socio-political context of locational decisions (e.g., property rights or constitutional and statutory limits on local government policy.[4]

Geographical approaches to conflict issues have been diverse.[5] A great wealth of case-study material has been assembled, including studies of community opposition to highways, mental health centers, and taverns.[6] However, there are many problems with these sources. For instance, each situation appears to be unique, being composed of individual actors in specific spatial settings that are unlikely ever to be replicated precisely. Moreover, there are few rules to guide the researcher's choice of what is relevant evidence, how to assemble that evidence "objectively," and how to construct theory from a given set of chronological events. While the trend toward such inquiry is to be applauded, it is nevertheless true that the recent rash of conflict case studies has been combined with a noticeable lack of generalizations based upon them. A theory of locational conflict has thus been slow to appear.

An alternative approach has been to develop methodologies which would permit cross-sectional comparative analysis of conflict situations. These studies have emphasized the need to recognize the common structural dimensions which characterize the conflict situation; to assess the full impact of a locational decision; and to determine the extent of any compensation merited as a consequence of that decision.[7]

A final approach, common in locational conflict studies, is to begin with existing theory and extend its application. Prime candidates here are a variety of theoretical constructs from sociology. Seley, for example, has explored the suitability of Dahrendorf's class-conflict model for the analysis of urban conflict,[8] while others have returned to the Marxian tradition.[9] More commonly, several attempts have been made to expand many of the fundamental concepts of spatial economic theory into a conflict setting. This is particularly true of the notion of externalities, which will be further discussed below.

The analysis of locational conflict almost invariably focusses upon public decision making. This is especially the case with planning decisions, which are a major source of land-use change. Moreover, even when private sector initiative is the source of conflict, public decision makers are frequently called in to arbitrate. The probability of conflict over public decisions is high. This is largely due to the different rules which apply once decisions are moved into the public (i.e., political) arena. Criteria such as fairness and equity become more important than traditional efficiency considerations. Moreover, there is ultimately some accountability to the public through the ballot box.

The shift from a private commodity market to a public political market has a profound impact on the decision situation. The "invisible hand" is replaced by a voting mechanism, public discussion, or citizen participation. The allocative criterion for political decisions should be client *need*, rather than demand, but the concept of "need" is highly ambiguous.[10] How is a decision based upon need to be determined? Which groups should pay for the good, so that other groups may benefit? It is hardly surprising that conflict is generated as answers to these questions are sought.

Conflict can arise over the type of goods to be provided, the group targeted to receive those goods, or the location of the facilities from which they are to be delivered. Parenthetically, it should be noted that we are not confining attention here solely to the range of "pure" public goods, which are a feature of economic analysis. Our categorization of public goods includes all goods which are produced or provided by government at public expense. For example, it could include pure public goods (an air pollution control system), as well as merit goods (a library).

Locational conflict, therefore, is usually generated with respect to the potential impacts of public decisions. It has been suggested, moreover, that it is associated with some sense of "illegitimate transfer," involving the impacted population.[11] Specifically, the locational decision will result in some unfair transfer of utility away from the impacted population. At issue in locational conflict, then, is some perceived discrepancy between existing environmental quality (or utility) and anticipated environmental quality, should the locational decision be implemented.

Two types of impact are important in generating locational conflict: direct and indirect. The former refers to those effects which are deliberately anticipated in a public decision. For instance, an examination of the provision of street, school, and library services in Oakland, California, suggested that those neighborhoods already well endowed with these services attracted a disproportionate share of funds being allocated for those purposes.[12] However, there is also a range of indirect effects from public decisions. These are unanticipated side effects (externalities) of the decision. They include: the wide range of uncompensated costs borne by displaced households in highway and urban renewal projects, and the appreciation of property value which accrues to residences in the vicinity of urban parks.[13] It is significant that locational decisions can have both a positive and a negative impact, as these examples demonstrate.

The study of conflict over locational decisions begins with the simple notion that the impact of these decisions is confined to a geographically limited area. In short, the greater the distance from the source of impact, the less is the degree of that impact. Hence, the (direct) benefits of a fire protection service are available only within a spatially limited catchment area, while the noise nuisance of an urban expressway (an indirect effect) is usually confined to a broad strip adjacent to the pavement. This basic observation is significant because each location in an urban area is unique, in the sense that it is the only point which has exactly that relationship to all other locations. Hence, *access* to a particular location can become an asset *or* a liability. As Williams has indicated, when the "social access" of one individual or group to a particular location becomes blocked by the action of another, conflict begins.[14] Harvey has suggested that much of the debate in the political arena can be viewed as an effort to manipulate to personal advantage the impact "fields" of locational decisions.[15] In practice, the effect has frequently been to saturate "soft" inner-city areas with noxious facilities because their community clout has been insufficient to prevent such locational decisions.[16]

Community Strategies

A crucial variable in locational decision making is power. This is a difficult concept, and we shall make no attempt at a formal definition.[17] Instead, we shall proceed inductively by examining the bases of the powers held by various participants in the public decision-making sphere. What is the power base of the three major groups of participants in the urban development game?

The basis of *government* power is, of course, the fact that it possesses the ultimate authority for decision making. This authority is backed by law. The power of *business* interests, on the other hand, is predominantly an economic power. Planners and other *professionals*, for their part, have the power of project initiation, design, and evaluation.

Community power is not overt in the way that politicians literally have the power to make choices or business groups have financial power. Instead, community power may be measured by its effectiveness in attracting or deflecting those impacts having desirable or undesirable characteristics. In short, *community power in locational conflict is manifest as a set of strategic options available in response to proposals of a group in authority.* The remainder of this section examines this set of strategic options. A perfectly general heuristic model is outlined. It should be emphasized that the model is not meant to describe the range of options facing every community group on all occasions (although this may frequently be the case). Instead, the model should be regarded as a tool for the systematic analysis of community response to locational decisions. It should be used in the way which we report it: as a methodology for structuring the cross-sectional analysis of several case studies. Only with considerable experience and refinement could it be regarded normatively as a true choice model.

In general terms, it is possible to recognize five strategies which may be available to community groups involved in locational conflict: exit, voice, resignation, illegal action, and formal participation (figure 5-1). In what follows, emphasis will be laid on groups in *opposition* to any particular proposal. In judging the efficacy of any strategy, we shall therefore be concerned with the extent to which individual or group can influence urban decision making.

Exit

Exit is what is assumed to happen in the market situation where, if a consumer is dissatisfied with a product, he/she ceases to purchase it, and either does without the commodity or finds an alternative supply.[18] Presumably, if the number of exiters is sufficiently great, the producers have an incentive to improve the quality of the goods being offered.

By analogy, exit is here considered to be the course of action adopted

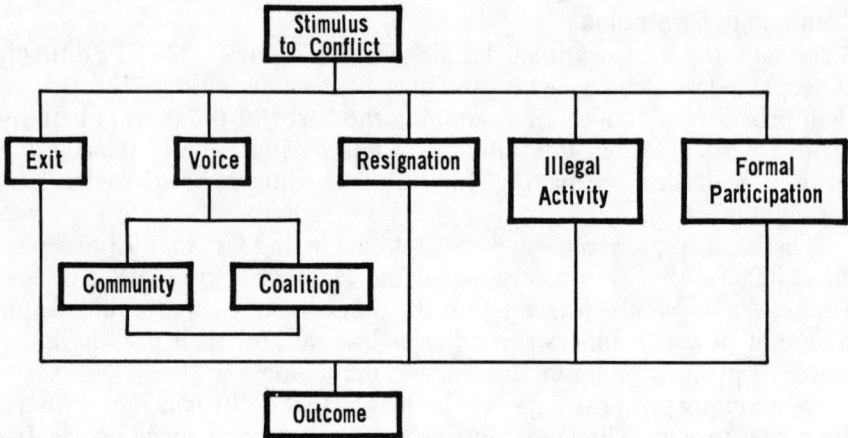

Figure 5-1. Community Strategies in Locational Conflict

by those who decide to leave their district for one they feel more nearly satisfies their needs.[19] From an individual viewpoint, this type of action almost certainly leads to an immediate improvement in the environment. However, it will not suggest to the government that something about the area is undesirable until a large number take this course. This limitation of exit's ability to produce a general solution might be insignificant were it not for the fact that some residents are restricted (e.g., financially) in their ability to exit. Moreover, in his original formulation, Hirschman assumed that the management would be both willing and able to respond to the warnings provided by its customers and that it was manifestly in its own interest to do so. Because of the multitude of conflicting interests within an urban area, however, it is by no means certain that a government will be willing to accommodate the demands of a particular group. Even when willing to act, the government may lack the wherewithal to do so.

In other circumstances, the exit message might not be clear because it is dampened by an inmigration of families who arrive to occupy the vacated accommodation. While this is the case, and exit is considered the only legitimate protest, inaction on the part of the government can be justified on the basis that the area is obviously serving an important need and should, therefore, not be changed. Hence, the exit option is *inexplicit.* If a person exits, it may well be a signal of dissatisfaction with the area, but it can hardly be expected to provide any detailed information as to the exact nature of the problem. Obviously, a move may be prompted by reasons other than dissatisfaction, but unless these occur with dramatic consistency within a particular area, government action would not appear to be justified.

Voice

In resorting to the voice option, the consumer tries to change the deteriorating conditions by articulating his interests, rather than by trying to escape from the problems.[20] This implies that residents stay to fight the problems of the area, rather than forsake it. Characteristically, voice has taken the form of gathering signatures for a petition; lobbying members of parliament, councillors or aldermen; writing letters to newspapers; and forming local resident groups to present a united front. Whereas it was asserted that exit was inexplicit, in that it merely demonstrated a vague dissatisfaction with something in the neighborhood, voice can be quite specific in pinpointing the nature of that something, even to the point of embarrassing the local authority. This must be counted as its most important advantage.

Inevitably, expectation of the success that voice will enjoy is an important determinant in the decision on what course of action will be taken. This is inextricably bound up with the cost of staying to voice. Voicing requires the expenditure of time, effort, and resources; and, while staying in a deteriorating area, the individual is foregoing better opportunities elsewhere, as well as paying taxes for inferior public goods.

The cost involved and, therefore, the likelihood of voice are affected by the length of time over which voice would have to be sustained to have the desired result. Whereas exit, insofar as the individual is concerned, will have an almost instantaneous effect on the personal environment, voice will take much longer. Even after voice has been effective and a decision has been made to improve the surroundings residents still have to wait for this decision to be implemented before they benefit.

Resignation

Just as exit can be expensive, voice is a process which consumes time and other scarce resources. Hence, one would not necessarily expect residents to use either strategy on every occasion they disapprove of some aspect of locational change. On all, bar the most important, issues a very large number will simply resign themselves to the situation.[21] However, even on the more important issues, there are two further reasons (apart from pure apathy) for active choice of the resignation strategy. These are alienation and free riding.

It is not surprising that a community whose voice is regularly ignored, or overruled, should learn resignation. Many people who disapprove of plans see the use of voice as a futile waste of time, and so resign themselves to having to adapt to new circumstances. These groups may be said to be alienated by the political process.

The second reason, based on the concept of "free riding," relates to the peculiar nature of the link between the individual and participation in collective action. If voice is likely to be a success, the individual may feel there is no point in acting, since the same benefits will be received whether he acts or not. On the other hand, if voice is going to fail, the individual may believe that his contribution would make no difference, anyway. Olson has demonstrated how individuals will discontinue their participation before the optimum for the group is attained; and the larger the group, the greater is the shortfall. This is particularly important when it is remembered that political power is generally assumed to increase as the numbers supporting a movement grow.[22]

Nevertheless, although not active in either voicing or exiting, the resigned group may play a significant role in conflict, since its acquiescence is invariably interpreted by the government as tacit approval of public policy.

Illegal Action

The fourth alternative considered here is that of illegal activity, which might be considered a subset of voice. It can be an eloquent means of displaying dissatisfaction and is undoubtedly designed to draw attention to the grievance in question. However, it should be regarded as a distinct class because, while voice is generally considered socially acceptable, the activities grouped here cannot be so classified. They include any illegal actions, such as personal violence, violence to property, and sit-ins.

The shortcomings of these actions are obvious, particularly as most people are reluctant to break the law, even when fully aware of the injustice of the situation. These strategies therefore rarely generate mass support. On the other hand, illegal action gains much when contrasted with the failings of more acceptable approaches. Goodman points out how direct action counters the usual feeling of hopelessness in poor neighborhoods and provides a focus around which community action can crystallize.[23] This is also a fundamental aspect of the Alinsky-style approach to political activism. For instance, Lipsky has commented on the use of protest as a strategy of relatively powerless groups in order to increase their bargaining ability.[24]

In the majority of cases in which illegal action would come under consideration as a tactic, it would probably not be considered as the means of bringing about a desired improvement directly, but as a means of improving a group's bargaining position. The predominant role of illegal activities seems to be to act as a *threat* of what could follow. We will return to the strategy of threat below.

Formal Participation

The final option in the community's repertoire of strategic alternatives is formal participation. It involves a discontinuous, or irregular, input into the decision-making process. Its important distinguishing characteristic is that it is initiated by government, as distinct from voice (which is community initiated). The most common kind of formal participation is institutionalized citizen participation in the planning process. This may take many forms, including appointed advisory councils or formal "information" sessions. This form of community strategy is strongly biased toward the decision makers, since it was made possible by them, and it can be withdrawn at any time, according to their discretion. In spite of the manipulative quality of formal participation, it is undoubtedly a major strategic alternative for many community groups.

Locational Conflict at Victoria Park

A full-scale empirical testing of the model described in the preceding section is beyond the scope of this paper. However, a brief summary of some earlier research will serve a dual purpose of (a) highlighting the utility of the strategy model; and (b) giving some indication of the analytical difficulties involved in its use.[25]

For the purpose of this paper we shall concentrate upon those respondents who indicated their opposition to the road-widening proposals, since those in favor would have no need of corrective action. Those who objected to the proposals were asked whether they had done anything to demonstrate their objection. On the basis of their response, they were divided into two groups: thirteen had chosen the *voice* option, and thirteen had chosen *resignation*. The significance of this division is that only the former would be recognized as opposing the current proposals; whereas, in fact, the number was twice that size.

In a discriminant analysis of the twenty-six voicing and resigning households, none of the variables representing residents' age, income, or length of residence proved to be significant discriminators. However, the voice/resignation groups showed interesting variation along two other discriminant dimensions. These were: (1) beliefs about the outcome of the widening proposal; and (2) attitudes towards planners and planning. Both variables proved to be successful discriminators (at the 95-percent level) for the voice and resignation groups. It would seem that the more pessimistic people are in their beliefs about the plan outcome, the more likely they are to voice. The less sympathetic attitudes of the voice group towards planners and planning may have two sources. It could be that, as a result of their abortive efforts to be heard, those trying to voice lowered their opinions of planners and planning. On the other hand, it may be that, because they already had these opinions, they felt it all the more necessary to voice. It is interesting, in passing, to note the superiority of the psychological variables, as discriminators, over the kind of variable more usually investigated in these issues.[26]

Since those interviewed still resided in the area, they were obviously not in the *exit* category. However, of those interviewed, 38 percent said that they knew families who had moved as a direct result of the proposals. Moreover, the number of houses being sold in the area, by half-year periods from 1973 to the beginning of 1975, had increased in this sequence: sixteen, eleven, seven, eighteen, forty-one. While these figures provide no firm estimates of the number of families choosing to exit, it is a clear indication that, even in a low-income area, exit is still potentially significant. It was impossible, in retrospect, to trace the group which had exited from York Street. This is but one manifestation of the analytical problems associated with the model presented here. In another study, Orbell and Uno tried to establish respondents' "propensity to move," but such measures tend to be biased toward the hypothetical.[27]

Although *illegal* activity was not witnessed in relation to the York Street widening, it did arise over a separate issue in the same area. The action of certain individuals in tearing down the fastball diamond fence clearly falls into this category. Unfortunately, by its very nature, it is impossible to document accurately this type of action. However, it is clearly a case where illegal activity was used to add volume to a voice already engaged in signing petitions and attending public meetings. One of the advantages of illegal action, when coupled with voice, is that it is easily understood and makes a dramatic point. It is also likely to gain media coverage, which provides a further platform for concomitant voice. However, the amount of illegal activity must be carefully calculated if it is not to be discounted as irresponsible. On this occasion, such illegality proved a relatively easy option, in physical terms; also, it was unlikely to engender a feeling of self-righteous indignation from the rest of the public.

It is interesting that, although the residents' strategies in the York Street issue were to no avail, it provided them with the experience necessary to protest the Victoria Park fence issue with more success. In fact, the core of the York Street Opposition Union also participated in this later issue. The use of illegal actions in the latter case was apparently effective, yet not used to counter the road-widening scheme, even when voice appeared to be failing, and it seemed that exit would be unlikely to act as a serious message of disapproval capable of changing the course of government action. Exit, in fact, simply facilitated city efforts to accumulate the land necessary for the road construction or else enabled developers to acquire land close to the new arterial for speculative purposes.

Finally, it is worth noting that some intriguing games appear to have been played under the guise of *formal participation* in the Victoria Park conflicts. One local businessman owning property on York Street, initially opposed to the plans for street widening, later changed his opinion. Being a prominent member of the local Italian community, he was able to swing a large portion of the residents into line with his new views. Popular information suggests that he was promised a "good deal on his property," and it seems highly unlikely that the government was totally unaware of his status within the community. In another development, public funding for a local community group was withheld until the various factions within the area decided who truly "represented" the community. It was during a particularly vehement conflict between the two major groups that the authorities moved to demolish half a dozen buildings which lay in the path of the proposed widening. This had the effect of adding to the "fatalistic" attitude of many residents with respect to the eventual outcome.

Temporal Considerations in Strategic Choice

The nature of a conflict will inevitably change over time. Both stress and inducements will affect an individual's relationship to it. Within a community, the degree of solidarity is subject to constant flux, as different coalitions materialize and disintegrate under pressure. Moreover, the nature of the conflict itself must be expected to change as a result of interaction between the parties and of changing expectations. Yet, any shifting of ground in a bargaining situation is seen as a weakness, likely to be interpreted as uncertainty or lack of commitment.[28]

The Learning Process and Sequencing of Strategies

The most significant temporal aspects of the Victoria Park conflicts were: (1) the community's learning process in moving from the urban renewal experience to that of the fastball diamond enclosure; and (2) the sequential, or simultaneous, use of strategic options by the community group.

It has long been established that groups gain experience from early battles, and this aids them in future confrontations.[29] Not only is social cohesion in the neighborhood strengthened as a result of confrontation with a common enemy, but the group also learns how to conduct future campaigns more effectively. These factors are important, since time is not generally on the community's side. For example, it is difficult to sustain interest in one issue within a community over a prolonged period of time, especially if major events are not regularly forthcoming. Even if they are, the whole process becomes wearing and energy is drained. This is particularly pertinent if a sizable group is involved. Prolongation of a conflict is often deliberately employed by decision makers as a strategy to defeat community groups. This procrastination can take many forms, from non-decision making to purposeful ambiguity.[30] Clearly, the government opposition may also learn from its experiences.

This last point emphasizes how important *government response* to community strategy is to the progress of any particular conflict. The formal participation option is open to the community only if government permits it. Moreover, participation is a form of cooptation in the face of opposition. This involves the public being persuaded to become formally involved in the existing planning structure, where they then have to play by the rules or forfeit the privilege of participating. Because of this concession, the residents now have something to lose and have thus placed themselves in a position where they can be more easily manipulated by the authorities. In circumstances such as these, the community is given the illusion of voice but not the voice itself; thus, opposition is stifled without policy being altered.

Not only does the community learn as the conflict matures, but the circumstances guiding its choice of strategic option must also alter. This raises the possibility of the sequential (or simultaneous) adoption of several conflict strategies. As a simple example, the execution of a violent act is almost always preceded by the threat of that action. In addition, the notion of *fatigue* in a community group is relevant if that group is forced to adopt a repeated sequence of, say, exit or voice.

It is possible to view the whole question of sequential strategic choice as an exercise in conditional probability. As Hirschman noted: "... the decision whether to exit will often be taken *in the light of the prospects for the effective use of voice.*"[31] If individuals expect that voice will be effective, then they may postpone exit, pending the outcome of voice. However, it is also possible for those who have exited to continue to participate via voice. Those persons, for example, who have had their property expropriated and thus have been forced to exit may feel strongly enough to continue to voice from afar.

Perhaps the single most important factor in determining a community group's progress through a locational conflict is their degree of success. Success is, of course, a difficult concept, implying many different things at various stages of a conflict. It is especially difficult for a group's leaders to report successful outcomes during a prolonged conflict. It then becomes important to examine the effects of defeats, real or apparent, upon the group. A strong group will typically *escalate* the conflict, as in the progression from voice, through threat of illegal action, to the sort of physical destruction of property reported in Victoria Park. Active groups will also attempt to *widen* their conflict to include others or to *intensify* the feelings of animosity within their own group. By contrast, a fatigued or coopted group is likely, in the face of setbacks, to become fragmented, failing to recognize its links with other groups of similar persuasion. Alternatively, they may internalize their frustrations, focussing on intra-group status conflicts and structural reorganization.[32] In Victoria Park, for example, a violent debate over which organization truly represented the community, effectively divided the opposition forces.

Additional Concepts of Threat and Slack

In order for a *threat* to be effective, the party issuing it must be seen to be irreversibly committed to carrying it out. In these circumstances the very lack of resources which precluded exit, and dulled voice, may prove to be an asset. The group may now seem to have little to lose by adopting a normally unacceptable strategy and is free to threaten a sequential use of progressively more damaging strategies. It is essential, of course, to ensure that the "last clear change" falls to the other party, so that the emphasis is left on them to retreat to a mutually beneficial solution.[33]

This inevitably raises the question of what threats the public has in its repertoire. The list includes the threat of political sanctions at election time and the withholding of tax or rental payments. A more potent threat, however, may be related to violence, but this poses the immediate problem: At whom should it be directed? Moreover, certain events may not be designed specifically as a threat but may be so construed. For example, in nineteenth-century Britain, it was the threat posed by the slums as a health hazard which prompted reform. Perhaps in the twentieth century, the threat of crime and violence issuing forth from the inner city may act as a spur to new reforms.

A further concept which is usually distinguished in relation to community strategy is the notion of *slack:* this is present whenever a component of the system is not working to its limit.[34] This may occur when, even in a deteriorating neighborhood, not all residents choose to protest. Those who resign themselves to the situation provide the governing authority with room to maneuver, since less pressure can be brought to bear by the depleted community group. This situation may persist unless the neighborhood deteriorates still further, at which point these slack resources may be brought into play. Thus, the resigned group represents an important reservoir of potential support which, if the opposition group can contrive to tap it, will lend considerable strength to their cause.

Conclusion

The approach of this paper is predicated upon the belief that a strong effort has to be made to develop a systematic theory of locational conflict. A general heuristic tool for the analysis of community response to locational decisions has been presented. The focus of this model has been on the choice variables: exit, voice, resignation, illegal action, and formal participation. The additional concepts of threat and slack were introduced, and empirical analysis suggested the importance of community learning and strategy sequencing over time. The progress of any conflict was constrained by government response to community strategies. The set of government strategies (e.g., cooptation) was important in defeating community groups. However, success in conflict could counter community fatigue, thereby avoiding problems of group fragmentation and internalization of frustrations.

The future research problems in this area are large. Although the model presented here seems fully testable, the methodological problems (e.g., of sampling the exit group) are considerable. Of the conceptual problems which remain, our major concern is the dichotomy between individual and group actions in the strategy model. Thus, decisions in favor of exit, voice, or whatever are intrinsically private; however, effective action in a conflict situation depends upon aggregate behavior.[35] Another major issue is the extent to which this model can be legitimately utilized in a wider conflict context.[36] We have used it in the analysis of a neighborhood-based protest movement. Would it be adaptable to a different scale; e.g., to a city- or regionwide problem? To what extent can it be used to analyze the behavior of a group in favor of a particular proposal, but that tends to appear in a later phase of the conflict cycle? And to what degree does intragroup conflict differ from the intergroup situation described in this essay?

Notes

1. See, for example, Kevin R. Cox, *Conflict, Power, and Politics in the City: A Geographical Approach* (New York: McGraw-Hill, 1973).
2. Anatol Rapoport, *Conflict in Man-Made Environment* (Baltimore: Penguin Books, 1974), p. 8.
3. Michael J. Dear, "Spatial Externalities and Locational Conflict," *London Papers in Regional Science* 7 (1976): 152–67.
4. Kevin R. Cox and Michael Dear, "Jurisdictional Organization and Urban Welfare," Ohio State University Department of Geography Discussion Paper no. 47 (Columbus, 1975).
5. These are discussed briefly by John Seley, "Toward a Paradigm of Community-Based Planning," in *Community Participation and the Spatial Order of the City*, ed. David Ley (Vancouver: Tantalus Research, 1974).
6. The Discussion Paper Series edited by Julian Wolpert ("Research on Conflict in Locational Decisions," available from the Regional Science Department, University of Pennsylvania) and Stephen Gale ("Research on Metropolitan Change and Conflict Resolution," available from the Peace Science Department, University of Pennsylvania) are representative.
7. John Seley, "Paradigms and Dimensions of Urban Conflict" (Ph.D. diss., University of Pennsylvania, 1973); C. Murray Austin, Tony E. Smith, and Julian Wolpert, "The Implementation of Controversial Facility-Complex Programs," *Geographical Analysis* 2 (1970): 315–29; Michael Dear, Ruth Fincher, and Lise Currie, "Measuring the External Effects of Public Programs," *Environment and Planning* 9 (1977): 137–47.
8. Seley, "Urban Conflict."
9. David M. Evans, "A Critique of Locational Conflict" (M.A. research report, University of Toronto, 1973); David Harvey, *Social Justice and the City* (London: Edward Arnold, 1973).
10. J. Bradshaw, "A Taxonomy of Social Need," in *Problems and Progress in Medical Care*, ed. Gordon MacLachlan (London: Oxford University Press, 1972).
11. Cox and Dear, "Urban Welfare," p. 63.
12. Frank S. Levy, Arnold J. Meltsner, and Aaron Wildavsky, *Urban Outcomes* (Berkeley and Los Angeles: University of California Press, 1974).
13. Anthony Downs, "Uncompensated Nonconstruction Costs Which Urban Highways and Urban Renewal Impose on Residential Households," in *Analysis of Public Output*, ed. Julius Margolis (New York: Columbia University Press, 1970); and T. R. Hammer, E. Horn, and Robert E. Coughlin, "The Effect of a Large Urban Park on Real Estate Value," Regional Science Research Institute Discussion Paper no. 51 (Philadelphia, Pa., 1971).
14. Oliver P. Williams, *Metropolitan Political Analysis* (New York: The Free Press, 1971), chap. 2.
15. Harvey, *Social Justice and the City*, chap. 2.
16. Julian Wolpert, Michael Dear, and Randi Crawford, "Satellite Mental Health Facilities," *Annals of the Association of American Geographers* 65 (1975): 24–35.
17. An excellent discussion on aspects of power may be found in Peter Bachrach and Michael S. Baratz, *Power and Poverty* (New York: Oxford University Press, 1970).
18. Albert O. Hirschman, *Exit, Voice, and Loyalty* (Cambridge: Harvard University Press, 1970), chap. 1.
19. John M. Orbell and Toru Uno, "A Theory of Neighborhood Problem Solving, Political Action vs. Residential Mobility," *American Political Science Review* 66 (1972): 471–89.
20. Hirschman, *Exit, Voice, and Loyalty*, chap. 1.
21. Orbell and Uno, "Neighborhood Problem Solving."
22. Mancur Olson, *The Logic of Collective Action* (New York: Schocken Books, 1971).
23. Robert Goodman, *After the Planners* (New York: Simon and Schuster, 1971).
24. Michael Lipsky, *Protest in City Politics* (Chicago: Rand McNally, 1970).
25. Jonathan Long, "Individual and Community Strategies in Public Issues" (M.A. research paper, McMaster University, 1975).
26. Cf. David C. Schwartz, *Political Alienation and Political Behavior* (Chicago: Aldine, 1973).
27. Orbell and Uno, "Neighborhood Problem Solving."
28. Thomas C. Schelling, *The Strategy of Conflict* (Cambridge: Harvard University Press, 1960), pt. 3.
29. Anthony J. Mumphrey, John Seley, and Julian Wolpert, "A Decision Model for Locating Controversial Facilities," *Journal of the American Institute of Planners* 37 (1971): 397–402.
30. Bachrach and Baratz, *Power and Poverty*, chap. 3; and John Seley and Julian Wolpert, "A Strategy of Ambiguity in Locational Decisions," in *Locational Approaches to Power and Conflict*, ed. K. R. Cox, D. R. Reynolds, and Stein Rokkan (New York: Halsted Press, 1974).
31. Hirschman, *Exit, Voice, and Loyalty*, p. 37 (italics in original).
32. Group fragmentation and group internalization are discussed as aspects of "idolatry" in David Ley, "Problems of Co-optation and Idolatry in the Community Group," in Ley, *Community Participation*, pp. 75–88.
33. Schelling, "Strategy of Conflict."
34. Hirschman, *Exit, Voice, and Loyalty*, chap. 1
35. Cf. J. Olives, "The Struggle Against Urban Renewal in the Cité d'Aliarte," in *Urban Sociology: Critical Essays*, ed. Christopher G. Pickvance (London: Tavistock Publications, 1976).
36. An interesting discussion of this point appears in Anthony H. Birch, "Economic Models in Political Science: The Case of Exit, Voice, and Loyalty," *British Journal of Political Science* 5 (1975): 69–82.

Chapter 6

MARKET RELATIONS
AND LOCATIONAL CONFLICT
IN CROSS-NATIONAL PERSPECTIVE

JOHN A. AGNEW

The notion that conflict over access to resources results from the form that social and economic relations take in market societies has recently emerged as a significant theme in urban studies.[1] As an assertion this clearly requires historical investigation. But analysis of contemporary market societies is not redundant. We can address the question: Do conflicts over access to resources in contemporary market societies arise from the market nature of these societies?

In this paper I wish to provide, first, some theoretical context for an understanding of the relationship between, on the one hand, conflict over access to *urban* resources—houses, parks, "good" schools, "good" neighborhoods, etc.—and, on the other hand, the property relations typical of market societies; and, second, an empirical examination of this relationship.[2] In order to assess the generality of the theoretical argument, a cross-national perspective is adopted. England and the United States serve as the market societies in question.

The paper is divided into three sections: The first comprises a discussion of the association between market relations and locational conflict. Locational conflict is defined as conflict over access to resources. The second section consists of a report on an empirical investigation of the relationship between market relations and locational conflict. The focus is upon conflict over public housing location in English and American cities. A final section provides a concluding statement.

Market Relations and Locational Conflict

A house or apartment complete with associated characteristics—physical form, social and locational ties—can be regarded as one of life's necessities. In this sense it takes on a use value. It supports life, and the occupier responds by holding it in esteem. He enjoys it to the extent that it lives up to his desires. Clearly, given the personal nature of this definition, the use value of a specific residence is not the same for all people, nor is it constant for the same person over time. In particular, life-cycle changes can be expected to generate different definitions of what constitutes a satisfactory use value.

In a market society, however, a residence must be purchased to be obtained. A price must be met in the form either of payment for ownership or of contract rent before the use value can be realized. The price is paid to those individuals and organizations—developers, builders, bankers, and landlords—who engage in the provision of housing. A monetary value, then, an exchange value, is returned for the necessary consumption of housing. Money income, typically earned, is traded for a place to live.

Those who provide housing and the rest of the "built environment" have a variety of interests.[3] Their major interest, however, is in exchange value.[4] The collection of exchange value—in the form of mortgage interest payments, contract rents, and immediate profits—and the market for existing properties set the conditions for the creation of new use values by indicating whether capital should be invested in new building, rehabilitation of old buildings, or an interest outside of real estate. If this means abandoning investments which cannot now produce a rate of return as high as elsewhere, then this is done.[5] Decisions concerning the provision of new use values and the destruction of old ones, then, are made by those whose goal is profit, not use. Use values are created and destroyed in order to realize exchange values.

The situation could not be otherwise in a "market society." By definition, objects in such a society must be traded as commodities in order for them to be provided. Profit serves as the incentive for producing and trading. In a housing milieu the distinction between providers and consumers in terms of goals may become blurred. Critically, consumers in pursuit of use values participate in the market when buying and selling and become concerned about exchange values. In the present context interest attaches to the extent to which consumers of housing, and other urban resources, see themselves as investors and the specific resource as a commodity to be traded. Not only the providers of the built environment, then, but also the consumers may see that environment in exchange-value terms.

In the early years of capitalism as a distinctive mode of production, labor and capital were well-defined categories of interests. In a housing context one could substitute the terms landlord and tenant for capital and labor, respectively. However, more recently these categories have become less easy to define.[6] In particular, labor is fragmented. This is important, for capital, though divided by specific goals, is still united in "principle" behind the ethos of private property and "possessive individualism."[7]

Labor, however, is divided into a variety of "housing classes"—most generally, homeowners and renters—one of which, homeowners, has become a "class of owners."[8] This development has important implications for the way in which properties are regarded. Specifically, it means that there is now a large group of people in market societies, such as England and the United States, committed to ownership of property.[9] Ownership entails a further commitment to the notion of private property and, given the monetary resources ownership requires, interest in preserving the savings invested. Sternlieb has gone so far as to suggest for the United States that:

> For all but the more affluent in our society, a house is not only a home, it is typically a major repository of capital investment and stored equity. As any imaginative architect will testify, houses are purchased to be sold, not to be lived in.[10]

This statement may exaggerate the extent to which homeowners have become solely concerned with exchange values. Obviously, preservation of savings is important to a certain degree. However, and more importantly, to quote Harvey:

> ... Every homeowner, whether he or she likes it or not, is caught in a struggle over the appropriation of values because of the shifting patterns of external costs and benefits within the built environment. A new road may destroy the value of some housing and enhance the value of other, and the same applies to all new development, redevelopment, accelerated obsolescence, and so on. ... Homeownership, in a very different way, invites a faction of the working class to wage its inevitable fight over the appropriation of value in a capitalist society. It puts them on the side ... of private property and frequently leads them to appropriate values at the expense of other factions of the working class.[11]

Conflicts over the location of new highways, schools, low-income housing, and the like, then, may largely stem from homeowners' integration into market relations which redefine use-value concerns in terms of the exchange-value concerns of private capital. This, moreover, is a general argument which can claim applicability in those market societies in which homeownership has become important. England and the United States are obvious examples.

The relationship between market relations and locational conflict has not been subjected to much analysis. A recent piece of research, however, provides a starting point. As part of a survey investigation of the sources and outcomes of conflict over public housing location, a sample of home-owners in one English city, Leicester, and one American city, Dayton, were asked about their interest in exchange values (exchange-value orientation).[12] The following question was used:

One of the reasons people buy houses these days is so they can sell later at a profit. In your particular case, would you say that this considera-tion was: 1. Very important; 2. Important; 3. Unimportant; 4. Very unim-portant.

There appears to be a vast difference between homeowners in Leicester and Dayton in terms of orientation towards exchange values (see table 6-1). The Dayton homeowners showed much more concern for exchange values than did those from Leicester.

Table 6-1. The Importance of Profit

	Very Important	Important	Unimportant	Very Unimportant
	%	%	%	%
Leicester	0.0	14.4	42.2	43.3
	(0)	(13)	(38)	(39)
Dayton	12.9	60.0	24.3	2.9
	(9)	(42)	(17)	(2)

One could argue, however, that the assertion of a between-city differ-ence in patterns of response is premature. The entries in table 6-1 may result solely from the composition of the sample. The fact that the Dayton homeowners were younger on the average than the Leicester ones, for instance, may be of importance. Certainly, one might expect younger homeowners with more years of investment ahead of them and more current mortgage debt to have a greater commitment to exchange values than older owners.[13] Similarly, the Dayton homeowners were also more likely to be nonmanual workers and identify themselves as "middle class."[14] These are attributes one would associate with greater concern for exchange values.

A check upon the impact of these compositional effects can be pro-vided by applying Multivariate Nominal Scale Analysis (MNA).[15] Table 6-2 presents the R^2 coefficients derived from analysis of responses to the

Table 6-2. The Importance of Profit, R^2 from MNA Runs*

All Variables Included		Excluding:	
.388		City	.275
		Age	.341
		Occupation	.328
		Self-rated Class	.311

*The number of categories for each variable is as follows: City, 2; Age, 3; Occupation, 2; Self-rated Class, 2.

"Importance of Profit" question when four independent variables were included. Attention focusses upon the ordering of the variables with respect to "marginal usefulness." The marginal usefulness of each independent variable is derived by subtracting the coefficient associated with its exclusion from the "All Variables Included" coefficient. The larger the difference between the two coefficients, the more important is the variable. Quite clearly, even with the inclusion of theoretically plausible control variables, the cross-national difference persists. The English (Leicester) homeowners were much less committed to their homes as investments than their American (Dayton) counterparts.

At this juncture it may be useful to point out that this contrast appears to be reflected in attitudes towards land-use changes. In the survey, respondents were asked if they would support or oppose the mixing of private and public housing; and, if so, why. Those opposing provided a variety of grounds, shown in table 6-3. However, it appears that among this group property values were more important for the American than the English opponents of mixing. Why should this be?

Table 6-3. Reasons Given for Answering "No" to Mixing

	Property Values	Use Considerations	Fairness Considerations
	%	%	%
Leicester	8.6	88.6	2.8
	(3)	(31)	(1)
Dayton	34.5	65.5	0.0
	(19)	(36)	(0)

While no adequate theory is at hand, some speculation as to what might produce this cross-national difference in conceptions of the home as an investment can be provided.[16]

The first speculation concerns the role of residential mobility. Available evidence suggests that the rate of residential mobility in England is about half that in the United States.[17] English homeowners, therefore, are less likely to sell their homes than are the more mobile American homeowners. In the absence of much involvement in real estate transactions, English homeowners may be less likely to see their homes in exchange-value terms.

A second argument involves the role of volatility in exchange values. When their future appreciation or preservation is uncertain, homeowners may show more interest in them. This uncertainty over the future of exchange values may be greater in the United States than in England. For instance, there is a widely acknowledged housing shortage in England (13,609,864 dwellings for 16,188,067 households in Britain in 1961). This compares with a situation in the United States which in recent times has been typified by a surplus of housing units (58,326,000 housing units for 53,021,000 households in 1960). Although local circumstances may differ, in general, exchange values should almost certainly appreciate in England, whereas in the United States the outlook is much less certain. Moreover, patterns of external costs and benefits are much more permanent in England than in the United States. In particular, the existence of, publication of, and relatively strict enforcement of comprehensive local land-use plans have acted to increase the lead time associated with changes in land use.[18] With patterns of land use set for relatively long periods of time, uncertainty regarding future fluctuations in exchange values should be reduced.

A final speculation concerns the extent to which the market ethos—the reduction of use values to exchange values—has penetrated into the two market societies. The United States is often characterized as a nation of individuals tugging on their bootstraps in the pursuit of individual—typically, monetary—gain. Certainly, few areas of national life remain untouched by market operations. Anything, and anybody, can be "sold." In contrast, English capitalism appears restrained and unadventurous. The American conservative writer George F. Will considers that:

> Far from being natural shopkeepers, the English have underdeveloped commercial instincts. The aggressive gospel of getting on has not taken root in their souls.[19]

English working-class consciousness and its mobilization in the form of a politically active labor movement have also perhaps served to restrict the operations of private capital and prevented the *embourgeoisement* of the working class, including that fragment owning their homes.

Clearly, there is little theoretical or empirical basis for preferring any one or any combination of these speculative proposals. They are presented in order to excite inquiry and the quest for suitable theory, not to offer definitive answers. Whatever the explanation, however, the finding that homeowners in Dayton are more interested in exchange values than are homeowners in Leicester has important implications for the incidence of locational conflicts in England and the United States. Given the close association between orientation towards exchange values and locational conflict posited above, two research questions can be suggested: (1) Is there, as one might expect, less locational conflict in England than in the United States?; and (2) To what extent is this difference explained by differences in exchange-value focus?

The Case of Conflict over Public Housing Location

The incidence of locational conflict and the role of exchange-value orientations in accounting for this incidence can be evaluated by examining local reactions to a specific land use: public housing. Public housing is in no way locationally "footloose" and free to locate anywhere within English and American cities in the sense that most private housing is.[20] The location of public housing is the result of a public decision-making process infused with conflict—conflict that appears to be engendered by expectations concerning the behavior of public housing tenants and the potential impact of this behavior on use values and exchange values in particular neighborhoods.[21]

Two questions are at issue in the present context: (1) Is there less conflict over public housing location in England than in the United States?; and (2) To what extent are the different reactions to public housing derived from differences in exchange-value orientations?

The Extent of Conflict

In order to estimate the relative extent of conflict over the location of public housing in American and English cities, a mail questionnaire was sent to city housing managers and housing directors in 100 American and 100 English cities with populations greater than or equal to 50,000.[22] Responses received during the mail survey period of January through July, 1975, totaled sixty-nine for the U.S. and eighty-one for England.

The major focus of the mail survey was upon housing manager perceptions of the presence and intensity of "controversy" over the location of public housing.[23] Two questions from the survey are particularly relevant for gauging the relative extent of locational controversy. They are the following:

Thinking about the selection of sites for public housing, which of the

following statements would best characterize the situation in your city in recent years (past ten years)?
1. There has been no controversy over site selection decisions.
2. There has been very little controversy over site selection decisions.
3. There has been some controversy over site selection decisions.
4. There has been a great deal of controversy over site selection decisions.

and;

With reference to complaints received about particular sites in recent years (past ten years), can it be said that there have been: 1. Many; 2. Some; 3. Few; 4. None; 5. Don't know.

As table 6-4 clearly indicates, American housing officials are more likely to relate the selection of sites for public housing to controversy than are their English counterparts. Also, American respondents are more likely to claim for their offices "some" and "many" complaints about sites than are the English respondents (see also table 6-5). In response to both questions, then, American respondents are more likely to note the presence of, and a greater intensity of, controversy over site selection for public housing than are the English housing officials. The cross-national difference persists when responses are tabulated by city size category, relative magnitude of public housing stock, and region.[24]

Market Relations and Locational Conflict

For investigation of the relationship between market relations and locational conflict, two cities, one in the United States and one in England, serve as research sites. An ideal research framework, of course, would include several different case study investigations in each of the two nations. This approach would mitigate the danger of facile generalization to the national situation. However, limited time and funds indicated otherwise. One American city, Dayton, and one English city, Leicester, were selected as case study cities.[25]

Within each city two areas of public housing were chosen in the vicinity of which face-to-face interviews could be conducted with local residents occupying private sector housing. The criterion of controversy over the location of public housing was not employed in the selection of study areas. The public housing areas selected complied, however, with three other criteria: first, that the public housing be of recent construction so that any controversy would be salient to local residents; second, that one area provide an instance of private construction prior to public, and that the other area provide an instance of public construction prior to private;

Table 6-4. Controversy in Your City, by Nation

	Great Deal	Some	Little	None
	%	%	%	%
England	0.0	19.8	53.1	27.2
	(0)	(16)	(43)	(22)
United States	17.4	36.2	23.2	23.2
	(12)	(25)	(16)	(16)

Table 6-5. Complaints About Sites, by Nation

	Many	Some	Few	None	D.K.	N.A.
	%	%	%	%	%	%
England	0.0	27.2	58.0	12.3	2.5	0.0
	(0)	(22)	(47)	(10)	(2)	(0)
United States	15.9	31.9	36.2	11.6	2.9	1.4
	(11)	(22)	(25)	(8)	(2)	(1)

and, third, that in order to maximize the incidence of homeowners among local residents, all study sites be located in middle-income, residential neighborhoods.[26]

For survey purposes, those households living in the immediate vicinity of the public housing were identified as the target population. On the grounds that consciousness of, and involvement in, controversy might be related to a household's distance from public housing, a distance-strati-fied, random sample design was adopted.[27] An interview schedule previously tested in both England and the United States was applied to the Leicester portion of the sample between January 2 and January 22, 1975. The Dayton part of the sample was interviewed between February 20 and March 2, 1975.[28]

Two attitudinal questions from the household interview schedule are pertinent in the context of this research. One is that relating to exchange-value focus presented earlier in this paper. The other relates to general attitude towards public housing location and is as follows:

Do you think that when council/public housing is being built, an attempt should be made to mix it up with private housing? 1. Yes; 2. No; 3. Don't know.

Responses to this question help to establish whether the case study situations reflect the different incidence of conflict in England and the United States noted earlier.[29] Apparently, this is so. Homeowners in Dayton were much more likely to oppose mixing than their counterparts in Leicester (see table 6-6).

Table 6-6. Attitude Towards Mixing Public and Private Housing

	Yes	No	D.K.
	%	%	%
Leicester	44.5	38.8	16.7
	(40)	(35)	(15)
Dayton	10.0	78.6	11.4
	(7)	(55)	(8)

A check on this interpretation can be provided by applying MNA, in table 6-7. The variables other than "City" are included as controls in order to provide some standard for evaluating the marginal usefulness of "City" as an explanatory variable. Each of these variables is included on theoretically plausible grounds. "Age" is included in the analysis on the grounds that younger homeowners with more years of investment ahead of them and more current mortgage debt are more likely to have a commitment to exchange value than are older owners. "Occupation" and "Self-rated Class" are included on two grounds: First, resentment at the income transfer implicit in public housing might conceivably be more characteristic of those with greater social distance from the public housing clientele: nonmanual workers and those identifying themselves as middle class. Second, one might expect homeowners who identify themselves as "middle class" or who are in nonmanual occupations to be more integrated into market society and, therefore, to show more of an orientation towards exchange values than others. Quite clearly, however, even with the inclusion of these theoretically plausible control variables, the cross-national difference persists. English (Leicester) homeowners, whatever their age, occupation, or self-rated social class, were more likely to approve the mixing of public and private housing than were their American (Dayton) counterparts.

Table 6-7. Attitude Towards Mixing Public and Private Housing, R^2 from MNA Runs

All Variables Included		Excluding:	
.423		City	.389
		Age	.401
		Occupation	.410
		Self-rated Class	.395

The critical question can now be addressed: How important is exchange-value orientation in explaining this difference in attitude towards mixing? If the pattern of responses to the "Importance of Profit" question reported in table 6-1 is incorporated as an independent variable into the MNA model outlined in table 6-7, a suitable model can be created. This model produces coefficients which indicate a considerable attenuation of the "City" effect noted in table 6-7. "Importance of Profit" (table 6-8) is now the most important variable in explaining attitude towards the mixing of public and private housing. This is a significant finding. We now have evidence for the association between market relations and locational conflict proposed in the first section of this paper. The direction of the association is indicated in table 6-9. Clearly, those regarding profit as important or very important are much more inclined to be negative about the mixing of public and private housing than those who place less emphasis on the home as an investment.

The MNA model of table 6-8, however, presents the impact of "Importance of Profit" in additive terms. Yet, when a control for "City" is introduced into table 6-9, an interaction between "City" and "Importance of Profit" is evident (see table 6-10 and figure 6-1). The effect of "Importance of Profit" in the MNA model, then, is not purely additive; there is a multiplicative effect stemming from the impact of "City" on the "Attitude Towards Mixing"/"Importance of Profit" relationship. In table 6-10, and as simplified in figure 6-1, therefore, we have summary presentations of the research findings: "Importance of Profit" differs among cities and this largely accounts for "Attitude Towards Mixing."

It can now be suggested, then, that not only is there a substantial difference between English and American homeowners with respect to exchange-value focus (table 6-1), but it is this difference that accounts in large part for the different degrees of conflict over public housing location in the two nations (tables 6-8 and 6-10).

Table 6-8. Attitude Towards Mixing Public and Private Housing, R^2 runs with Importance of Profit Included as an Independent Variable

All Variables Included	Excluding:	
.467	City	.443
	Age	.452
	Occupation	.458
	Self-rated Class	.439
	Importance of Profit	.421

Table 6-9. Attitude Towards Mixing Public and Private Housing, Cross-tabulated with Importance of Profit

	Mixing		
	Yes	No	D.K.
Profit	%	%	%
Very important	0.0	88.9	11.1
	(0)	(8)	(1)
Important	5.5	85.5	9.0
	(3)	(47)	(5)
Unimportant	32.7	43.7	23.6
	(18)	(24)	(13)
Very unimportant	63.4	26.8	9.8
	(26)	(11)	(4)

Table 6-10. Attitude Towards Mixing Public and Private Housing, Cross-tabulated with Importance of Profit Controlling for City

	Leicester			Dayton		
	Mixing					
	Yes	No	D.K.	Yes	No	D.K.
Profit	%	%	%	%	%	%
Very Important	0.0	0.0	0.0	0.0	88.9	11.1
	(0)	(0)	(0)	(0)	(8)	(1)
Important	23.0	54.0	23.0	0.0	95.2	4.8
	(3)	(7)	(3)	(0)	(40)	(2)
Unimportant	31.5	44.8	23.7	35.3	41.2	23.5
	(12)	(17)	(9)	(6)	(7)	(4)
Very unimportant	64.2	28.2	7.7	50.0	0.0	50.0
	(25)	(11)	(3)	(1)	(0)	(1)

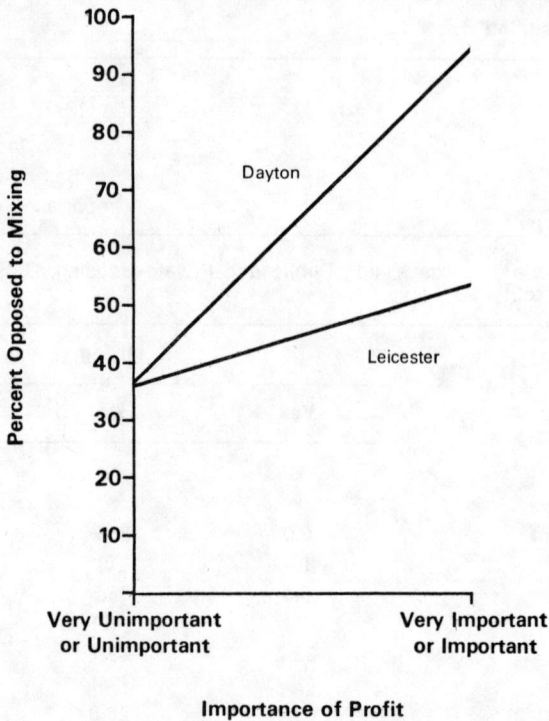

Figure 6-1. Illustration of the Interaction Between City and the Importance of Profit

Conclusion

Although more evidence must be collected before any definitive conclusions are in order, some preliminary judgments can be made. First of all, there is evidence that in different market societies different conceptions of the home as an investment may prevail. Specifically, in England, homeowners are much less likely to see their homes in exchange-value terms than are homeowners in the United States. Further, and to all appearances, the incidence of locational conflict is largely a function of conceptions of the house as an investment. Hence, conflict is more widespread in the United States, where the home is more likely to be viewed as an investment.

A suitable conclusion to this paper would be that locational conflict appears to be largely a function of market relations, but market societies differ in the extent to which these relations have penetrated all aspects of social life. Hence, market societies differ with respect to the incidence of locational conflicts.

Notes

1. See, for instance, David Harvey, *Society, the City, and the Space Economy of Urbanism* (Washington, D.C.: Association of American Geographers Commission on College Geography, 1972); and Manuel Castells, *La question urbaine* (Paris: Maspero, 1972).

2. "Urban resources" are equivalent to the elements in Harvey's "built enviornment." See David Harvey, "Labor, Capital, and Class Struggle Around the Built Environment in Advanced Capitalist Societies," chapter 1 of this volume.

3. This is true only when providers are regarded as individuals, rather than as representatives of interests.

4. Some writers, however, suggest that goals other than the enhancement of exchange value per se (such as the quest for security) may motivate *individual* providers. For instance, see B. Elliott and G. McCrone, "Landlords in Edinburgh: Some Preliminary Findings," *Sociological Review* 23, no. 3 (August 1975): 539–62.

5. There is now a substantial literature on this. See, for example, Michael S. Stegman, *Housing Investment in the Inner City: The Dynamics of Decline* (Cambridge, Mass.: M.I.T. Press, 1972); David Harvey and Lata Chatterjee, "Absolute Rent and the Structuring of Space by Governmental and Financial Institutions," *Antipode* 6, no. 1 (April 1974): 22–36; and James Little, *The Contemporary Neighborhood Succession Process*, (St. Louis, Mo.: Washington University Institute for Urban and Regional Studies, 1975).

6. For example, there is now considerable dispute over where to place "managers"—both private and public. Should they be included under capital, which they represent, or under labor, because they work? On this issue see, for instance, Raymond E. Pahl, *Whose City?* (Harmondsworth, Middlesex: Penguin Books, 1975), chap. 13; Robin Blackburn, "The New Capitalism," in *Ideology in Social Science*, ed. R. Blackburn (London: Fontana, 1973); and Peter Norman, "Managerialism—A Review of Recent Work," in *Proceedings of the Conference on Urban Change and Conflict*, ed. Michael Harloe (London: Centre for Environmental Studies, 1975).

7. Landlords seek rent, builders seek immediate profit, and financiers seek interest. However, all are seeking in different forms the same thing: exchange value and dependence upon it for the provision of use values.

8. The term "housing classes" was first used, although in a different general context, in John Rex and Robert Moore, *Race, Community, and Conflict* (London: Oxford University Press, 1967). The increased extent of homeownership in England and the United States owes much to government subsidy of providers and consumers. Consumers have been subsidized through income tax breaks on property tax and mortgage interest payments. Providers have been subsidized by secondary mortgage activities, depreciation allowances against income taxes, mortgage guarantees, and government-sponsored "homeownership" programs.

9. Some recent survey research carried out in one American and one English city provides evidence that property ownership does tie people to the property rights status quo. This survey is described later in the paper. Of the owners, 53.2 percent interviewed agreed or strongly agreed that "the main purpose of government should be to protect the private property of its citizens." Only 16.3 percent of the renters were of similar opinion. This contrast between homeowners and renters persists when responses are subjected to multivariate analysis. Tenure status and age of respondent are the two most important explanatory variables. Whatever the nationality, therefore, ownership appears to imply a greater commitment to the property rights status quo. For details see John A. Agnew, "Public Policy and the Spatial Form of the City: The Case of Public Housing Location" (Ph.D. diss., Ohio State University, 1976), pp. 229–31.

10. George Sternlieb, "Death of the American Dream House," *Society* 9, no. 4 (February 1972): 39.

11. Harvey, "Labor, Capital, and Class Struggle," chapter 1 of this volume.

12. The same survey alluded to in note 9 (above) and described below.

13. This relationship is suggested by the results of a survey reported in "Homing In on the Homing Instinct," *Business Week* (October 14, 1967), pp. 104–9.

14. For a detailed breakdown of the survey sample, see J. A. Agnew, "Spatial Form of the City," chap. 5.

15. The basic reference work on MNA is Frank M. Andrews and Robert C. Messenger, *Multivariate Nominal Scale Analysis* (Ann Arbor: University of Michigan Research Center ISR, 1973).

16. The only relevant theoretical argument known to this author is that concerning the mediating role of "local interests" in relating market relations to locational conflict. See Kevin R. Cox, "Local Interests and Political Processes in American Cities" (Paper presented at Symposium on Land Use and Public Policy, University of California at Riverside, June, 1975).

17. For the United States, total movers as a percent of total population has remained a fairly constant 20 percent per annum since 1947. See Eric G. Moore, *Residential Mobility in the City*, Association of American Geographers Commission on College Geography Resource Paper (Washington, D.C., 1972), p. 2. For England the most recent rate of total movement is for 1971, when 6.7 percent of the total population of England and Wales moved. *Census of England and Wales* (1971), table 4.

18. However, the introduction of vaguer "Structure Plans" may disturb this certainty. Many of the letters written by "concerned citizens" to the Leicester and Leicestershire Structure Plan Inquiry in 1975, for instance, contained reference to the "instability" that the lack of detail in the new plan might produce. (Thanks to Chris Geere of Leicester Planning Department for showing me the letters.)

19. G. F. Will, "The English Malady," *Newsweek* (February 23, 1976), p. 96.

20. This, of course, is a matter of degree. Private apartment buildings and new, single-family homes can meet with a similar, if more muted, response from established homeowners.

21. On the United States see, for example, Martin Meyerson and Edward C. Banfield, *Politics, Planning, and the Public Interest* (New York: The Free Press, 1954); on England, see Peter Collison, *The Cutteslowe Walls* (London: Faber, 1963).

22. The housing managers of all English cities with populations of 50,000 or more were therefore contacted. Given the greater number of cities in the U.S. with populations in excess of 50,000, some selection was necessary. The cities in the U.S. whose housing directors were contacted were selected on the basis of enhancing representativeness with respect to city size and region.

23. The term "conflict" was eschewed, given that it might alienate potential respondents from answering the survey.

24. J. A. Agnew, "Spatial Form of the City," chap. 4.

25. Some justification for the selection of these cities is appropriate. Of primary importance, both Dayton and Leicester were logistically convenient for the author, and both cities match closely in terms of population size and occupational composition. Also, in an extensive correspondence (separate from the mail survey) with housing officials throughout the United States and England, the housing directors for Dayton and Leicester proved exceptionally cooperative in providing information. Finally, neither Dayton nor Leicester has, by respective national standards, a controversial or particularly unusual public housing program. In particular, the respective relative locations of Dayton and Leicester are such that extreme regional stereotypes are avoided. This is especially important in England, given the "council housing and working-class" image of many northern cities, such as Leeds and Sunderland, and the "suburban and bourgeois" image of many southern cities, such as Reading and Oxford. Dayton and Leicester can be regarded as reasonably good examples of "typical" or "average" situations in their respective national contexts.

26. The second criterion was included in order to introduce some control for the impact on attitudes of the sequencing of development.

27. Around each of the four public housing areas, three distance bands, each approximately 250 yards wide, were drawn. Then, using the *1974 Register of Electors for Leicester* and *Polk's 1973 Directory of Dayton,* a sampling frame was drawn up for each distance band. Using a uniform sampling fraction of one-sixth of the total population of households in each distance band, a random sample of households was drawn. This produced a total sample of 203 households: 101 in Leicester and 102 in Dayton. Ninety of the Leicester and seventy of the Dayton respondents were homeowners.

28. Only nineteen refusals were experienced: eighteen in Leicester and one in Dayton. These households were replaced by substitutes selected for each distance band at the initial sampling.

29. However, the question from the household survey involves the assumption that, in Fishbein's words, "Knowledge of an individual's attitude toward some object will allow one to predict the way he will behave with respect to the object." Clearly, this may not be the case. Martin Fishbein, "Attitude and the Prediction of Behavior," in *Readings in Attitude Theory and Measurement,* ed. M. Fishbein (New York: Wiley, 1967), p. 472.

Chapter 7

CONFLICT IN THE LOCATION OF SALUTARY PUBLIC FACILITIES

DAVID R. REYNOLDS

REX HONEY

Conflict over the locations of public facilities frequently arise in market societies. This is because, in addition to jurisdictional benefits (which accrue to everyone within the jurisdiction providing a service), many public facilities also generate local effects, which impact only the immediate vicinity of a facility. Noxious facilities—those with negative local effects—have frequently been the subject of geographical studies.[1] This paper broadens the scope of the public facility location literature by addressing the converse problem: locating and relocating salutary facilities whose local effects are positive. In market societies, local effects can be expected to enter the decision calculus for public facility locations. We use a geographical variant of public choice theory to deduce distribution of support for, and opposition to, salutary facility locations in market societies.

Noxious and Salutary Facilities

The noxious facility location decision requires a strategy for imposing a facility which reduces the locational satisfaction in one neighborhood so that residents of other neighborhoods in a jurisdiction may benefit. If subjected to approval of the neighborhood receiving the facility, the noxious facility likely would not be built without a side payment: perhaps a salutary facility. The decision maker is tempted to locate where resistance is low or, minimally, where resistance is less than elsewhere. Resistance also tempts the decision maker to locate as few noxious facilities as possible. Locational costs would thus be concentrated in the few neighborhoods receiving the facilities: likely, lower-income neighborhoods with low levels of participation or political acuity.

Locational conflicts are different for salutary public facilities which include publicly provided or maintained amenities; e.g., parks and beaches, as well as facilities with frequent and widespread use, the foremost example being schools. Locational benefits from salutary facilities increase the desirability of nearby residences and thus may enhance property values. To the extent that increments to value are greater than increments to property obligations, the household near a salutary facility may obtain a capital gain in addition to any gain in personal satisfaction.

Given the desirability of salutary facilities, the locational problem becomes one of denying competing sites, rather than of finding areas of least resistance. Individuals distant from facilities would appeal for nearby ones, possibly tempting decision makers to authorize more than are necessary on technical efficiency grounds alone. On the other hand, households near existing facilities may oppose additional sites, either on the grounds of needless expenditure (which may or may not be the case) or because this would decrease the value of their own property, since these areas already have capitalized the benefits of the facilities near them. Resistance would be even greater if closing or relocating one were proposed. Understanding support for, and resistance to, changes in a set of salutary facility locations requires consideration of localized capitalization benefits, as well as the more direct jurisdictional benefits. One way to understand the behavior of households with regard to salutary public facilities is to examine their demands for them.

Public Choice Implications for Locating Salutary Public Facilities

It is not difficult to determine the "goods" demanded from local governments by urban residents. A large literature points to items such as: housing; pleasant physical and social environments; accessibility to production and consumption activities; "good" public services, such as education and personal and property protection; and, importantly, the ability to alter the levels at which some or all of these "goods" are supplied as incomes and needs change. The distinguishing characteristic of these items is that decisions pertaining to their supply are collective or political, with the inherent result that conflict is the rule, rather than the exception. The essence of collective decision making in urban areas is determining what people want, understanding the constraints imposed by scarcity, ascertaining the conflicts between desires and constraints, and finding some means of resolving conflict. Yet this must be done by maximizing the satisfaction of individual demands without also maximizing the cost imposed on others.[2]

The study of alternative means to satisfy demands for local public goods, to resolve conflicting demands, and to trade off demands for

different public goods has become the focus of a large and growing literature loosely referred to as "public choice theory." The alternative means
identified include: political activity (voting, lobbying, even litigation);
relocating in an area with more desirable public goods; or turning to the
private market (for example, transferring children from public to private
schools). Political processes, residential relocation, and use of private
markets are imperfectly substitutable and, hence, have comparative advantages in different institutional contexts and for different groups of
people. Unfortunately, public choice theory as developed in economics
has been preoccupied with the latter two options, particularly residential
relocation. Important exceptions include: Buchanan and Tullock; Haefele;
and Bish and Nourse.[3]

Local governments, however, clearly serve an important role in the
allocation of public goods to individuals within their jurisdiction. They
decide what goods and services will be provided through what institutions,
how public goods will be financed, and where public facilities will be
located. If one looks at either the government production, financing, or
location decisions, one finds that the theoretical basis for making these
decisions is relatively well worked out. For the production decision, the
theory of the firm provides conceptual guidance; for the financing decision, public finance theory is useful; for the locational decision, location-
allocation models are increasingly practical.[4]

However, theoretical models of the demands for publicly provided
goods and services are underdeveloped and tend primarily to provide
negative guidance. For example, according to public choice theory, the
jointness-in-consumption property of public goods, coupled with the relative lack of markets for these goods, precludes public officials from directly observing the preferences of their constituents. Furthermore,
individuals may be reluctant to express true preferences for public goods.
An individual who does so risks bearing the full marginal cost of provision
because it might then be possible to finance the good through direct
benefit taxation. By masking his true preference, he can participate as a
free rider or as "partial-payment" rider in the consumption of public
goods.

In short, the lack of an empirically relevant theory of demand for public
goods implies either that local governments must use indirect means to
ascertain community preferences and develop a local social welfare function upon which to base collective decisions, or that they must simply
refuse to entertain any public good supply decisions that are thought
(erroneously or not) to engender community conflict sufficient to endan-
ger their tenure in office. The focus in this paper is on the latter of these
two alternatives. In particular, we analyze expected patterns of citizen
support for a variety of salutary facility expenditure and locational propos-

als and attempt to deduce the one which local officials would choose, given certain assumptions regarding their behavior.

Theoretical Demand for Educational Expenditures

Analysis of local public service demands becomes more tractable and considerably less abstract if one is willing to build more institutional and geographical structure into the problems; for example, by making realistic assumptions about local taxation, the means through which collective decisions are reached, and the geography of private benefits from public services. In subsequent subsections of this paper we will deduce statements pertaining to the spatial distribution and levels of aggregate demand for expenditures on a local public good. Our example is public education. The focus will be on the demand for educational expenditures and capital expenditures for schools, rather than on demand for some common and altogether hypothetical unit of educational output.[5]

Unless indicated otherwise, the following assumptions will be made throughout the analysis:

1. Expenditures for education, including the costs of transporting distant students to and from schools, are financed entirely through general property taxation (on land and improvements) within a given school district.
2. All households own property.
3. All school children are assigned to the nearest school.
4. Households prefer to minimize their distance from a school.
5. School officials prefer the expenditure and location policy which, at any point in time, will maximize the total number of households which will support it.
6. Incomes of households vary, but no household's income is so low, nor its attachment to its present residential site so great, that it is geographically immobile.
7. Households are economically rational.
8. Households can derive four types of benefits from educational expenditures:
   a. "user" benefits which are independent of school locations;
   b. "user" benefits which decrease monotonically with increasing distance between the household's residence and the nearest school;
   c. districtwide capitalization benefits due to the general educational reputation of the district vis-à-vis its residential competitors; and
   d. local capitalization benefits which, like the "user" benefits in (b), also decrease monotonically with increasing distance from a school. All households receive districtwide capitalization benefits, if any

exist, but whether a household obtains any of the other benefits is dependent on its location within the district and on whether it is a user or nonuser of the educational programs provided.

Assumptions 1–4 and 7 simplify exposition, yet introduce a modicum of realism into the analysis; 1 and 2 are strong assumptions, but the effects of their relaxation in the subsequent analysis are straightforward. The remaining assumptions warrant further discussion. Assumption 5 ensures that school officials do not engage in "slate making" designed to forge a minimum-winning coalition of households in school elections and that they weigh the political support of households equally. Its welfare implications are obvious, but its "realism" is questionable. Its general normative value suggests that it may be a useful first approximation to the political behavior of school officials. Assumption 6 is also not particularly realistic in most contexts but is included so as to highlight the potential impact of geographical mobility on household demand for salutary public facilities.

Assumption 8 represents a significant departure from assumptions typically made about local education benefits by public choice analysts in economics.[6] As explained below, three of the four types of benefits described in this assumption are deducible from public choice theory and our other assumptions but are included to lend intuitive meaning to the residual concept of "user" benefits independent of location. Theoretically, those user benefits dependent on school location are similar to local capitalization benefits: the former refer to the amount in increased "rent" a household would be willing to pay, *but does not pay*, at its present location for being accessible to a school with a certain level of educational expenditure; the latter refer to that portion of the *market* value of a residential site attributable to its accessibility, again, to a school with a certain level of educational expenditure.

Standard public choice theory suggests that it is the individual marginal benefit and tax price of the public service which determines a consumer-voter's true demand for a service.[7] But, ever since the seminal article by Tiebout, public choice theorists have given lip service to the fact that the mobile household in a decentralized system of local governments in a market economy always has the option of selling property holdings in one community and moving to another when confronted with unsatisfactory levels of preferred local public goods or, more generally, whenever the economic welfare of the household can be enhanced.[8] Ironically, public choice theory as it presently stands fails to recognize that such a household will be concerned with the effects of local public service supply on the pecuniary terms on which it can leave the community; i.e., on its property values, as well as—or perhaps even instead of—the marginal benefit and cost of the service.[9] Therefore, we are led to hypothesize that anticipated wealth or capitalization effects should play a role in determining household demands for public expenditures. Cross-sectional evidence of the capitalization of educational expenditures into property values at school district level is presented by Oates; Edel and Sclar; and Sabella.[10] As pointed out by Bloom and Jackson,[11] however, with high levels of household mobility, capitalization is likely to be a short-run phenomenon.

> Households who want good schools, but who are not able or willing to pay the necessary premium to locate in a particular town, may locate in another town and over time vote to raise the level of schooling. It is easy over time for a town to raise taxes and provide better schools if that is what the people want. When this happens in enough towns, the premium people will pay for housing in the first town will decline because of the competition from additional towns with good schools. Housing prices will reflect only service level differences for the period required for other towns to build up their schools and establish their educational reputations.[12]

However, we argue that within an individual school district, local capitalization benefits from educational expenditures can have a high degree of permanency if the locations of schools remain fixed and the quality of education provided is not allowed to deteriorate. This follows from the simple geography of the situation (all households cannot be equally "near" a school) and from our assumption that all households prefer to minimize "distance to a school." In addition, local capitalization benefits and location-dependent user benefits will decrease with increasing distance from a school.

Although educational expenditures are likely to be capitalized into local property values in a locationally systematic manner, however, this does not imply that within a school district households which are relatively distant from a school fail to enjoy other private benefits from these expenditures. Otherwise, only the minority of households near schools would support public education. The benefits "distant" households obtain are districtwide capitalization benefits, if they are nonusers of the school, and both districtwide capitalization *and* location-independent user benefits, if they are users.

Given the theoretical similarity between location-dependent user benefits and local capitalization benefits, it is possible to simplify subsequent analysis, without much loss in generality, by referring to the sums of these two benefits as *locational benefits*. Also, for the sake of brevity in exposition, location-independent benefits from educational expenditures will be referred to as *user benefits* (unless otherwise noted).

Empirical Demand Model for Educational Expenditures

A simple model for the estimation of household demand for levels of local school spending has recently been proposed, and a modification of it tested successfully by Peterson.[13] Under the assumption of simple constant elasticity, it can be written as:

$$L_i = aY_i^\alpha \left[\frac{H_i(N)}{T} \right]^\beta s^\delta n_i^\varepsilon \tag{1}$$

where L_i = household i's desired level of local school spending;

where Y_i = household i's income;

where H_i = value of household i's property tax base (property value);

where T   = total tax base of the district;

where N   = total number of pupils in the district;

where s   = amount of state aid received per pupil by the district;

where n_i = number of public school children in household i;

and a, α, β, δ, and ϵ are constants.

Simplifying (1) to render it more consistent with our assumptions and Peterson's empirical work, we may write:

$$L_i = aY_i^\alpha \left[\frac{H_i(N)}{T} \right]^\beta \tag{2}$$

The bracketed term can be interpreted as "tax price," and α and β as income and tax-price elasticities, respectively. Given our arguments concerning local capitalization benefits, one would clearly expect to encounter specification problems in estimating the parameters of the model if calibrated at the household level within a single school district. Furthermore, one must question the assumption of constant elasticities. This is granted. However, for our purposes, the relevance of Peterson's model is that despite these shortcomings, it provides an impressive fit to empirical data. Peterson calibrated the model by utilizing cross-sectional school district data and analyzing voting in school tax referenda. In all cases he found α to be +1 or greater and β to be negative (varying between −.25 and −.83). This suggests two things: First, the negative elasticity of L_i with tax price is as posited by public choice theory. Second, demand for local school spending appears to increase directly with household income. We will utilize these findings in our analysis.

Analysis and Implications

In the following analyses the consequences of applying public choice principles to school location issues are deduced from our eight initial assumptions and relaxations of them in specific locational contexts. We begin by looking within a jurisdiction in order to gauge the effects of locational benefits. The first analysis assumes identical user benefits and consequently results in everyone wanting to be near a school so that those benefits can be obtained. The resulting conflict is more readily resolved in the second analysis, when the identical user benefit assumption is relaxed. The consequences of this are extended in the third analysis to show that a dual housing market—higher- and lower-income individuals competing for different residences—may result. The fourth analysis examines the public choice and locational implications of our assumptions in the context of rapid population growth. The last analysis turns to interdistrict problems, so that the combined effects of locational and districtwide benefits may be examined.

Analysis I: Identical Marginal User Benefits— Single Jurisdiction

For the purposes of exposition, let us assume initially that all households in a school district enjoy identical marginal user benefits with increasing educational expenditures (indicated by the lines DE and AB figures 7-1 and 7-2, respectively) and that the locations of all schools in the district are determined simultaneously and remain fixed. Let us also assume that districtwide capitalization benefits are nonexistent (this assumption is relaxed later) and that all expenditures are allocated equally across schools on a per pupil basis. Then, given our previous assumptions (1–8), the following are obtained:

First, the tax prices confronted by households "close" to a school (indicated by IJKL in figure 7-1) *increase* with increasing school expenditures over time until that level at which marginal locational benefits equal zero, while the tax prices of households "distant" from a school (indicated by CDEF in figure 7-2) decrease with increasing expenditures until the locational benefits of the "close" households are exhausted. For further marginal increases in expenditures, the tax prices of the two "types" of households are constant (see figures 7-1 and 7-2). Second, the relevant marginal benefits (demand) curve for the "close" household is the sum of its locational and user benefits curves (FGHE in figure 7-1). Since locational benefits from educational expenditures are (by assumption) small or nonexistent for the "distant" household, its relevant marginal benefits

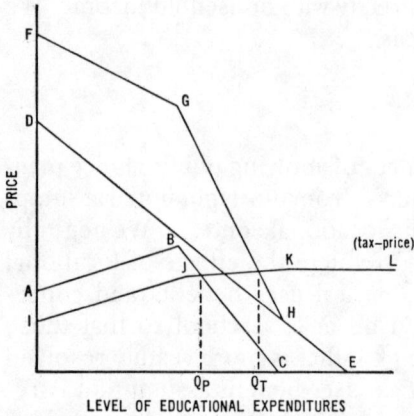

Figure 7-1. Demand—Tax-Price Relationships: "Close" Household

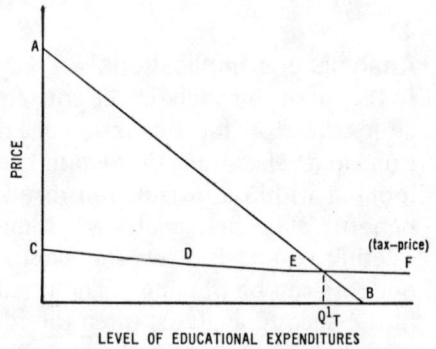

Figure 7-2. Demand—Tax-Price Relationships: "Distant" Household

curve is the user benefits curve (AB in figure 7-2). Third, the existence of locational benefits for at least some of the households in the school district ensures (by assumption 5) that the level of expenditure will be at least Q_T in figure 7-1 or Q^1_T in figure 7-2, whichever is smaller.

We are led to conclude that, under these assumptions, households close to schools will always prefer levels of expenditures higher than would households farther away for all levels where their marginal *increases* in tax prices are less than the marginal *decreases* in tax prices of those farther away. This would be the case when the school district is geographically large and the number of schools is small. When the number of schools is large (i.e., when more households are "close" to schools), good location vis-à-vis a school is a less scarce resource. Hence, one would expect that the magnitude of increases in locational benefit and decreases in tax price would be less with increasing levels of school expenditure. In the extreme case of a school in the backyard of every household, the capitalization component of locational benefits from education would be nonexistent. Furthermore, one would hypothesize that the total level of expenditures in the district would be lower than it would be with fewer schools (ignoring, of course, any scale economies). This also leads to the interesting possibility of there being more public support for increases in educational expenditures, the fewer the number of schools in a district.

If educational expenditures are not capitalized in a locationally dependent manner, households would prefer to maximize the number of schools in a district subject to a relevant production function. However, if capitalization is pervasive but decreases with distance from a school, households would prefer to minimize the number of schools, subject again to a relevant production function and to the condition that the number of households supporting a locational pattern of schools is maximized. All households would, of course, prefer to be close to one of the schools, with the result that conflict is not over the level of expenditures per se, but over the location of schools. Furthermore, this locational conflict is not easily resolvable under our assumptions. For any given number of schools the locational pattern which would maximize citizen support would be the one which minimized the total distance of all households from their nearest school. However, there would be a large number of patterns which would muster *approximately* equal levels of support, with the result that the levels of community conflict would be high and the locational deliberations of public officials lengthy.

Analysis II: Unequal Marginal User Benefits— Single Jurisdiction

When the unrealistic assumption of identical marginal user benefits is relaxed, the locational conflict identified above can be resolved (or at least minimized) relatively easily. Referring again to figure 7-1, it can be seen that even if "close" households obtain no user benefits from educational expenditures (e.g., they have no children and do not utilize school facilities for recreational or other purposes); they would prefer an expenditure level of Q_p (where the marginal increase in their local capitalization benefits equals their tax price). If this household also derives marginal user benefits that are positive at expenditure levels greater than Q_p, then its preferred level of school spending will be still higher. This implies that locational conflict in school politics will be minimized when schools are located in low user-demand neighborhoods. Given Peterson's evidence that the user demand of low-income households is lower than that for higher-income households, there are distinct welfare *and* political advantages to locating schools in relatively low-income neighborhoods. It is not politically efficacious to locate schools in high user-demand neighborhoods (under our assumptions) because households in these areas will support "high" levels of expenditure, anyway. Locating schools in lower-income areas is politically and (in a traditional welfare maximization sense superior) to one which simply minimizes aggregate student travel in the school district. It does not, however, lead to a stable equilibrium set of school locations if low user-demand households will sell their property to higher-demand households. If the former relocate elsewhere in the district, they will presumably not favor further increases in educational expenditures that do not entail the relocation of schools to their new neighborhoods. Instead, the above arguments suggest that the concept of a stable pattern of school locations is inappropriate in a market society characterized by democratic public choice, where: resources are limited; households, mobile; and capitalization effects, pervasive.

Analysis III: The Possible Formation
of a Dual Housing Market

In the previous two analyses we have addressed the question of what would be the preferred pattern of school locations within a district comprised of taxpayers with differing benefit streams from education expenditures under the implicit assumption that once school locations are determined through the political process, they remain fixed. In this brief analysis we retain this assumption, but relax the requirement that expenditures be allocated across schools on an equal, per pupil basis and allow new schools to be located.

Recall the population redistribution implication of analysis II: that low user-demand households (perhaps lower-income households), in order to realize locational benefits, will sell their properties to higher user-demand households and relocate to residences less accessible to schools (where housing costs are lower). These households consequently become opponents of any additional public investment in education unless new schools are located near them. It is clear, however, that the higher user-demand households (which have, in effect, "paid" for school accessibility) will oppose new school construction which can result in a perceptible decline in market value of their "new" residences. Again, the school district is confronted with locational conflict that cannot be reduced to zero, but can be minimized through a strategy whereby new schools entailing per pupil expenditures lower than those in existing schools are allocated to low user-demand neighborhoods. In order to maximize citizen support, the expenditures in these new schools must be at a level high enough for households near them to realize capitalization benefits from the competition of low user-demand households for residential sites, but at a level low enough so that high user-demand households do not enter the competition. If we can assume that our classification of high and low user demands are the result of marked income differentials, then it can be seen that the school location-allocation process can contribute to the formation, or at least the maintenance, of dual housing markets (dual in terms of income, not race—the lower-income residents are simply not competing for the same residences). It is important to note that this result obtains largely because of our assumption that school officials are attempting to maximize citizen support in their selection of school policies. If this assumption is, say, replaced by the assumption that officials attempt to form minimum-winning coalitions, then school location-allocation policy can contribute to the maintenance of a single housing market from which low-income households are simply excluded. Under these circumstances, the welfare implications of our maximization assumption are more ambiguous than they might appear otherwise.

Analysis IV: Effects of Rapid Growth

Consider a city (district) which is experiencing population inmigration and territorial growth. To avoid congestion and keep transportation costs down, one would expect strong public support for the construction of new schools. If we make the additional and realistic assumption that the inmigrants consist largely of young families with high user demands for education, the total number of households supporting additional capital expenditures will likely be maximized if the proposed locations of new schools will result in no reduction in *existing* locational benefits and yet increase the property value benefits of as many households with low user demands as possible. As before, if income is a major determinant of the demand for education, one is led to a policy of proposing school locations in existing, relatively low-income areas of the district.

Alternatively, those responsible for locating schools could, in this instance, attempt to locate new schools so as to minimize the aggregate travel of existing students or the travel of some projection of future students without relocating existing schools. This approach is not devoid of geographical "reasonableness" but would be politically inferior to that above in that it would: (1) lose the support of households in older residential areas with schools because older housing is, in general, less attractive to households than newer housing and, hence, the property value advantage of areas would decrease; and (2) lose the support of low user-demand households in older residential areas whose children are presently being transported to schools in other neighborhoods because they, too, would prefer to enjoy enhanced locational (property value) benefits. Clearly, an unconstrained travel minimization approach entailing the relocation of existing schools would result in an even greater reduction in support. This approach would likely have the support of developers, speculators owning developable land on the periphery of the city (district), and those households in the recently developed areas. If this approach were somehow implemented, school officials could be accused, quite justifiably (by households residing in older residential areas), of contributing to the residential decay of central city neighborhoods by subsidizing suburban sprawl.

Indeed, the only easily conceivable urban growth context in which a minimum aggregate travel solution is politically dominant over those based on user and locational benefits is when inmigration to a school district is so rapid that the property values of existing households inflate due to the failure of the *new* housing market to keep pace with the demand for housing in general. However, it should be pointed out that if school officials are not constrained to maximize total support (as they are in our fifth assumption) but must merely secure simple majority support, then their tendency to pursue a strategy of minimizing travel distances should be increased.

Analysis V: District and Locational Benefits

In the preceding analyses the emphasis has been on locational benefits with districtwide capitalization benefits held constant. Let us expand the analysis by looking at the consequences of considering both types of benefits simultaneously. Assume a region with two school districts, each with an urban center and surrounding rural area. Within each district, schools are located in the urbanized areas with locational benefits decreasing outward from them. Assume also that one district—call it District A—has better schools than the other—call it District B. District A, therefore, enjoys districtwide capitalization benefits. Consistent with the preceding analyses we can assume that District A's greater school expenditures follow from income higher for its residents than that of residents of District B. As long as the districts remain as they are, no school location decisions are considered.

Consider the case, however, when migrants move into the region. For purposes of explication, assume that the migrants have the same high incomes and propensity to pay for education as do residents of District A. The differences between the districts will affect the attractiveness of the districts to citizen-consumers and the attitude of the districts toward meeting any increased need for school space. All else being equal, citizen-consumers will prefer the district with better schools, so that new development is concentrated in that district. Officials of District A have three options: (1) simply to construct new schools where growth is occurring; (2) to construct new schools in the older neighborhoods (as in analysis IV); or (3) to expand existing facilities. Those in new areas would doubtlessly prefer the first option, which is often standard operating procedure. The second and third options allow residents of the older area to maintain their locational benefits in exchange for allowing newcomers to obtain districtwide benefits. Clearly, the second or third options would be preferred by those already residing in the district. Without bringing in more contextual assumptions regarding, for example, the rate and levels of inmigration and the relative cost of expanding old facilities or building new ones, it is not possible to determine which of these two options would be preferred. Therefore, let us simplify analysis by asserting that conditions are such that older residents prefer to expand existing facilities, at least initially. If we also assume that school officials are concerned with maximizing the support of existing residents, rather than that of some future set of constituents, they will follow the preferences of existing residents and expand existing facilities, rather than build new ones. Ironically, even the new inmigrants should be supportive of this policy if they believe that at some future date they will be sufficiently numerous to have the political clout to have new schools built near them because this would enable them to enjoy locational benefits without completely paying for them.

Under these conditions and our earlier assumptions, the distribution of locational and districtwide benefits leads to a spatial sequencing of development as newcomers maximize their benefits and existing residents respond. The newcomers build on the urbanizing periphery of A until the sum of benefits (both districtwide and locational) falls below that obtainable in the older residential areas of B. They then buy homes in B until exhausting locational benefits to the point that the districtwide benefits of A are the greatest available. The existing lower-income residents in District B are willing to sell—obtaining capital gains in the process—and build new residences on the periphery of District B, just as was the case in analysis III.

But what happens to District A after this point? Is there an incentive for building new schools? Yes, if a failure to build schools creates an incentive for low-income residents (formerly in District B) to move to the periphery of A. The lower-income residents would not support the same high level of expenditures for schools, thus jeopardizing District A's districtwide benefits. To protect their districtwide benefits, those in District A would then be willing to build new schools, so that new development was occupied by inmigrants sharing the propensity, extant in the district, to spend on education. In effect, District A would be building schools for exclusionary purposes, so that districtwide benefits could be maintained. Alternatively, the leaders of District A could try other exclusionary options, such as minimum zoning regulations, to effect the same result.

Discussion and Conclusions

Additional analyses based upon our initial eight assumptions can, of course, be conducted. Indeed, we intend to do so in future papers. But the basic thrust of our public choice argument should be clear: Given a market society characterized by well-entrenched concepts of private property and high levels of geographical mobility, the demand for local public expenditures may be quite divorced from any notion of user benefits. This pertains because, in a market society, housing is more than just a necessity. It can also be a capital investment appreciable through the location-allocation policies of local and other governments. In short, we have argued that at least some of the benefits from the location of salutary facilities are purely private or pecuniary and occur in the form we have referred to as jurisdiction-wide and local capitalization benefits. The existence of jurisdiction-wide benefits is quite well established in empirical studies, but the possible existence of local capitalization benefits remains largely uninvestigated. Obviously, carefully designed empirical studies of local capitalization benefits need to be undertaken.[14]

If our assumptions regarding benefits are realistic, and our other assumptions have empirical support and/or normative value, then one important implication of our analyses is that property taxation for the provision of education and perhaps other local services is, at least in part, "benefits" taxation. It should not, therefore, be abandoned completely as a source of revenue. Insofar as the location of salutary public facilities increases the property value of certain sites within a jurisdiction and/or enhances property values on a jurisdiction-wide basis, property taxation provides an efficient means for the public appropriation of such "windfall" benefits. Complete elimination of property taxation would not only increase the difficulty of taxing those who benefit from capitalization but could also result in public policy being determined even more by the pecuniary self-interest of citizens than would otherwise be the case.

In several of our analyses we deduced locational conflict resolution strategies with at least mildly progressive income-redistribution implications. Of critical importance in these analyses was our assumption that public officials select policies which maximize citizen (household) support. Departures from this assumption, in all the cases examined, led to regressivity in redistribution and, in a locational sense, to the urban center subsidizing the urbanizing periphery. Therefore, a second implication worthy of future analysis stems from the possibility that mechanisms can be found which compel policy makers to abandon location-allocation policies, forging the equivalent of "minimum-winning coalitions," in favor of those which *approach* maximum (i.e., unanimous) citizen approval. If so, then considerably more income redistribution can take place at the local scale than is recognized by researchers following the standard public choice paradigm of economics. In recent years, urban economists have argued for the implementation of marginal cost-pricing schemes to pay for the outward expansion of public service infrastructure and delivery systems. The prescription is, of course, based on the normative assumption that those who benefit from expansion should pay for it. Even if these marginal costs could be measured with relative ease, and marginal cost-taxing systems could be instituted, the result would only "correct" a regressivity in the local redistribution of income. Marginal cost taxing would not produce the progressivity possible under the political process assumptions employed in our analyses.

We have limited our analyses to instances in which all households are geographically mobile. However, our approach can easily be extended to the situation in which some households have initial incomes so low as to exclude them from housing markets: namely, any capitalization benefits they might obtain through facility location go unrealized because they are unable to afford "replacement" housing (even after capitalization). In terms of our previous models, these households would respond politically only to the user benefits they might obtain, contingent upon the relevant tax price entailed in any expenditure proposal. If tax price exceeded benefits, immobile households should be opponents of the proposal. Their opposition simply would be ignored by decision makers responsible for framing policy as long as they are a smaller group numerically than that consisting of relatively low-income, yet mobile, households (that can realize capitalization benefits). Similarly, even if immobile, low-income households pay no local taxes (and, hence, support all expenditure proposals), facility location policy, as in our previous analyses, should be determined largely by the locations of mobile, low-income households. Any system of direct, nonlocal income redistribution which renders the immobile poor more mobile also greatly enhances their political efficacy in the local location-allocation, decision-making process.

The analyses presented in this paper are highly simplified and clearly speculative. Our hope is that our theoretical probings help to stimulate the development of a less simplified and more explanatory public choice theory of locational conflict. Public choice theory offers a promising, albeit rudimentary, framework for the analysis of conflict situations in market societies. Like most varieties of economic theory, however, public choice theory developed aspatially, except in the sense of choosing among jurisdictions, with the variable being the bundle of services, rather than jurisdictional delimitation or location, within a jurisdiction. Geographers and other locational analysts can extend and refine public choice theory by bringing locational considerations (in a juxtapositional sense) more sharply into focus. As we have argued, the number and location of facilities may be as much a part of local political conflict as the level of service provided.

Notes

1. John Seley and Julian Wolpert, "A Strategy of Ambiguity in Locational Conflicts," in *Locational Approaches to Power and Conflict,* ed. K. R. Cox, D. R. Reynolds, and Stein Rokkan (New York: Halsted Press, 1974), pp. 275–300; also see C. Murray Austin, "Avoiding Conflict in Metropolitan Planning," *Geographical Perspectives* 35 (Spring 1975): 26–30.

2. John E. Jackson, "Public Needs, Private Behavior, and Metropolitan Governance: A Summary Essay," in *Public Needs and Private Behavior in Metropolitan Areas,* ed. J. E. Jackson (Cambridge, Mass.: Ballinger, 1975), pp. 1–29.

3. James M. Buchanan and Gordon Tullock, *The Calculus of Consent* (Ann Arbor: University of Michigan Press, 1962); Edward T. Haefele, *Representative Government and Environmental Management* (Baltimore: The Johns Hopkins University Press, 1973); and Robert L. Bish and Hugh O. Nourse, *Urban Economics and Policy Analysis* (New York: McGraw-Hill, 1975).

4. Allen J. Scott, *An Introduction to Spatial Allocation Analysis,* A.A.G. Commission on College Geography Publications Research Paper no. 9 (Washington, D.C., 1971); and Bryan Massam, *Location and Space in Social Administration* (London: Edward Arnold, 1975).

5. Efforts to define units of educational output have failed to the point that most studies of school efficiency have measured only educational expenditures.

6. Werner Z. Hirsch, Elbert W. Segelhorst, and Morton J. Marcus, *Spillover of Public Education Costs and Benefits* (Los Angeles: University of California Institute of Government and Public Affairs, 1964).

7. Tax price is defined as the decrease in the value of private good consumption which accompanies a marginal increase in public good supply. It is implicit in any given tax system; e.g., the individual's share of the tax base times the aggregate marginal cost of public good provision.

8. Charles Tiebout, "A Pure Theory of Local Expenditures," *The Journal of Political Economy* 64 (1956): 416–24.

9. R. Deacon and P. Shapiro, "Private Preference for Collective Goods Revealed Through Voting on Referenda," *American Economic Review* 65 (December 1975): 943–55. To our knowledge, Deacon and Shapiro are the only other researchers who have suggested that property value effects may influence public good demand.

10. Wallace E. Oates, "The Effects of Property Taxes and Local Spending on Property Values: An Empirical Study of Tax Capitalization and the Tiebout Hypothesis," *Journal of Political Economy* 77 (December 1969): 957–71; Matthew Edel and Elliott Sclar, "Taxes, Spending, and Property Values: Supply Adjustment in a Tiebout-Oates Model," *Journal of Political Economy* 82 (September/October 1974): 941–54; and Edward M. Sabella, "The Effects of Property Taxes and Local Public Expenditures on the Sale Prices of Residential Dwellings," *The Appraisal Journal* 42 (January 1974): 114–25.

11. Howard S. Bloom, H. James Brown, and John E. Jackson, "Residential Location and Local Public Services," in *Public Needs and Private Behavior in Metropolitan Areas,* ed. J. E. Jackson (Cambridge, Mass.: Ballinger, 1975), pp. 73–98.

12. Ibid., p. 79.

13. George E. Peterson, "Voter Demand for Public School Expenditures," ibid., pp. 99–119.

14. However, given that our assumption regarding local public officials attempting to maximize *total* citizen support in expenditure and locational policies has little empirical support, there may be few empirical contexts in which the hypothesis of distance-dependent capitalization benefits could receive a rigorous test. For example, if school officials attempt to maximize *parental* support, schools can and will be located so that total student travel is considerably less than it would be if officials maximized total citizen support (see analysis IV), with the result that schools could be sufficiently numerous and sufficiently close to other schools for local capitalization benefits to be indistinguishable empirically from districtwide capitalization benefits.

PART 3

Locational Outcomes

Overview

The papers presented in this final section concern two of the most obvious of the spatial outcomes of urbanization in market societies: suburbanization and residential segregation. Richard Walker's paper is ostensibly historical in character and treats the initial emergence of what he calls "the suburban solution" and the specialization of land uses in the nineteenth-century city. The other two papers focus more on the contemporary city. Oliver P. Williams and Kent Eklund discuss recent changes in levels of residential segregation in a major American metropolitan area (Philadelphia), while Ken Young and John Kramer are concerned with the exclusionary policies of independent suburbs in the London area that are attempting to limit the influx of lower-income households from central London. Despite the disjunction in time between the latter two papers and the first, however, Walker does provide a framework which allows us to place all these aspects of changing spatial form in context.

The specific context at issue in Walker's paper is that provided by capitalist development. Urbanization, he argues, is an expression of capitalist development: As capitalism evolves, so urban form will evolve in a way that will overcome, albeit temporarily, the contradictions immanent in that development. Changing urban form represents the consecutive "solutions" capitalist societies create to further accumulation and prevent social and political crisis.

More particularly, Walker contrasts the characteristic form of the large American city at the beginning of the nineteenth century with that which was starting to emerge after 1840, approximately. In what he calls "the petty commodity mercantile stage of accumulation" (1790–1842), the major cities are characterized as presuburban. They had little of that functional separation of land uses associated with cities today, and separation of work place from place of residence seems to have been the unusual rather than the norm: Most businesses were small and the owner would often live over the business. In an age when the independent artisan was more typical than the wage laborer, therefore, there was little scope for social segregation. Significantly, residential desirability appeared to *decrease* with increased distance from the center of the city. The city center was the cultural center; the wealthy did not as yet feel threatened by any incipient working-class movement; and, in an age where business control was often of a personal nature, ready access to business was most important.

With the evolution of capitalism, the emergence of the factory, and the increasing separation of the worker from the means of production, all this changes and we see the emergence, albeit in embryonic form, of spatial "solutions" which have continued to dominate the city to the present day.

Most significantly, factory production and the displacement of the independent artisan by the wage laborer spelled the demise of the spatial identity between work place and place of residence.[1] Henceforth, the place of living would be separate from the place of work. At the same time, the factory created a relationship to nature and one of man to man that were as alienated as they were exploitative. Here, therefore, we have the initial seeds of new residential arrangements: the suburb for the business classes who had both the time and income to afford commuting by horse-drawn streetcar; and the industrial slum for those who did not. The industrial slum, moreover, created its own problems from which the dominant classes were anxious to escape. On the one hand, overcrowding and congestion in inner areas of the city provided favorable conditions for the typhus and cholera epidemics of the nineteenth century.[2] On the other, the degrading condition of the wage laborer, both in the work place and the living place, was associated with threats to civil order and a bourgeois fear of the working class. Appropriately, the first municipal police forces and penitentiaries appear at this time.

About this time, also, we find the emergence of new social ideals associated with the suburban solution. In particular, Walker draws attention to the arcadian ideal: "Beginning rather suddenly in the 1830s and 1840s, the bourgeoisie sought the solicitude of nature in the landscape for their recreation, home life and literary fancy ..." (see chapter 8, p. 196). Walker identifies this as a substitute for relations to nature and man that could no longer be obtained in the city. Consequently, it can be regarded as a form of social and aesthetic escapism.

But the fundamental motivation for suburbanization is the desire of the dominant classes to put distance between themselves and the working class. And this motivation has to be seen within the context of fundamental structural changes in capitalism; in particular, the emergence of the factory and the wage laborer and the separation of work place from living place.

Walker's paper provides a useful framework for placing the substance of the other two papers in perspective. Williams and Eklund draw attention to the increasing levels of residential segregation across municipalities in the Philadelphia metropolitan area and identify those municipal policies—exclusionary zoning, in particular—likely to create this segregation. Young and Kramer, on the other hand, examine the defensive policies of outer London suburbs confronted with the threat of public housing for newcomers.[3] In the case of both papers, therefore, a basic mechanism of residential sorting is assumed to be the exclusionary policy of the municipality. Yet such exclusionary policies receive virtually no mention in Walker's treatments of suburbanization and the emergence of residential segregation. Nevertheless, Walker's framework does provide a basis for understanding the emergence of exclusionary policies.

Given the conditions of production to which Walker refers, the distance which the dominant classes were able to put between themselves and the city was a distance which, in cost terms, and possibly more importantly, in terms of time, the working class could not afford. Changing conditions of production have altered all that. The suburbanization of employment, mass automobile ownership, and shortening of both the workday and the workweek have reduced the real costs of commuting. The desire "to open up the suburbs," therefore, seems to have a reality above and beyond federal rhetoric.[4]

Consequently, the analyses of Williams and Eklund and of Young and Kramer not only complement that of Walker, they confirm it. The exclusionary behaviors which they highlight have been necessitated by that diffusion of personal mobility which allows the syndrome of "social escapism" to percolate still further down the social ladder. Everyone wants to put distance between himself and those lower in the social hierarchy, but distance can no longer be the preserve of the few. It is that, above all, which accounts for the essentially twentieth-century nature of local exclusionary policies.[5]

NOTES

1. This, of course, had implications for conflict in that it led to a separation of work-based and community-based conflict. See David Harvey, "Labor, Capital, and Class Struggle Around the Built Environment in Advanced Capitalist Societies," chapter 1 of this volume.

2. A consciousness of the medical geography of the nineteenth-century city is a consistent theme in the statements of contemporary observers and in the public postures of politicians of the time. It is, for example, a persistent idea in the arguments surrounding the operation of nineteenth-century railroads in Britain. On the one hand, it helped to remove opposition to the demolition of inner-city residential areas for the construction of central terminals and approach routes ("ventilating the slums" was the expression used); and, on the other hand, it was a persistent point in the arguments of those trying to facilitate working-class suburbanization by procuring cheap workman fares on the railways. See John R. Kellett, *The Impact of Railways on Victorian Cities* (London: Routledge and Kegan Paul, 1969). It is also a constant in discussions of the housing problem: see F. W. Lawrence, "The Housing Problem," in *The Heart of the Empire,* ed. C. F. G. Masterman (London: T. Fisher Unwin, 1901), chap. 2.

3. This is not regarded as inconsistent with the assertions in chapter 4 of this volume regarding the relative incidence of exclusionary policies in Britain and the U.S. The exclusionary policies noted by Young and Kramer are both quantitatively and qualitatively different from those encountered in the U.S., where, for example, suburban policies have aimed at excluding public housing altogether. This is not true in the London area, where independent suburbs have public housing stocks (as a fraction of their total stocks) that would flatter most American central cities. In addition, one will look in vain for evidence of those educational, public safety, and property value concerns that are so significant for American exclusionary policies.

4. A recent analysis of requests to move by Greater London Council housing tenants shows that the strongest demands are for moves from central to more suburban areas. This seems especially associated with the desire for a house (as opposed to an apartment). Houses are more readily available in suburban council estates. See Heather Bird, "Residential Mobility and Preference Patterns in the Public Sector of the Housing Market," *Transactions of the Institute of British Geographers,* n.s. 1, no. 1 (1976): 26–27.

5. And, we might add, this also demonstrates the essentially escapist character of the arcadian ideal. The concern of the exclusionary policy makers in outer London suburbs, therefore, is, according to Young and Kramer, to preserve a reality expressed in an image of their surroundings. And that image is, among other things, ". . . a lingering rurality, symbolized by wildlife, trees, agricultural remnants, and the immediacy of the protected countryside—the symbolically potent 'Green Belt.' "

Chapter 8

THE TRANSFORMATION
OF URBAN STRUCTURE
IN THE NINETEENTH CENTURY AND
THE BEGINNINGS OF SUBURBANIZATION

RICHARD A. WALKER

Introduction

Theories of urban structure have too long been in the grip of neoclassical, Von Thünen models of the Alonso-Muth-Mills variety.[1] While these models recommend themselves on the strength of their apparent mathematical rigor, a closer look at first assumptions casts serious doubt on their explanatory power. This is not the place to enter into a systematic critique of neoclassical economics, but certain salient objections can be raised in order to point out what new directions need be taken.

Neoclassical location rent models involve essentially minor additions of new variables to the conventional neoclassical theoretic framework in order to simulate space. These additions have to be simple in order to allow the complex mathematical calculations of equilibrium solutions to be made.

A first objection can be raised concerning the treatment of space. Here space reduces to a linear distance between two points and to the cost of overcoming this distance. This conception of relative space, as Harvey has shown,[2] ignores the fundamental aspects of *absolute* space, where private property reigns in service of purposes such as procuring rents or defending one's home-as-castle; or *relational* space, which presupposes the rich relationships among people and land uses operating outside the market altogether. This leads, for one thing, to an extremely limited conception of urban rent, a problem which I have considered elsewhere.[3] It also

The author wishes to thank Sy Adler, David Harvey, and Kevin R. Cox, the editor, for their critical readings of an earlier manuscript. This paper is based on a portion (especially chapter 3) of an unpublished doctoral dissertation, "The Suburban Solution: Urban Reform and Urban Geography in the Capitalist Development of the United States," The Johns Hopkins University, 1977.

corresponds to the convenient assumption of a featureless plain and to perfect substitution of one location for another, a conception which ignores not only the variations of nature, but also the more important fact of an urban built environment. Space is void of the real clutter of buildings, and the model is relieved of the need to account for how they got there or how they are adapted to new uses.

But the problems go deeper than the conception of space. Conventional location models also begin from the standard consumer choice and production function paradigms of neoclassical economic theory. The first objection to this approach is that the two sides of urban life, production and consumption, exist in splendid isolation from one another. But more important is the way in which these processes are conceptualized in order to produce a model which "explains" the apparent centrality and declining gradient of the urban rent field. On the one hand, consumer choice theory assumes a world of individuals without social relations, loves, fears, conventions, and the like; they are, instead, a set of autonomous atoms with preexisting and fixed "tastes" for commodities. The origin of these tastes does not interest these theorists.[4] People relate only to their commodities, and space is simply another commodity consumers invariably want more of. The result is an unquestioned assertion that people desire space per se and purchase more as they grow richer, *ceteris paribus*. The purpose of this rather strong assumption is, of course, to reproduce in theory the observable movement of richer people to the suburban fringe in contemporary American cities.

Production, on the other hand, is depicted essentially as an extension of exchange, rather than as an internally related, but fundamentally different and socially dominant, process as in Marxist theory.[5] It consists of commodity relations instead of social relations, equality in place of class domination, and an infinite smoothness of substitution in place of the discontinuity of technical change.[6] The picture of the city drawn on the basis of such a theory lacks any semblance of conflict or change emerging from the sphere of production.[7]

Furthermore, in order to reproduce the apparent centrality of cities, all production must be lumped by assumption into the central business district (CBD), or else it is said that a significant portion of the city's commodity flow must pass through the center in the process of exchange, whether for internal marketing or for export and import. The reasons for these assumptions are that either economies of agglomeration in production are realized at the center, or it is in the nature of transportation to concentrate the transfer of goods, owing to scale economies or transshipment costs. These are not unreasonable assumptions, but they leave certain questions unanswered: Under what circumstances are agglomeration economies really vital to production costs? Under what conditions of production and consumption, and with which modes of transportation, does transport play such a crucial role? Have cities always been centralized? And are cities in fact centralized for reasons of *commodity* production and circulation?

This brings up a final and most essential objection to the neoclassical models: their ahistorical nature. The same causal factors are assumed to have prevailed since the beginning of time and for all humanity. But cross-cultural and historical studies show clearly that present-day American patterns, such as the preference of the wealthy for the urban fringe, have simply not always existed nor do they hold for all modern forms of urbanism. And even if these theorists know full well the historical limits of their models, the latter provide no insight into the process of historical change of the qualitative, rather than quantitative, sort and thus help not at all in developing an understanding of how we came to our present urban condition, whether it need be as it is, and from what direction change is likely to spring.

A small but growing body of historical and geographic literature now exists to show that the spatial structure, or internal morphology, of American cities has changed rather considerably over time. A most profound alteration, for example, in the morphology of the large cities of this country has been observed between, roughly, the first and second halves of the nineteenth century. The purpose of this paper is, first, to describe the nature of that shift and, second, to provide a systematic framework to help account for the change. It is hoped, in particular, that from this a clearer understanding of the origins of suburbanization—or rather certain dimensions of urbanization presently associated with that term—may emerge to supplant the naive view that suburbanization is a "natural" outcome of (1) increasing affluence of consumers with a taste for space and (2) disembodied technical change in transportation and production.[8]

This is an interpretative essay rather than an accounting of new historical evidence. But a fresh way of looking at existing data can make them appear as new. A certain familiarity with the outlines of American urban history is presumed, so that only the relevant highlights will be emphasized. Admittedly, the available data are not so numerous or sufficiently precise as to permit uncritical confidence in any explanation of urban transformation in the nineteenth century. One hardly need say that the conclusions reached in this paper need further study. On the other hand, a virtual consensus exists among urban historians and geographers on many points concerning the profound realignment of the internal structure of the leading cities of the United States during the last century: that the years from about 1830 to the Civil War were a crucial time of change is undisputed, if for no other reason than the observably vast difference in the way cities appeared between the first and last quarters of the cen-

tury. But accounts of timing, cause, and process in this change are sufficiently gnarled so as to demand an effort to venture into the bog of
history, theoretical sword in hand, in hopes of cutting through the tangle
and laying the essence bare.

Prefatory Remarks on the Theory Under Which We Labor[9]

Urbanization and Capitalism

Modern urbanization is taken here to be part and parcel of the larger
process of capitalist development, a process of great apparent complexity
and constant flux. But beneath the superficial complexity and movement,
it is possible to discern an underlying stability—an eye of calm at the
center of the storm—owing to certain fundamental social relations. The
pivotal relations of capitalism arise in production, centering around the
capital-wage labor relation. From this relation flow the most essential
dynamics of capitalism: economic, social, environmental, and so forth.
The three most important are: (1) production, appropriation, reinvest-
ment, and **expansion of surplus value** or the accumulation of capital; (2)
the **antagonism between the working class and the bourgeoisie** engendered by **the latter's control over the means of production** and, hence,
over the product and process of social labor; and (3) the transformation
of nature into commodities under the domination of the bourgeoisie and
the pressures of accumulation. Yet the analogy to the hurricane is misleading for the eye of the storm is, in this case, also the cause of the storm,
the fundamental source of contradiction in capitalist society. It is the
tension arising from below—the drive for the accumulation of capital (and
the self-contradictory nature of this drive), the struggle among the classes,
the limits to the exploitation of nature—which provide the chief driving
forces for historical change under this system.

Capitalist urbanization partakes of the contradictions and movements
of capitalist development. Urbanization is not, of course, a mere reflection
of an organic totality, but rather an internal relation of the whole of
capitalism. It thus adds its own wrinkles to the whole and cannot be
collapsed to a simple identity with it. It is strongly structured, but not
determined, by capitalist development; the latter sets the problems and
the possibilities for capitalist cities. The mode of production makes certain demands on urbanization and must also supply the means for meeting
them. Capital works at both ends at the same time.

Capitalist accumulation, or production as a whole, depends on a functional working out of the various moments of production, circulation,
distribution, and consumption over definite periods of time. Urbanization

must facilitate this process and the relations among its parts. Similarly, capitalist social coherence depends on the mitigation of class struggle; and here, too, urbanization plays a necessary mediating role in the reproduction of capital. Urbanization therefore forms part of the "solution" which ongoing capitalist societies create of necessity to further accumulation and keep the body politic from being irretrievably rent apart. Every age of capitalism has its distinctive "urban solution."[10]

But the solutions which capitalism devises—urban and otherwise—are never permanent. Social strife and economic crisis break out periodically as the underlying contradictions of capitalism force their way to the surface anew. Thus, the solution of every age of capitalist development ultimately contains contradictions, including those of the mode of urbanization.

Nor are urban solutions uniquely determined. American cities are widely credited, for instance, as the most suburbanized in the world, for better or worse. This distinction flows, no doubt, from the special character of American capitalism and out of the particular conjunction of class forces, ideology, government structure, and the like operating here. But a recognizable suburban movement actually occurred earlier in England than in the United States, and the cities of Europe have taken on an increasingly "American" and suburban look in the postwar era. So, despite differences in national cultures and institutions, capital appears to be working in similar ways on both sides of the Atlantic, creating an undeniable convergence of many aspects of the "suburban solution" to the problem of advanced capitalist urbanization. This—and the fact that other wide-ranging changes in urban form, such as the rise of the central business district, took place with the rise of capitalist cities on both continents and have evolved continually ever since—leads one to believe that the choice of urban "solutions" is sharply circumscribed by the structural imperatives of the capitalist mode of production.

Urbanization and Accumulation

Accumulation proceeds in distinct cycles of growth and crisis. For Marx the periodic crises of capitalism were not to be explained as a series of accidents or random fluctuations, but as recurrent contradictions arising from the logic of accumulation itself. Marx points out a number of sources of crisis in *Capital*. Suffice it to say that they depend on internal conflict: conflict between buyer and seller, between workers and capitalists, between the present and the past embodied in fixed capital, among fellow capitalists, and so forth. At the same time, accumulation must be internally consistent for a time, or it would not succeed at all. At a given moment within a cycle of accumulation, one can discern a definite and necessary arrangement of the moments of production as a whole—primary production, circulation of commodities, circulation of money, consumption, distribution—and of the superstructural institutions which guide these arrangements in everyday life. Put another way, there will be a particular *growth ensemble,* or growth path, under which accumulation proceeds successfully. The mode of urbanization is an essential part of the growth ensemble.

Capitalist growth ordinarily builds up from a stable base at the beginning of a cycle and becomes increasingly rapid in absolute terms until the limits and contradictions of the existing growth ensemble result in checks to further growth along existing pathways; yield increasing instability; and lead to the onset of crisis. The upshot of encountering limits to growth and destabilizing forces is, in the first instance, an overproduction of capital (in any of its forms as money, commodities, and labor power). That is, there is no insurance that reequilibration of the system will take place in the face of its own contradictions before a major accumulation crisis takes place. This, like accumulation itself, is owing to the force of competition, which drives individual capitalists to seek to expand their own capital, despite the adverse collective impact of such anarchistic actions. David Harvey calls this phenomenon "overaccumulation," and it has occurred at the end of every major accumulation cycle, with varying degrees of severity.[11] Yet, equilibrium must be restored, so the ultimate result of the crisis will be a forced rationalization of the economy. This will be carried out by the automatic processes of the market (e.g., bankruptcy), the class-conscious reform efforts among capitalists, and the help of the state. In the end, both overaccumulation and forced rationalization help the economy get back on a new growth path. Surplus capital pushes into "new economic space," and forced rationalization adjusts the institutional arrangements of the growth ensemble. Here lie decisive forces for change in capitalist society, forces which greatly overshadow the usual considerations of spontaneous innovation, entrepreneurial guile, and the prick of competition.

As a consequence of growth within an ensemble followed by overaccumulation and crisis, accumulation and social change are decidedly lumpy, allowing us to speak of definite cycles or stages of accumulation and of pivotal eras of reform and change. Urbanization and change in urban structure relate directly to the succession of cycles. These are not just fluctuations imposed on urbanization, but they actually describe the mode of urbanization.

Two major cycles can be discerned from the multitude of lesser fluxes and general "background noise" in the business climate. The first cycle is that of the Kuznets waves, lasting from fifteen to twenty-five years. It has been identified in a wide variety of economic indicators and by a wide assemblage of eminent economists and other investigators.[12] The second, and more controversial, period of growth is the fifty- to seventy-year movement first discerned by Kondratieff, for which I prefer the name "stage of accumulation."[13] The evidence for Kondratieff stages is highly debatable, given the scale of events and our limited experience with them, but they appear to explain major differences among historical eras as well as the three profound periods of social upheaval and change—the Jacksonian era, the Progressive era, and the 1930s, which separate the major eras.

In this paper we will focus on the first two Kondratieff waves, or stages, of accumulation after the American War of Independence, circa 1780–1842, 1842–1896, the transition between them, and the distinctive style of urbanization attached to each. A finer lens would force us to look further at the steps of development marked out by the Kuznets cycle, without which the story must necessarily sound hollow; but, as this is beyond the scope of a single paper, reference to these cycles must be confined to special points of emphasis.

Finally, real cities of wood and stone must actually be constructed. City building requires investment in fixed and immobile capital, such as buildings, roads, and the like. This requires a level of accumulation sufficient to support the real cost of labor, tools, and materials which go into the built environment. But fixed capital investment is not strictly synonymous with primary production; it is introduced to deepen capital and increase productivity (or lower costs). It is itself a sign of growing overaccumulation in the primary circuit of capital.[14] It has thus been observed that fixed capital investment is concentrated at the end of the Kuznets cycle.[15] As a result, construction of cities tends to occur in waves peaking just before depressions, and normally accompanied by excessive land speculation.[16]

The creation of fixed and immobile capital in the form of a city creates a number of problems for capitalist urbanization which cannot be pursued here. But the most important one is that the built environment is not perfectly, nor instantaneously, flexible. Cities create their own decidedly non-featureless plain. In terms of the model of accumulation cycles just outlined, this comes into play because today's fixed capital investment literally freezes the image of the present into concrete and asphalt, and this image can become a barrier to accumulation in the future.

Urbanization and Suburbanization

What is suburbanization? This question is certain to cause a vigorous falling out among any collection of urban scholars. Unfortunately, the historical work on suburbanization remains in both its theoretical and empirical infancy, to which this essay offers no final solution.[17] Today suburbanization in the United States is typically known by reference to a number of salient characteristics, such as peripheral growth, low density, and functional segregation of land uses. Automobiles, trucks, and the ubiquitous highway tie together this far-flung urban space, particularly by mediating the lengthening journeys to work and to market. Large areas of the suburbs are devoted exclusively to residential use, particularly on the outlying fringes, but equally noticeable are the nodes of commerce (shopping and office centers) and industrial districts. The mode of residential life seems to follow the lead of the wealthier trend-setters or at least to follow the dictates of the "proper" middle-class lifestyle, simultaneously growing out of a worried glance cast back over the shoulder at the inner city with its lower-class, nonwhite populace. That lifestyle is deeply grounded in homeownership, home-based consumption, family life, and the detached house sitting in its small garden plot; but almost as important as this private mode of living is the small-scale collectivity of consumption achieved through social homogeneity of the community, attention to local schools, and other public services.

Both the private and collective aspects of consumption depend heavily, it should be added, on the highly fragmented form of the state at the level of local suburban governments and on their various tools for taxation, spending, and police powers. The suburbs appear to be a kind of uneasy compromise between country and city, the city spilling out over the countryside and the countrified landscapes incorporated into the city. More features could undoubtedly be added to form a picture of the suburban ideal type, with diminishing rewards for developing an understanding of the suburban process.

Where did all this come from and when did it begin? It is by now widely understood that suburbanization did not begin with the close of World War II. Although the postwar period has some new features (and the very recent past points to some radical alteration in the suburban pattern), the roots of suburbanization go very deeply into American history. The greater part of the postwar pattern of city building was fully worked out by the 1920s. The achievements of that decade rest in turn on forces that emerged first during the Progressive era and which were based on the crucial structural changes in capitalism centered around the depression of the 1890s. It can be argued, then, that a distinctive twentieth-century form of urbanization and suburbanization corresponds to the stage of modern corporate capitalism.[18]

But the twentieth-century pattern of urbanization qua suburbanization was built on the foundation of movements under way in the nineteenth century. Certain aspects of urban structure which we think of as "modern" and recognize as characteristically "suburban" appear very early in capitalist development. In particular, a bundle of decisive changes coincides with the coming of the United States Industrial Revolution, a process pivoting on the transition from the era of petty commodity production

(1780–1842) to the era of generalized industrial production (1842–1896) and emerging fully over the course of the later period. It is this story that we take up now.

Presuburban Cities of the Petty Commodity Mercantile Stage of Accumulation, 1790–1842

The initial half century or so of American history after independence is often treated as a kind of halfway house between colonial society and industrial society. While this is a truism, the era deserves to stand on its own as the mature stage of the petty commodity mode of production.[19] This was the dominant mode of production within the social formation of the northern states, although a true capitalist mode, epitomized by the textile industry, was rapidly expanding in its midst. (We ignore here the fortunes of the distinctive slave mode of production in the South, which also reached its apogee in the social formation of the U.S., as a whole, during the first half of the century and which was central to the process of proto-capitalist accumulation.) The post-colonial era was the high tide of expansion for the system of small, independent proprietors, farmers, and artisans, producing for the market but owning their land, homes, and basic tools.[20] Post-revolutionary America was a thoroughly commercial order, proto-capitalist in all respects: a money economy of private property, individual mobility and acquisitiveness, generalized exchange, and rapidly accumulating capital. Under these powerful solvents, residuals of colonial life, such as subsistence farming, the centrality of religion, hierarchical stratification, and communal social ties, rapidly dissolved. But the quantity of free land and rich resources ensured that the central core of producers was not yet divorced from the means of production.

This mode of production presupposes a certain development of trade, finance, and manufacture: in short, a mercantile order. Along with this came a mercantile class structure of merchants and small masters on one side and casual day laborers on the other.[21] Significant inequality in wealth and concentration of ownership were most marked in the areas of greatest commercial penetration near the urban centers.[22] It also presupposed British capitalism and substantial European economic domination. Yet, political independence did allow this mode to break free from restrictive British mercantile policies and develop to its limits. Nor were domestic attempts at mercantile restriction emanating from eastern merchant, manufacturing, and finance capital markedly more successful in stemming the agrarian tide across the Appalachians or the political high tide of Jeffersonian and Jacksonian Democracy. Nonetheless, the petty commodity mode of production held within itself the seeds of its own transformation to industrial capitalism, and as it unfolded the true independence of farmers, artisans, and household production became increasingly problematic.[23]

The productive base of the time was still decisively agriculture, where eighty-one percent of the work force still labored as late as 1810.[24] The landscape was overwhelmingly rural. Nonetheless, urbanization picked up very rapidly with rates as high or higher than at any subsequent time in American history. The percentage of the total population residing in places of greater than 2,500 persons grew from 5.1 to 10.8.[25] Furthermore, the concentration of population within the urban system was extreme. The four great seaports—New York, Philadelphia, Baltimore, and Boston—towered over the lesser towns.[26] Our chief concern here lies in the internal structures of mercantile cities. At the same time, however, it is essential to consider the characters of a special class of small towns, which carried the seeds of revolutionary change: the industrial mill towns of the Northeast.

The national economy grew quite rapidly during the petty commodity stage of accumulation. The most dramatic advances were registered in the areas of southern cotton, western settlement, and mercantile fortunes made in international trade.[27] Manufacturing, including the beginnings of modern factory production, developed more or less in the background of national affairs, gaining its first decisive foothold during the period of the Embargo and the War of 1812 and making decisive strides in the 1820s and '30s. Despite its small size, however, domestic manufacturing growth appears to have set the pace of the business expansion during the Kuznets cycles of 1808–1822 and 1823–1824. Each successive upswing in the economy after the Revolution surpassed the last in strength, as well as in the excesses of overaccumulation which topped off the wave of expansion. The 1830s closed the era on a note of severe overaccumulation in which a growing weakness of manufacturing profits was lost in the general euphoria of land speculation, urban construction, and internal improvements. When, at last, the overheated economy collapsed, the country settled into the worst depression it had thus far experienced and one of the deepest in American history (1839–1842).[28]

The Industrial Revolution came to America during the petty commodity stage of accumulation but did not revolutionize it at that point. By 1840 the proportion of the labor force occupied in manufacturing had risen only to just under nine percent, while that in agriculture was still over sixty percent.[29] Textiles and shipbuilding were virtually the only large-scale manufacturing processes, and, along with large-scale construction of canals, turnpikes, and railroads, acted as "the backbone of the strictly industrial component" of this era, according to Schumpeter.[30] Factory production dominated only one industry: textiles. Independent artisans and small masters were still the rule in most branches of manufactures, and normally they sold their commodities as well, though there was some minor use of the putting-out system.

The development of industrialization was checked by a number of closely related factors.[31] The most important of these were: British competition flooding the market with cheap goods; the lack of a significant, "free" labor force willing or compelled to leave other occupations; poorly developed domestic markets and overland transportation; and an unwillingness of merchant capitalists to invest in manufacture (considered fourth best behind trade, land, and public works).[32]

What did all of this mean for the internal structure of cities during the first stage of accumulation? The large port cities of the Northeast, which so dominated the urban scene, remained almost wholly consistent with the mercantile and petty commodity economic basis of the time. As Pred has observed: "The factory and industrial capital had not as yet become the cornerstone of metropolitan growth."[33] The only urban places which were created in the image of industrial capitalism at this time were the mill towns, and even they had features rather different from later industrial cities. We will consider the two modes of urbanization in turn:

In the mercantile cities, functional separation of land uses had not proceeded very far owing, principally, to the still uncentralized nature of production. In the first place, the place of work and the place of residence were ordinarily the same for the artisans, small masters, and, oftentimes, even the great merchants. "Often their stores or workshops were on the first floor of their houses, their living quarters on the second. Junior partners, journeymen, or apprentices might 'live in' as part of the employer's family."[34] In New York as late as 1840 only about one-fourth of the labor force worked outside the home.[35] Separation of home and work place was prevented, above all, because the means of production had not yet become concentrated under the ownership of the capitalist class, and production had not yet been brought, for the capitalists' benefit, under a single roof in the factory. For much the same reason, merchandising was highly decentralized in tradesmen's shops or small retail establishments. As a result of these decentralized conditions of production and circulation, everyday commerce, production, and living were interwoven through the mixed fabric of the city in a fashion quite alien to the strategically zoned cities of today.

Some wage labor did exist and these people needed to reside close to places of employment, accessible by foot. But only a handful of employers were large enough to require any significant amount of space—creating a distinct use zone aloof from the fabric of the city—or to exert a substantial gravitational force on the districts nearby.

The centralization of activity and employment that existed in the mercantile cities derived chiefly from exchange. The great cities were all ports, and the docks provided an essential focus for economic life:

> The chief business of the great seaports was commerce; the location of the wharves determined the focus of activity. Warehouses and countinghouses, the establishments of great merchants, and the retail outlets of petty tradesmen, the taverns and grogshops all crowded close to the waterfront, and the longshoremen, hustlers, clerks, shiphandlers, sailmakers, and coopers lived nearby.[36]

This description was meant to apply to the situation circa 1800. Over the course of the mercantile stage of urban growth, distinct wholesaling and retailing districts broke off, and wholesaling even began clustering into specialized subdistricts. The former movement began in New York around 1780 and in Boston by 1800, while the latter began in New York between 1795 and 1800. The first intentional luxury retail areas appeared in New York by 1805 and Boston in the 1830s. The big ports also developed small, but clearly defined, financial districts before 1840. New York pioneered here once again with its Wall Street aggregation, which formed between 1805 and 1910.[37] Then, along with these commercial centers, the mercantile cities ordinarily had distinct administrative loci, where a state building or city offices might be found, and all had their "better" neighborhoods, consisting of the fine houses of wealthy merchants and other persons of moment, for whom a central location bespoke status and provided access to the cultural and economic pulse of the city.[38]

These subcenters related to each other closely both in space and in function, creating an early sense of centrality and even of a central business district. But the degree of centralization of urban economic life, especially *production,* does not begin to compare with that achieved in the cities of the industrial era to follow.

If "functional" separation of land uses was not yet highly developed, neither was "social" segregation. Unfortunately, our understanding of class distinctions and conflict and the way these worked themselves out spatially in this period are not terribly good. But clearly an *industrial* class structure had not yet arisen, with its focussed confrontations in the work place or vast gulfs of wealth. Since wage labor was not yet generalized, it is best to speak of laboring *classes,* divided among casual day laborers, artisans, journeymen, apprentices, and so forth.[39] While the varied work relations of these laborers before the age of the factory precluded anything like the collectivity and class antagonism of the later industrial proletariat, they also seem to have precluded the same intense divisions which later developed within the working class. That is, before the era of mass immigration began in the 1840s, racial and religious conflicts do not appear to have been so severe among the laboring classes as they later became, nor were stratifications among different skills a strong divisive force. Those in the crucial artisan class certainly did not consider themselves particularly alienated from the social order and, alternatively, allied with the masters and the unskilled laborers.[40] All this accords with descriptions of the cheek-by-jowl residential mixture of the mercantile city.[41] Nonetheless, this picture should not be overdrawn because even by the late eighteenth century, distinct, segregated residential patterns could be discerned.[42] For example, eighteenth-century Philadelphia's first suburb, Southwark, numbered among its population chiefly artisans connected with the sea trade, and blacks in that city were more frequently found on the urban fringe.[43]

The latter is one indication that "decreasing desirability of location corresponded with increasing distance from the center."[44] The dominant classes, merchants and small employers, and professionals did not yet feel a strong need to put space between their homes and the city, as the following description indicates:

> At the center of the metropolis clustered the churches, the public buildings, and the homes of the most prominent and well-to-do citizens. Nearby lived lesser merchants and leading craftsmen, their residences frequently intermingled with commercial buildings.[45]

Reasons which may be surmised for this behavior are that the city center was the cultural center of urban society, that the wealthy did not feel threatened by their social inferiors, and, probably most important, that the dominant classes wanted ready access to their place of business, since control was still largely personal in nature; many still carried on their business affairs in their homes. As a reflection of this confidence in their urban roots, Boston merchants of the early nineteenth century, for example, complained of the "country look" of their city and adopted a consciously grand urban style: the Georgian townhouse of London.[46]

Nonetheless, new social conditions began to create marked tensions within the mercantile city. Concern for controlling and inculcating work discipline in the laboring population became intense following the Panic of 1819 and again in the mid-1830s, showing up as reform movements to make the poor laws harsher; temperance movements; and the proliferation of large, authoritarian, and highly ordered institutions for the poor, criminals, orphans, and the insane. Riots in Boston during the mid-thirties led to the creation there of the first modern professional police force to secure order.[47]

At the same time, the first signs appeared in the second quarter of the century that the upper-class love for the city as a living space was beginning to erode. Country seats, summer traveling, and a Romantic view of the country became the rage: "So many prominent men retired to the country that living in the country became the fashion."[48] More important the 1830s brought, for the first time, an effort to blend the country into the city within the rounds of everyday life, as some of the big bourgeoisie started commuting by steam railroad or ferry, and the first countrified, Romantic parks made their appearance in the somewhat bizarre form of the "Romantic cemetery." Some of the lesser elite—petty bourgeois, job-bers, clerks, and skilled workmen—moved to more peripheral locations within the city and began commuting by omnibus: a horse-drawn wagon on a fixed schedule and with a flat fare.[49] But the modest extent of this movement, which should not be exaggerated, is indicated by the relative obscurity to which the omnibus boomlet has been relegated by urban historians.

Other tendencies which characterize modern urbanization/suburbani-zation were better developed. Unplanned growth was already the domi-nant mode of urban settlement and expansion.[50] While speculative land conversion on the urban fringe is a weak index of suburbanization, it does contrast with the relatively unitary, preplanned, or segmental building of mill towns at the same time.[51] This tendency became stronger throughout the petty commodity stage of accumulation, indicating the progress of accumulation and, concomitantly, overaccumulated capital seeking outlets in the city-building process. It also bears witness to the fact that the free market in land operated more thoroughly in the United States at the beginning of the nineteenth century than it would in some European countries in the mid-twentieth century.[52]

In addition, it was already commonplace by the 1830s for the fastest growing areas to lie outside the existing political boundaries of the cities; this tendency, too, became more marked as the century progressed.[53] But, unlike today, annexation soon brought these early "suburbs" into the political fold.[54] It should be clear from the preceding discussion that these early suburbs were not, to any measurable degree, residential bedroom communities for well-to-do commuters to the central city, and their class character was more likely to be common than elite.[55] It is difficult to impute any intentional escape from the political jurisdiction of the city motivating this type of satellite development; it seems, rather, to be a case of low-level polynucleate growth to which political boundaries normally adjusted in time. Early surburban polynucleation appears to be owing partly to the mercantile division of labor and partly to a relatively undif-ferentiated process of satellite town growth in the vicinity of larger cities.

Urban density and density gradients—whether of population, floor space, or rent—are potentially helpful indices of changing urban struc-ture, but adequate data for the nineteenth century are rather scarce. It is well known that mercantile cities were quite compact compared to today's cities. The urban-rural fringe was usually quite abrupt. Since the prevail-ing mode of travel was by foot, there was little of the modern sort of "leapfrogging" development involved in the urban expansion process, and the prevailing building style was row-type housing.[56] In Philadelphia, peak densities of population may have been reached during the first half of the nineteenth century, and certainly by 1860, but this is probably atypical; Chicago reached its highest densities in 1890; and New York, in 1900.[57] On the other hand, Philadelphia's population *gradient* steadily declined from 1830 (perhaps sooner), and in this it was undoubtedly typical of all big cities.[58]

It should be clear from what has been said that it is not sufficient to explain the density or spatial structure of mercantile cities by reference to their being chiefly "walking cities."[59] There was as yet little reason for putting space between classes, races, work and home, and so forth. Nor would new means of transport be available without the means to pay their fares or the capital to invest in them, which required, first, a definite level of accumulation; and, second, a wave of overaccumulated capital seeking outlets in "internal improvements." The latter was forthcoming in vast quantity at last during the 1830s; and, not surprisingly, the boomlet in omnibus service corresponds to the general building-transport cycle (part of the Kuznets cycle).[60] The case against explanation by transportation technology is sealed by the fact that omnibuses (and later horse-drawn streetcars) were both technically feasible for decades before their general adoption. Indeed, the first horse-drawn transit system was tried in Paris in 1662, only to fail for lack of demand. In the 1860s, horse-drawn streetcars, already the rage in the United States, would be introduced to London and fail there, too.[61]

Mill Towns

American industrialism had its origins in a handful of textile mills, established first in New England in the 1790s and soon proliferating over the northeastern countryside during the petty commodity era.[62] The location of the mills and the character of the so-called "Arkwright villages" built to house their workers reflect the basic conditions of industrial production of the time. The first thing to note is that industry grew up in the countryside, not in the towns, just as it had in England; but, unlike England, it remained there much longer, because the big cities lacked two essential factors of production: good sites for waterpower and a significant, free-laboring population willing to work in the new factories. Nonetheless, the mill towns were normally clustered within the vicinity of the great ports, to which their products flowed and from which the long arm of merchant capital reached out.

Pioneer industrialists, such as Samuel Slater of Rhode Island, had to solve the labor shortage problem by devices such as hiring entire families, including the children, and building housing for the workers.[63] This housing was not only substantial, but also was oriented directly about the mill, which figured as the center of village life. This was both a convenience and a social statement.

Most of the mill towns were quite small (as befits the subordinate position of industry at the time), with one exception being the city which became known as "the American Manchester": Lowell, Massachusetts.[64] Following the scheme begun in nearby Waltham (founded 1814), mill complexes in Lowell (founded 1821) integrated all phases of textile production at one location, bringing together what was otherwise scattered all over the New England landscape. Lowell's spatial structure was by no means a revolutionary departure from that of the smaller mill towns; however, it grew up in segments which retained their focus on the mills, making this "a city of cells rather than a countryside of cells."[65]

All mill towns had to be planned, in a sense, since they were built directly for the mill owner as a necessary part of creating a viable factory operation. No free market operated in the development of land or the building of worker housing. Lowell was remarkable in that it was the first attempt to build a *model* industrial town in America. In this, the correct moral order for the laboring people (the great preoccupation of the age) figured very largely. The merchant capitalists of Boston and Kirk Boote, their agent, took care to build a proper social life into their town. They installed a decidedly paternalistic, hierarchical, and even familial social order in the boarding houses built to house the female workers drawn from the New England countryside. Indeed, the famous mill girls of Waltham and Lowell themselves represented a significant innovation in industrial labor. These women were employed not only because they represented one of the few sources of available labor, but also, no doubt, because of their presumed tractability in the face of a novel work situation. The cultural life of the mill girls outside the factory and the residence— such that it was, given the long hours of work and strict domestic oversight —was also carefully provided for, from the exclusion of entertainments of ill repute to the subsidization of a literary journal, the *Lowell Offering*.[66] It is interesting to note, however, that with all this careful devotion to the factory workers' lives, casual day laborers employed in construction were not provided for at all in the Lowell plan and had to fend for themselves in a shanty town on the outskirts of the town.[67]

Lowell was widely considered to be, in the eyes of the bourgeoisie, the ideal urban solution of industrialism, the "American" solution to the evils of British-style industrialization. But despite careful planning, the social order of Lowell offered no special resistance to the crisis which beset the economy in the 1830s and '40s. The mill girls were driven out by the pressure to reduce wages and rationalize the work process in response to deteriorating profits, and they were replaced by more malleable immigrants. Lowell even became something of a focus of working-class agitation for the ten-hour day.[68] Just as in the ill-fated model town of Pullman fifty years later, the failure of the Lowell ideal undoubtedly warned the dominant classes against undue optimism about the possibilities of planned cities where the relations between work and home life and among classes were too readily apparent.[69]

Urbanization and Suburbanization in the Industrial Stage of Accumulation, 1842–1896

The Transition from Petty Commodity Production to Full Industrialization

The second half of the nineteenth century is generally acclaimed as the period of the full industrial revolution in the United States. The crucial forces making possible a generalization of this revolution appeared with the first severe crisis of overaccumulation in the late 1830s, the deep depression of 1839–1843, and the next burst of accumulation and overaccumulation in the 1840s and '50s. Turning on the pivot of the depression, the American economy shifted from one stage of capitalist accumulation to another. It was in the full industrial stage that capitalism transformed completely the face of the landscape and the character of social life. The nature of the change from one era to another was clear by the eve of the Civil War.[70]

In the long Kuznets wave swing from 1842 to 1859 manufacturing clearly replaced cotton as the leading sector of the economy. The strong revival of manufactures after the depression of the early 1840s indicates their new role, and a remarkable increase in output and labor productivity took place in the decade 1844 to 1854. The rise of nearly seventy percent in these figures was the largest decennial growth rate in the entire nineteenth century.[71] Furthermore, the range of commodities partaking of this growth had broadened considerably from the traditional leaders, such as textiles and shoes, to include, especially, some capital goods industries, such as iron and light machinery.[72] Douglass North emphasizes the contrast with pre-depression conditions, remarking that:

> Manufacturing growth throughout the Northeast during the 1830s gave evidence that this development was under way. But it was during the 1840s and early 1850s that the pace of industrialization accelerated to the degree that the Northeast could unequivocally be called a manufacturing region.[73]

Three influences stand out as the cause of the great leap forward: The first was the broadening of the national market.[74] This was owing, above all, to the lowering of transport costs and internal integration brought about by the canal system built at the end of the previous boom.[75] Canals in the East and the canal-steamboat traffic in the West formed the initial basis for what George Roberts Taylor calls the "Great Breakthrough" into a national market.[76] But it should also be emphasized that a truly national market was by no means a fact before 1860; it had to await further waves of railroad building, the standardization of railroads in the 1870s, and, of course, the conquest of the South and of the western plains. Forging a national market was the business of the whole of the industrial stage of accumulation, not only its first cycle.

A second and far more fundamental source of industrial advance proceeded through an attack on labor that lowered real wages, rationalized the labor process in the factory, and undermined the independent artisan. In the textile factories the assault on labor began as early as the first downturn in prices in 1834, shattering the paternalistic harmony of capital and labor in the Lowell mills.[77] The attack consisted of cutting wages and intensifying work and was aided by the application of improved machinery, hiring of scab labor from among newly arriving Irish immigrants, blacklisting and other strike-breaking methods, and the creation of unemployment.[78] Pressure increased during the depression, precipitating a wave of strikes in the mills, but the owners were victorious. As a result, profits in the mills picked up rapidly in the years 1844 to 1847, although wages and labor conditions did not.[79] When textile prices slumped again in 1848, the attack on labor began anew.

Norman Ware has traced a similar pattern of degradation of the mechanics, laborers, and household workers in a variety of trades outside the factory system, showing the same pattern of declining real wages: increasing competition from mechanization, immigrants and child labor; desperate intensification of work in an attempt to stem the tide; increasing loss of control to outsiders; and the angry outbreaks of strikes, riots, and political protests (most of which were failures).[80] Again, the process of decline began during the overproduction of the 1830s, peaked in the hard times of the depression, and continued sporadically throughout the 1840s and 1850s. It is fair to say that the back of the independent mechanic's resistance was broken in this period. Union membership fell between the 1830s and 1860, and during the 1850s a new form of labor struggle, the craft union, emerged as dominant.[81]

At the same time, the factory system was widely adopted outside the textile industry during the 1850s.[82] The proportion of wage laborers rose dramatically at the expense of independent artisans and household manufacture, even though the average size of all manufacturing establishments remained quite small (8.5 persons).[83] By 1870 the number of self-employed or employers outside agriculture amounted to only 8.6 percent of the manufacturing labor force. Independent farmers amounted to an additional 24.3 percent, making the total number of independent proprietors equal to 32.9 percent of the labor force. Against this, 67 percent were wage laborers, 28.7 percent were in agriculture and 39 percent were outside agriculture (additionally only 7 percent of the latter were "white-collar" workers).[84]

On the side of capital, certain rationalizations were also taking place to facilitate the above changes. Most important was the spread of the limited liability corporation, facilitated by the change made by state legislatures after 1837 in passing general, rather than special, incorporation acts.[85] This development not only aided in financing industry, but also accompanied the shift to a hard-nosed management policy through a separation of ownership and control, rare in the mercantile period before 1840.[86]

The third major factor speeding the advance of industry was the course of accumulation in agriculture. Overproduction in cotton and the newly opened grain fields of the Northwest dropped the price of agricultural staples for industry and workers. Transportation investments during the boom of the 1830s also helped lower costs of staples.[87] The glut of cotton in the South, carrying over into the 1840s, aided the revival of textile manufacturing in the East and abroad. Western agriculture also increased its demand for eastern manufactures, owing to the beginning of the first agricultural mechanization revolution. New agricultural machinery began to be invented and introduced in the 1830s (e.g., Cyrus McCormick's reaper) and was adopted for the first time on a large scale in the first cycle of the second stage of accumulation.[88] As a result of this—rather than the marvelous richness of prairie soils—agricultural productivity showed its first significant jump at this time.[89] The era of the 1840s and 1850s is commonly known as the period of the "first agricultural revolution" in the United States, and this revolution was clearly tied to the progress of the Industrial Revolution at the same time.

The most important effect of agricultural expansion through mechanization was to make labor redundant, rather than to absorb potential labor from the industrial sector. Marginal farmers were now being forced out by competition under conditions of overindebtedness, overproduction, and periodic depressions. The first to go in this country (beginning in the 1830s), were the Yankee farmers of the New England hill country.[90] But the process of agricultural expulsion at the margins was advancing on a world scale, and the combined impact of expansion in the United States and Argentina, plus the revolution in agriculture in Europe, produced a revolutionary effect on this country and the world just before mid-century: the beginning of the great European migrations to the "empty lands" of the earth. The greatest beneficiary of this tide of humanity was the United States.[91]

The first trickle of Irish laborers in the 1830s joined with the New England hill people in beginning to undermine the position of the mill workers.[92] But the trickle became a flood from 1845 to 1854 and fundamentally transformed the conditions for industrialization in this country. For here, at last, was the ready supply of surplus labor power which the factory system demanded.[93] The Irish, in particular, were destitute and without craft skills. Arriving at the eastern ports and unable to move on, they stayed to form a gigantic pool of cheap labor in those cities and throughout the Northeast.

> The availability of the immigrants in the labor force accelerated economic growth and assisted in the process of industrialization. Their unprecedented numbers, in addition to causing seriously crowded living conditions in eastern population centers, also provided a supply of cheap labor abundant beyond immediate needs.... A tremendous increase in labor supply encouraged industrial development and made a major contribution to the outburst of economic productivity in the decade or two before the Civil War.[94]

Not surprisingly, the total effect of immigration, the growth of industry, and so forth was to produce the fastest rate of growth of urban population in American history during the 1840s (93.1 percent) and the second fastest during the 1850s.[95]

Growth in the Second Stage of Accumulation
The American economy continued to grow prodigiously during the balance of the nineteenth century, expanding along the lines established before the Civil War.[96] The industrial stage of accumulation consisted of three Kuznets cycles, roughly from 1842 to 1859, 1860 to 1877, and 1878 to 1896. Each cycle repeated the now familiar mode of growth: steadily expanding output capped by a burst of overaccumulation showing up as: fixed capital formation; especially intense railroad building and residential construction; land speculation; pyramiding of credit; and, finally, a financial panic led in every case by a failure of railroad securities. The expansion of output was associated with rapid population growth, the assimilation of waves of new migrants from farms and foreign lands, and growth of the industrial wage labor force (which was increasingly employed in factories and located in cities).

This was the age in which the business firm with a national market, typically a single-purpose, family-owned corporation, became the dominant form of business organization, and the factory replaced the workshop as the form of labor process organization.[97] Industrial factory production expanded with the aid of: an increasing use of the corporate system of finance and management; a pool of cheap labor from which to draw; the rapid assimilation of mechanical innovations; the growing use of coal and steam power; and the steady growth of the market through population growth, urbanization, rising incomes, and national integration—all of which made feasible the adoption of techniques of mass production. Manufacturing firms also steadily freed themselves from reliance on merchant wholesalers (jobbers) and experimented with new methods of mass retailing.

Urban landscapes spread across the country as industrialization advanced; people were drawn into the urban-industrial centers, and waves of fixed capital in the form of factories, houses, and offices were laid down. This was the era of the rise of great industrial cities and the creation of the basic urban network in the United States. The population growth of cities was marked, rising from 1,845,000 to 22,106,000, or from 10.8 percent of total population in 1840 to 35.1 percent by 1890. The number of great cities of over 100,000 persons jumped from two to seventeen.[98] Rates of fixed capital formation were also extraordinarily high—higher than they would be in the twentieth century.[99] Chicago was the "shock city" of the age, indicative of the spread of industrialization to the Midwest.[100]

All the preceding factors meant not only the rise of cities, but also the decline of preindustrial ways of life and production. The golden age of independent proprietors was passing. From here on they would exist only in the interstices of corporate capitalism. In their place stood the mass of industrial workers facing a small number of owners of industrial and financial capital.

Urban Centralization of Production and Circulation

Within the major industrial cities growth was accompanied by internal rearrangement of space, as a new kind of urban system unfolded, one which we now think of as characteristic of nineteenth-century industrial cities. Behind the enormous complexity of this developing urban structure, a three-fold movement can be discerned: first, a concentration of production and circulation in and around the central business district, associated with an interwoven concentration of working-class residential areas; second, an outward thrust of the residential areas of the dominant classes, led by the big bourgeoisie; and, third, a dramatic increase in the economic and social differentiation of urban space.[101] The resulting land-use pattern is what E. W. Burgess later tried to capture in his familiar "concentric ring" model of urban structure, although this model was formulated at a time when the reality of urban structure was already being dramatically transformed by the rise of modern corporate capitalism after the turn of the century. Each of the three movements will be taken up briefly, beginning with the primary force of centralization of economic life; for what occurred in the second half of the nineteenth century was, above all, a vast "implosion" of the economic and social landscape of the United States and a parallel centralization within the burgeoning cities, notwithstanding the continued growth of nonurban places and the urban periphery.

The urbanization of production and circulation took a major step forward in the 1840s and '50s and was paralleled to a large degree by the growth of the central business districts of the great cities. This was owing, above all, to the great wave of immigrants trapped in the eastern port cities, where they provided an unprecedented pool of cheap labor. It was this supply of surplus labor that attracted capitalist industry back into the old cities.[102] In addition to being plentiful and cheap, the new recruits to the industrial labor force were also a good deal more docile and eager to take up whatever employment they could find than was the earlier generation of workers, who had become increasingly troublesome to employers. Certainly the eagerness of the employers to replace fractious native workers with immigrants is well evidenced in the old textile mills and in various trades, and there is every reason to believe that this exercised an influence on locational decisions as well.[103] Then, once the new locational pattern became established, it drew subsequent streams of migrants to the industrial cities where employment opportunities were greatest.

Steam power for driving machinery became practicable in the 1840s, freeing the factories from the need to locate near good waterpower sites out in the countryside.[104] Expensive coal had been the main obstruction to steam power in the first stage of accumulation, owing to poor transportation and inefficient steam engines. Only Pittsburgh and Wheeling used much steam power in the 1830s. But after 1840 the canals and railroads of the 1830s began to pay off in the delivery of cheap and abundant coal to the coastal cities, while technical improvements in the engines and the railroads built in the 1850s sealed the matter.[105]

The big cities also offered their attractions as market centers and transshipment points, both of which became more important with the advance of capitalist development. The progress of internal transport and the growth of the internal markets normally went hand in hand, with the cities as hubs of the system. Market growth came about not simply through growth in population, production, and national integration on a preexisting basis, but also through the radical transformation from one mode of production to another, particularly the penetration of capitalist production and market relationships into the rural hinterland, leading to the replacement of household and handicraft production by urban manufactures; i.e., the growing division of labor between town and country.[106]

At the same time, with the increasing social division of labor within production, and between production and circulation (as compared with the era of hand manufacture and simple commodity production), access to "the market" meant something different than it had before. It meant access to sellers and purchasers of specialized intermediate goods; to wholesale intermediaries capable of organizing the large-scale movement of commodities; to major capital markets for financing; and to a growing variety of specialized professional services, such as law, architecture, insurance, and real estate brokerage. These things, too, cities and systems of cities offered as advantages for industrial location. Urban agglomeration shortened transport linkages, creating threshold demands for specialized production and labor services, valuable personal contacts for businessmen, and so forth. It also provided the essential physical infrastructure of buildings to house business and labor, along with a rapidly growing category of public service infrastructure (schools, sewers, water supply, gas lines, etc.).[107]

In short, the urban system offered that variety of advantages normally lumped together under the heading "economies of agglomeration." But it is essential to recognize that these economies were not universally in force; they depended on a certain level of capitalist development, including industrialization, division of labor, concentration of ownership, and the like. Furthermore, these economies probably had their greatest impact before factory production, integrated corporations, and transportation-communication techniques were so far advanced as to internalize many of the external economies of urban concentration or to render them no longer necessary.

Most of the preceding factors drawing industry to the big cities similarly operated to concentrate production and circulation in the central business district. The central business district offered proximity to the port and railway terminal facilities and to the labor force, to other producers, merchants, financiers, and so forth at a time when foot travel was still the primary mode of transport for workers, and horse-drawn wagons, the principal intracity method of moving goods. Spatial proximity also offered face-to-face contact among an increasingly large, disparate, and residentially far-flung bourgeoisie. These considerations of business location obviously hastened the movement of residential location; the departure of the dominant classes from the central city; and the collection of the working class near the center, the locus, of employment. These will be taken up below.

Additionally, the business district offered a most important type of building: the warehouse.[108] Particularly in the early part of the industrial stage of accumulation, before large-scale factory production predominated—and wherever it did not penetrate thereafter—these largely undif-ferentiated shells of buildings provided great flexibility for setting up small machine manufacturing operations in newly mechanized handicraft industries, mercantile transactions, and in jobbing, as well as for providing storage. Warehouses had, of course, been a major part of the urban scene during the mercantile period, but after 1840 the warehousing district expanded very rapidly to fulfill its new, productive role. This physical development, it should be added, reflected the retention by the merchant intermediary of considerable influence over the organization of production. And it was aided technically in the face of greater demands for center-city space by innovations such as the cast iron frame (1848) and the elevator (1853).[109] Warehousing dominated central city land uses during the second stage, while large factories—less bound by forces of agglomeration than were their smaller brethren—tended to locate more loosely around the edges of the waterfront and business district, even on the edges of the built-up area in rapidly expanding Chicago, for example.[110] After about 1870 the dominance of warehousing began to be challenged, indirectly, by the increasing organization of production on a large scale in factories and directly, by competition for center-city land from retailing and financial-administrative-professional functions.[111] Yet manufacturing and warehousing remained the dominant central city land uses up to 1900.

The several factors (by no means exhaustive) just enumerated, operating to centralize production and circulation in cities and within cities, probably exerted their force on location in the order given, although this is an empirical question for which data are not available. It would be inappropriate, however, to indulge in the search for first causes in this sort of factoral analysis, since such pursuits invariably lead at some point to arguing in a circle. The first point is that we necessarily find an array of factors, of greater or lesser importance, making up a distinct urban-industrial growth ensemble.[112] Second, within the factoral array, or growth ensemble, we find that the changing conditions of *production* are more important than exchange factors in accounting for the concentration effect, in contrast to the suppositions of neoclassical urban theorists. The old forces were rapidly giving way, making for relatively dispersed location of production and circulation—especially the role of the independent artisan, master, and farm family producing and selling their own goods typically within their own homes. In their place appeared locational considerations of the industrial age, such as availability of wage labor and the needs of larger workshops and factories in the social division of labor and growing market penetration. Finally, at a level deeper than even these production and location factors, we can identify a structural shift from one mode of production to another—petty commodity production to capitalist industrialization—marked by a fundamental alteration of the social relations of production: the concentration of the means of production in a few hands, on the one side, and the formation of a propertyless class of wage laborers, on the other.

The Formation of the Slums

Around and through the central business district and nearby manufacturing zones of the industrial city were crowded the residential districts of the working class: the classic "slums" of the nineteenth century.[113] Before one can discuss the specific factors operating on the location of working-class housing, however, it is necessary to consider the preconditions for a "residential location decision" to be made at all. In the first place, working-class housing became separate from the place of production in a fashion quite unlike that of the old mercantile city or the early mill towns. Although the distance separating home and work was not great, the social division in people's lives between production and consumption, working and living, was to have profound implications.[114] James Vance comments perceptively that, "Probably few events in economic history have had more fundamental effect on the shape of the city than the physical parting of the residence from the work place."[115]

The separation of the work place from the home came about in the first instance because of the growing control over the means of production secured by the capitalist class and, second, because of the reorganization of the labor process under the factory and workshop system. This not only ended home-based manufacture by the independent artisan, small master, or cottager, but created as its opposite the class of wage laborers. In the era of the mill towns, this process had not gone much beyond the immediate employees of the mills, and there was not yet a large body of free laborers. The resulting scarcity of labor made it mandatory for the mill owners to provide housing, which was in most cases both solid and oriented directly to production.

By the 1840s a fundamental change had taken place: the workers were cut free by capital to fend for themselves in the matter of housing.[116] Along with a growing free market in labor came a generalized free market in working-class housing. A most instructive case of this can be found in the first new, large-scale mill town established in New England in the industrial stage of accumulation: Holyoke (1847). The Hadley Falls Company, which founded Holyoke, was principally a speculator-developer corporation dealing in water and land, not production. The mills were to be built by lessees and housing was to be provided by private builders. The company thus had as its interest the appropriation of rent and, because of the inflated land values created by expectation of rents, the company was able to create an artificial scarcity of land. Poor Irish workers who needed work crowded together to make do, with the result that housing conditions soon became appalling. Holyoke became the first mill town with a true industrial slum.[117]

The appropriation of rent was joined by three other effects—perhaps conscious aims of the capitalist class—of creating a "free market" in housing. The first was to lower the reproduction costs of labor by allowing workers to crowd together in substandard housing, instead of providing good housing as a part of the employment package.[118] Second, generalization of the housing market corresponded to the generalization of the labor market, whereby the optimal location of a worker's home would be made in view of having several possible employers for different members of the family or for one member over a period of time; this worked to the benefit of employers, as well, who wished to take advantage of a mobile and diverse labor pool. Third, a new mystification of class relations came into being to replace the lost paternalism of Lowell and the mill towns, which had failed to stave off class conflict. The free housing market served this purpose, introducing a new set of intermediaries between capital and labor and injecting the illusion of independence of the worker in this sphere of his/her life.[119] The way in which this operated in the large cities was much more complex than at Holyoke. A highly fragmented group of landlords, real estate operators, and builders mediated the housing relation, with many of these people being drawn from the working class itself, ones who hoped to get ahead by the petty bourgeois route.[120]

The result was everywhere usually the same as in Holyoke. Working-class housing conditions deteriorated, densities rose, and the industrial slums were born.[121] In some wards in New York City population density was already in excess of 300 persons per acre in 1860, triple what it had been twenty years earlier.[122] The workers were literally being expelled from the earth as a dwelling place, as Marx put it.[123] The "congestion" and "poor sanitation" consequent to this pressure on workers would be discovered by bourgeois reformers soon enough, though in forms distorted by their class position and ideological predilections.

But more than housing was involved in the creation of the so-called "slums" of nineteenth-century industrial cities. Capital not only withdrew direct provision of working-class housing, it also withdrew from the kind of direct oversight of working-class life attempted by the Boston merchants at Lowell. This left the working class much freer to begin developing its own culture, in the same manner as pointed out by E. P. Thompson for the English working class of the early nineteenth century.[124] It also appears that the bourgeoisie began withdrawing from city politics as early as the 1830s, leaving the field open for the development of the classic nineteenth-century "machine" form of political rule.[125] This, too, was similar to the political independence of some English working-class towns before 1850, with profound implications for potential radical threats to bourgeois hegemony there during the Chartist period.[126] Finally, these developments took place within a definite space which the dominant classes had abandoned to the workers in their flight to the suburban periphery. In the process they had created—again like the British bourgeoisie—a "vast terra incognita," as Gareth Stedman Jones has described it, which they dubbed "the slum."[127] Thereafter, whenever the dominant classes heard rumblings from below, they had to reenter this strange land to discover its secrets and its evils—from bad housing to bad politics—to be expunged.[128]

The question remains, however, as to why the American working class crowded near the city center instead of, for example, taking up residence on the fringes of the city, as was the South American pattern. To begin with, given a preexisting locus of employment at the center, immigrants would tend to locate nearby, since workers at this time could not afford to commute from any distance because of low wages, long and often irregular hours, or the need to be close by for casual employment opportunities.[129] These criteria, of course, presuppose a generally low level of social production which cannot support high wages, short hours, and a far-flung commuting system. But this explanation gives absolute priority to industrial location before residential location; it does not hold up, since, as we noted previously, industries were attracted to cities as sources of labor. Clearly, the location of production and of working-class residence developed symbiotically, once the pattern of centrality was established. The origin of the pattern is thus strongly historical, probably owing to the previously developed focus of the port and the tendency for new arrivals and people seeking employment to congregate near it.

Furthermore, certain relations of class reinforced the locational pattern emerging in production and circulation. On the one hand, the dominant classes did not hold their ground in the city center, but fled to the periphery for a variety of reasons (to be taken up below). From precapitalist institutions and culture there was no resistance (as in so many European cities) to the urban center's wholesale transformation in the pursuit of mammon, and its necessary accompaniment of laboring people. On the other hand, this escape meant that the working class was effectively trapped in space, prevented from effectively demanding peripheral housing by the competition of wealthier people.[130] More important, the workers' relative freedom to create their own political and cultural life in the slums resulted in a support network which attracted working people and which many would not voluntarily abandon.[131] This, too, must have acted as a force for reproducing the spatial structure of the industrial city.

The Beginning of Residential Suburbanization

The geography of the classic nineteenth-century industrial city involved, on the one side, an implosive bringing together of production, circulation, and the labor force, while, from the other, it involved a radical separation of people and activities in space. This separation proceeded especially along the lines of the division of labor in production, between production and circulation, work place and living place, and among classes and national cultures. As in a centrifuge, this separation of the urban solution was led by its outermost elements, the cream seeking the top. The suburbs were launched at the pole opposite from the slums and the central business district, but as part of the same dialectic of urbanization under capitalism.

The suburban movement began in the 1830s, became a major force in the leading cities during the 1840s and 1850s, and was thoroughly generalized after the Civil War.[132] The "suburban solution" was chiefly a residential phenomenon, highly restricted in numbers and income, which retained its focus on the highly centralized industrial city. It represented the "solution" of the dominant classes to the emergent contradictions of capitalist production as it took root firmly in the urban landscape, manifest in the areas known as the central business district and the slums. And, again, this movement cannot be imagined without the simultaneous revolution in the mode of production which picked up speed so quickly from 1830 to 1860 and increasingly dominated urbanization thereafter.

The big bourgeoisie led the suburban movement by commuting by rail and ferry. Behind the truly wealthy, on the fringes of the built-up area of the city, came the "middle classes" of small employers, merchants, lawyers, and the like; and even nearer the center were the homes of some skilled workers, clerks, shopkeepers, etc.[133] Boston was the leader in railroad commuting, and it has been calculated that by 1848 some twenty percent of Boston's businessmen already traveled to work daily on the steam railroads, and perhaps the majority of them did so by the early 1850s.[134] In New York and Philadelphia greater opposition to steam engines operating on city streets (often promoted by omnibus interests) meant that the omnibus retained its leading position in commuting.[135] In New York, ferries also carried many people to work from Brooklyn and New Jersey. The expense and time put this commuting beyond the reach of the vast majority. But, among the dominant classes, the journey to work began to lengthen rapidly, as has been shown for Philadelphia merchants and bank presidents between 1829 and 1860, and New York attorneys between 1825 and 1915; the key period for the latter was from 1835 to 1845.[136] Qualitative accounts of the suburban trend are also common from mid-century onward. For example:

> The movement of the affluent toward Germantown in
> Philadelphia and Chesnut Hill near Boston was duplicated
> in other metropolitan areas. In San Francisco, the city's

bankers, merchants, and doctors moved away from the downtown areas between 1850 and 1860 and put their new homes on the heights of Fern (Nob) Hill and Russian Hills. And, after the establishment of steamboat and ferry service on San Francisco Bay, Oakland and Alameda joined the competition for citizens and quickly garnered a reputation as "steamboat suburbs." Because of the competition from Brooklyn, newspaper editors in New York were complaining as early as 1849 of "the desertion of the city by its men of wealth." In Chicago, most of the high-grade residential areas were still very near the center at the time of the Civil War, but a tendency for the fashionable to move toward the periphery was already apparent. In almost every large city, the merchant princes and millionaires were searching for the hilltops and shore lands to build country estates; crowded cities offered fewer attractions with every passing year.[137]

The early phase of residential separation, particularly that based on the omnibus, was soon overshadowed by the horse-drawn streetcar in the 1850s. The streetcar mania hit New York, then Boston, then Philadelphia and other major cities in the late 1850s.[138] The streetcars have justly been associated with transforming urban morphology, creating, in Sam Warner's felicitous phrase, "streetcar suburbs." This process accelerated in each of the three Kuznets cycles of the second stage of accumulation.[139] In New York City the number of passengers increased from seven million in 1853 to thirty-six million by 1860.[140] Given its revolutionary impact on urbanization, we may ask, with George Rogers Taylor, "Why, despite the obvious advantages of the streetcar, was its general adoption postponed until the 1850s?"[141] Taylor tries, rather unsuccessfully, to answer his own question in terms of conservatism, corruption, and the like, but we should, rather, look to the fundamental forces of capitalist production, social conflict, and accumulation for the origins of the demand for, and supply of, streetcar suburbanization, recognizing that the urban-industrial system began to gel very quickly in the period between 1835 and 1855 and had altogether triumphed over preindustrial capitalist modes of life by 1890, as was previously argued.

On the demand side of the suburban equation we must provide an alternative explanation to the purely a priori assumption found in Alonso's neoclassical model of location, which says that people (particularly rich people) desire space for its own sake. Or, as Alonso puts it, "We are not concerned with how these tastes are formed, but simply with what they are."[142]

Several factors can be identified to fill this analytical void. First of all, there must be the economic possibility of separating the work place and the home, with the consequent need to commute. This presumes, at the least, a certain level of wealth, but this factor was probably only significant for those among the skilled trades and petty bourgeoisie taking up the rear of the suburban vanguard.[143] The most important development for the big bourgeoisie was the diminished need to supervise personally the work process and to be on call at the work place.[144] The other side of this freedom for the elite was the growing role of hierarchical forms of management characteristic of capitalist industry.[145]

A second factor inducing suburban escape was that the areas of production at the center came to be regarded as undesirable places in which to live. The usual things identified among the "disamenities" of the industrial city were traffic, noise, dirty air, filthy grounds, and visual ugliness of the factory districts. Undoubtedly, the physical changes commensurate with advancing industrialization (such as coal burning, steam railroads—witness the fear of the first commuter engines on city streets) and massive construction projects could alone account for a desire to put space between oneself and the center of productive activity.

But the negative aspects of production included more than physical affronts. Surpassing these were the kinds of social relations people—even those near the top—experienced in their work role: competition, exploitation, antagonism to—and degradation of—other human beings. Furthermore, the alienating, exploitative relations of production took on a tangible existence in the form of the working class and its degraded living districts. An increasingly fluid, unruly, and possibly threatening proletariat had already become a concern of the dominant classes by the 1830s, and they had sought to deal with this contradiction of capitalist life in a variety of ways, such as penitentiaries and professional police forces.[146] The threatening behavior of workers appeared in various forms, from petty crimes to riots, such as those hitting Boston from 1835 to 1836, Philadelphia from 1834 to 1849, and New York in 1863.[147] Perhaps more threatening than overt misbehavior by workers was the biological result of their degraded concentration. The appearance of the classic industrial slums in Europe and America also marked the major era of the cholera epidemic.[148]

A most direct "solution" to these problems was to put space between oneself and the workers. This removal was in large part a "blowout" from the center similar to the present-day rush to escape black inmigration; and, to continue the parallel, nineteenth-century class antagonism was joined by no small measure of racism against the foreign born. Streetcar suburbs joined the rise of American nativism and the politics of the Know-Nothing Party in the 1850s as answers to the foreign peril.[149]

The choice of spatial separation as a solution to class contradictions does not, of course, recommend itself uniquely on all counts. Many instances can be found in history where the rich and the poor have cohabitated districts or even buildings. Fear of contagion is one standard explanation for nineteenth-century suburbanization, and one not without considerable merit. But contagion has not always generated this particular response, so it would appear more likely that the demand for space had more to do with changing class relations; the increased size, antagonism, and mobility of the working class; and a fear that sufficient alternative social controls on threatening behaviors were lacking. The massive influx of foreigners to the United States may partially account for uncertainty as to the power of conventional social controls on the laboring classes. Certainly the clichés of great spatial mobility and lack of hierarchical deference among Americans have some weight, particularly in light of the relative triumph of petty commodity democracy and the lack of strong feudal antecedents in this country. It is not surprising that, during the first half of the nineteenth century, the American bourgeoisie were among the leading innovators of "modern" asylums—penitentiaries, insane asylums, and juvenile homes—as methods of social control and of inculcating "correct" individual behavior.[150] Furthermore, spatial removal had figured quite largely in managing deviancy in the early history of the U.S. colonial towns which regularly banished miscreants from their locale, while an important aspect of the later asylums was removal from normal urban social life. Indeed, the first asylums were typically founded in suburban locations, near the city but overlooking the countryside.[151] Since, as industrialism advanced, it was no longer possible to banish a few deviants from the city, the dominant classes chose instead to remove themselves.

A fourth factor driving the dominant classes from the central city is the truism that land values were rising steeply, making central locations dearer. Concomitantly, land uses were being converted very rapidly in the interests of production and housing the workers.[152] Yet, the operation of the land market is by no means a sufficient cause for suburbanization, nor even a necessary process. As mentioned previously, the dominant classes in the United States were singularly unwilling or unsuccessful in resisting the pressures for the concentration of production in the industrial city. One important cause that may be adduced for this is the remarkably advanced state of market relations in the U.S., even before the age of industrialization. So thorough was the commercialization of society, especially in matters of private property in land, that almost no restraints operated in the land market.[153] As a result, open bidding for urban land drove up values, few people were willing to resist the temptation to make money for some higher cause or tradition, and the consequent high prices and rapid turnover—which created insecurity as to who tomorrow's neighbors would be—drove out the unwilling.

A similar and complementary force making the suburban move a financially attractive one was the rising property tax rate necessary to support urban public services. And with the advent of rapid urbanization and, more so, with urban industrialization, the infrastructural support demanded of city governments grew very rapidly in areas such as water supply, sewerage, street maintenance and gas lighting. These expenditures increased markedly in the industrial stage of accumulation.[154] Nonetheless, suburbanites wanted certain public services for their homes. Around mid-century in Philadelphia, "numerous districts and borough governments had been created to offer, for example, rudimentary urban services to the early suburbanites."[155] Unlike the twentieth-century situation, the central cities continued to annex these outlying areas after they had built up, often because the city could offer better services.

A sixth aspect of the suburban lure was what Warner calls the "pull of the rural ideal."[156] This apparently simple "ideal," however, involves a more subtle ideological response to urban industrialism bearing deeper consideration than Warner gives it. For what was involved here was no longer a true agrarian idealism of the Jeffersonian type, characteristic of the age of petty commodity production; but, rather, as Peter Schmitt has shown, a shift to an *arcadian* ideal, more amenable to the realities of urban industrial life. "As a place, it lay somewhere on the urban fringe, easily accessible and mildly wild."[157] Beginning rather suddenly in the 1830s and 1840s, the bourgeoisie sought the solicitude of nature in the landscape for their recreation, home life, and literary fancy, and this movement drew more adherents and became more vulgarized by its proponents as it trickled down to the masses over the course of the nineteenth and early twentieth centuries.[158]

A similar process can be observed in the advance of suburbanization itself, as country seats gave way (by the post-Civil War era) to "garden suburbs," with their studied emulation of winding countryside, and thence to the generalization of the detached frame house, set on a small lot. As Sam Warner has observed of the late nineteenth-century Boston suburbs, only the top five percent of the populace "got the setting that the ideology of the rural ideal demanded," while the bulk of the "lower middle-class" migrants to the inner suburbs had to settle for "cramped suburban streets of three-deckers [which] stand as an ugly joke against their models: the picturesque houses set on garden lots."[159]

The great ideologists of urban landscaping of the Romantic and arcadian style were Andrew Jackson Downing, who died in 1852, and Frederick Law Olmsted, Sr., whose career spanned the whole of the industrial stage of accumulation. Their ideas concerning nature's relation to social problems epitomized the bourgeois goals of the "rural ideal." Downing believed in the power of "art, Romantic nature, and beauty in refining and stabilizing the disorderly and individualistic society of Jacksonian America." What Downing admitted to valuing most highly was "the love of order, the obedience to law, the security and repose of society, the love of home," things which appeared sorely lacking in the 1830s and 1840s.[160]

Olmsted's argument for city parks was that they would offer open and peaceful rural vistas (though highly stylized ones) which were to be "suitable for the distinctly rural recreation of people, as a relief and counterpoise to the urban conditions of their ordinary life."[161] Olmsted saw parks as a source of relief from the exhaustion, irritation, and depression of contemporary urban life, a problem chiefly afflicting, in his mind, the "middle class," but extending to other classes as well. Moreover, parks could function to bring the various classes of people into contact in a sort of "democratic community." Parks were, therefore, another kind of "reintervention" by capital, a new form of mediation of class relations by means of landscape evocations of rural life and a relation to nature, which capitalism had overthrown. Capital would readmit, by the back door, what it had cast out by the front: rural life, a sense of community, economic equality, an unalienated relation to nature, etc.

While sylvan parks in the midst of the city provided a direct contrast to urban life, suburbia represented an even more satisfying form of reconciliation of people to nature, a new form of "middle landscape" between town and country. Olmsted extolled the suburbs for their balance of the two, a balance which allowed "the more intelligent and more fortunate classes to seek the special charms and substantial advantages of rural life" in their homes, without any "sacrifices of urban conveniences."[162] Olmsted and Vaux designed Riverside, Chicago's first garden suburb, in 1868. As Olmsted makes eminently clear, this middle landscape was, for the time being, the province of the dominant classes.

Rural or arcadian ideals have played an important role in American life, but we must be cautious not to divorce these ideas from the material relations of social class and the mode of production, setting them up as the "cause" of phenomena such as suburbanization and the parks movement. Among the favored members of society with the power to turn their ideas into material forces, the ideal of social harmony through landscape manipulation and through consumption and recreation, rather than production, was the motivation to create urban parks and Romantic suburbs. The parallels to the creation of the famous eighteenth-century English country estates by a new capitalist agrarian gentry are striking. We can do no better than to quote Raymond Williams' perceptive commentary on the latter:

> It was that kind of confidence, to make Nature move to an arranged design, that was the real invention of the landlords. *And we cannot, then, separate their decorative from their productive arts*; this new, self-conscious observer was very specifically the self-conscious owner. The clearing of parks

as "Arcadian" prospects depended on the completed system of exploitation of the agricultural and genuinely pastoral lands beyond the park boundaries. There, too, an order
was being imposed: social and economic, but also physical.
The mathematical grids of the enclosure awards, with their
straight hedges and straight roads, are contemporary with
the natural curves and scatterings of the park scenery. *And
yet they are related parts of the same process—superficially opposed
in taste, but only because in the one case the land is being organized
for production, where tenants and labourers will work, while in the
other case it is being organized for consumption*—the view, the
ordered proprietary repose, the prospects. Indeed, it can
be said of these eighteenth-century, arranged landscapes
not only, as is just, that this was the high point of agrarian
bourgeois art, but that they succeeded in creating the land
below their windows and terraces what Jonson at Penshurst
had ideally imagined: *a rural landscape emptied of rural labour
and of labourers; a sylvan and watery prospect,* with a hundred
analogies in neo-pastoral painting and poetry, *from which
the facts of production had been banished.* ... But it is a com-
manding prospect that is at the same time a triumph of
"unspoiled" nature; that is the achievement: *an effective and
still imposing mystification.* [163] [Emphasis added.]

   In exactly the same fashion the new urban-industrial city of American
capitalism was laid out predominantly in mathematical grids organized for
production and profit. It was here that the primary relation to nature, the
labor process, was concentrated. The sylvan parks and rural homesteads
created by the industrial bourgeoisie were meant to banish the ugly facts
of the urban-capitalist production process from the scene in the same way
that the rural capitalist production process was eliminated by the English
landlords. Here, in the realm of consumption, a secondary relation to
nature, to one's fellow men—in short to living—could be established and
idealized in an effort to compensate for the less than ideal condition of
"ordinary life" in the cities. In the suburbs, the dominant classes could
escape the debased social relations and environment of the primary production process as well as the working classes (who personified this debasement) and could try to create an enclave of beauty and harmony—all
with the benefit of surplus value extracted from the laborers. The suburbs,
then, were in a fundamental sense an "imposing mystification," and they
have remained so ever since.

   The suburban solution also offered the home and family, in addition
to its landscape, a place of refuge and a mystification of human relationships. The home was something to be owned as private property, the rock
on which one built a life of respectable domesticity and consumption.
While all of this came easily to the big bourgeoisie, it was a matter of
desperate earnestness to the petty bourgeoisie and other members of the

"middle class" striving for respectability, as suggested by Sennett in his study of Chicago's Hyde Park in the post-Civil War era of growing class tensions.[164] These people stood in terror of sinking back down into the mire of the city and the working class. Their family lives show the marks of this tension in the fragmentation of social life and repressive atmosphere surrounding them. Sennett's unflattering conclusions about these middle-class lifestyles speak boldly to the contradictions of this aspect of the "suburban solution" and to the pervasive myths that family life *is* social life, that the nuclear family is a means of upward mobility (rather than a defense against downward mobility), and that the image of the happy, two-child family in the suburbs is reliable. Although precise timing of this fundamental change in the role of the family is beyond our scope here, nineteenth-century industrialization was generally accompanied by the rise of a "cult of domesticity" and a decline in the previous productive role of the household.[165]

A final factor to be considered in relation to suburbanization and the lengthening commuter transport network is the *supply* of urban space. Not only must people have wanted to put space between themselves and the central city, but they must have had the means by which to do so. This required not only the individual ability to pay for transport, but, more fundamentally, the *social* ability to support a far-flung urban system (since the cost of overcoming distance is not insignificant) and a successful process of private and state investment in the fixed capital of the built environment. These necessary conditions of suburbanization were dependent on the advances in capital accumulation made possible by the industrial revolution and thus were fulfilled on a significant scale for the first time in the Kuznets cycles of 1822–1842 and 1843–1859, and on an ever-expanding scale after that. In particular, construction of housing, transportation, and utilities depended on overaccumulation and the gigantic waves of fixed capital investment which duly put in their appearance toward the end of each "Kuznets."[166] Looking only at the transit revolution, which appears to have "created" suburbanization, we see that the establishment of omnibus companies coincides with the investment booms of the 1830s and early 1850s, and that the horse-drawn streetcar took the country by storm during the fixed capital investment cycle of the 1850s.[167] In answer to George Rogers Taylor's question, then, it was not the idea of the streetcar that was lacking, but the money for it, which apparently reached sums that would do justice to modern freeways.[168]

Nor were streetcars alone in their cyclic pattern of investment (and overinvestment) in creating the suburban built environment. Residential construction, land values, speculative subdividing, and outlays for public utilities all waxed and waned with the cycles of capital accumulation. Homer Hoyt, for Chicago, and Sam Warner, for Boston, have documented the way in which nineteenth-century urban expansion took place through a "growth coalition" of all the major participants on the supply side, including the local governments, private utilities, landowners, real estate promoters, subdividers, investors, brokers, and builders.[169]

What is significant, but normally overlooked in discussions of suburbanization prior to the post-World War II era, is that the supply of urban infrastructure was, to a degree, independent of demand and instrumental in creating some of its own demand through overexpansion and submarginal cost pricing. The urban center and the economy in general, then, actually subsidized suburbanization.[170]

There is evidence of overinvestment in suburbanization and transit systems in each of the Kuznets cycles. For example, Taylor reports that by the early 1850s ". . . the railroad managements found that, with growing expenses, the commuter passengers did not cover their added cost at the low season ticket rates. Despite vigorous public protests, the railroads substantially increased commuter fares."[171] This suggests, at least, that commuter railroad lines had been overbuilt in the 1830s and 1850s. Omnibuses also were overproduced in the 1850s, with hypercompetition forcing down rates thereafter.[172] The streetcars appear to have been profitable investments in the 1850s, but they nonetheless created demand by charging flat-rate fares instead of marginal cost and were occasionally extended beyond the area of settlement in hopes of creating demand for outlying properties held by the company.[173] This became much worse after the Civil War, when they were built in an unremunerative fashion well in advance of building activity and had to retrench during the depression of 1873–1877. In the next building cycle, housing appears to have caught up with the horse-car lines again, at a distance of about another mile or more from the city center; but even as this was occurring, a frantic search was under way for a faster mode of transit. This search included experimentation with cable cars and finally came up with the electric streetcar. Thereafter, in the 1890s and 1900s, electric streetcar lines were once again overextended beyond the limits of settlement and financial soundness.[174] The point is that supply, pushed by overaccumulating capital, may outstrip demand and even create its own demand in ways not appreciated by neoclassical theorists. Demand-only theories, such as those of Alonso and Muth, are not sufficient to account for the *building* of real urban space, as opposed to a featureless plain. Again, it must be emphasized that capital, in the urbanization process, works at both ends at once.

Spatial Specialization

The third basic movement encompassed by the rearrangement of urban structure in the industrial stage of accumulation was functional and social segregation, or spatial specialization. Some of the essentials of this movement have already been touched upon. Functional land-use separation is presupposed in the growing separation of residential and industrial areas and the lengthening journey to work, mediated by the omnibus, steam railroad, and streetcar modes of rapid transit. But this areal specialization has a finer grain than we have yet given it. Unfortunately, the detailed processes of spatial separation are very poorly understood or documented today, let alone for the nineteenth century.

To begin with, the concentration of production and circulation in the industrial cities was accompanied by an increasing social division of labor among different manufacturers. As mentioned previously, the warehousing district signified a rather low development of this division and a greater need to agglomerate as a result. True factory production, as it evolved in the nineteenth century, created a more dispersed pattern of production and a partial polynucleation of employment and attendant working-class districts.[175] And as the century wore on, accumulation of capital in expanding financial institutions and concentration of commodity sales created a more marked division between financial, retailing and manufacturing districts within the general CBD.[176] While all these tendencies ripened within the industrial stage of accumulation, especially in its declining years, the qualitative turning point in the character of the CBD and industrial decentralization did not come in the 1870s, as David Ward and others have supposed, but rather in the 1890s, when capitalism entered its modern corporate stage.[177]

The major spatial division between the residences of the dominant and working classes has already been discussed, but the process of social subdivision went much farther. The working class was divided within itself by the polynucleation of the social division of labor, as previously noted. It was also being divided in another way, by the detailed division and hierarchy of labor within the work place. The capitalist organization of production encouraged the growth of job specialization and of hierarchical gradations in industry for purposes of increasing output and controlling the workers.[178] Workers finding themselves in differing circumstances with respect to income, skills, authority, and job location, among other things, might be expected to seek out differing places of residence. And this residential differentiation, it has been argued, is likely to be encouraged for reasons of profit making by financial investors and real estate entrepreneurs in the land/housing market, and for its functionality in reproducing a labor force with appropriate schooling, behavior, standards of living, and so forth.[179]

We know that the residential pattern of the working-class districts was much more complex than the general and ideological term *slum* connotes; but we do not have much documentation as to how the pattern actually looked.[180] One overworked division is that between the "native" American workers and recent immigrants. But ethnic districts were not so clearly defined as the idea of the classic ghetto would lead one to believe; immigrants were often quite dispersed and well integrated into existing residential neighborhoods.[181] So far as immigrants were divided into subgroups, it was probably more likely to be by job specialization, not by culture.[182] Then, too, immigrants were likely to make up the bulk of unskilled laborers, whose focus of work was different from that of skilled craftspeople.[183]

Culture per se, of course, came into play *in relation to* the dynamics of employment. Divisive forces came decisively into play from the 1830s and 1850s.[184] As more and more Irish poured into the country and were used to undermine the position of existing mill and handicraft workers, racial and religious tensions were inflamed. This process has been investigated in detail in the dramatic instance of the 1844 Kensington weavers riots in Philadelphia.[185]

Workers were an important force in the nativist movement of the 1840s and 1850s.[186] The early part of the industrial stage of accumulation stands out as one of considerable ethnic tension, not equaled again until the opening of the modern corporate stage of accumulation in the 1890s, for reasons that do not depend on an inherent tendency to racial antagonism whenever new cultural groups mix—if, indeed, the cause of immigration can itself be separated from the process of capital accumulation on a world scale.

Labor was also being redivided along broad, new lines of skilled and unskilled workers, as illustrated by the radically different type of union organizations that arose out of the defeats of the 1840s.[187] Residential differentiation in the 1850s appears to reflect the growing schism between the mass of the unskilled and members of the new crafts unions, who were again winning certain gains. Means of transport came within reach of some craftspeople as fares fell, wages rose, and working hours became limited.[188] Unskilled workers were more closely tied to the CBD in terms of the division of labor, variety of employments, long work hours, low wages, and irregularity of tenure.

Finally, other kinds of functionally discrete land uses, such as urban parklands and railway facilities, came into being or were expanded dramatically during the second half of the nineteenth century. Each of these, too, has its distinctive history and relationship to the evolution of industrial capitalism. Developments with this great an impact on urban structure cannot simply have arisen from the personal achievement of the inventor of the steam engine or the creative genius of landscape architects, though these played their part. As has been argued throughout this essay, the evolution of the capitalist mode of production must constantly be taken into account as the dominant force making modern urbanization and its internal spatial structure both possible and likely, if not uniquely determined.

Conclusion: Suburbanization and the Twentieth Century

Certain characteristics of modern American suburbanization were firmly established during the second stage of accumulation: the preference of the dominant classes for the urban periphery; the ideal of blending the country and the city; the lengthening journey to work and commutation by rapid transit; the escape from the disamenities of production, the working class, and the foreign born; the search for lower land values and taxes at the periphery; the fragmented, speculative, and dramatically cyclic extension and hyperextension of the urban fringe; and so forth. Some of these tendencies began in the 1830s, or perhaps somewhat earlier, which is understandable since capitalist development and the growth of industry were already advancing briskly during the petty commodity stage of accumulation. Some others, such as the detached house or the Romantic suburb, developed significantly only after the Civil War. Other, lesser aspects of the suburban trend, such as rapid peripheral growth, growth outside central city political boundaries, and declining density gradients were certainly well established in the first stage. More quantitative research needs to be done in several areas in order to refine our understanding of changing urban structure in the nineteenth century and to make possible a more sophisticated specification of the relations between capitalist development and urban evolution in the United States. But existing evidence points overwhelmingly to the period from 1830 to 1860, pivoting on the depression of 1839–1842, as the time when suburbanization was launched in America.

The era centering around 1840 marked a dramatic hastening of capitalist industrialization which deserves to be recognized as a qualitative shift in the mode of production from a domination by petty commodity production to domination by modern industry. Coinciding with this came the change from an urbanism made up of mill towns and mercantile ports to one characterized by the classic industrial city. Focussing on this pivotal era allows us to see more clearly that the pattern of urbanization in this country has not been a smooth evolution to the conditions of the present, but has been marked by major transformations from one kind of city to another. At the same time it shows that the roots of the present suburban-dominated forms of urbanization go very deeply, even to the character of capitalism itself. For it is the capitalist industrial revolution gaining momentum and entering the big cities after 1840 which induces a suburban movement that is recognizably modern.

Suburbanization cannot be understood in terms of consumer demand theory in which people's social relations are reduced to autonomous "tastes" for space arising in a vacuum, without reference to what is happening in the central city, nor in ignorance of the process by which the city is actually built. Indeed, this grounds itself in the ideology of suburbia, the place from which production is banished; the lower orders of society, excluded; and harmony with nature and one's fellow man, presumed to reign supreme. What is required is a theory which is dialectical and structural, and one which situates capitalist production, classes, and accumulation at the center of a complex web of unfolding economic and social relationships.

Suburbanization was chosen less for itself than produced by its antipodes: the concentration of production, the concentration of the working class, the degraded relations to nature in the work place, the investment process in fixed capital (flowing, no doubt, through the central business district), and so forth. In turn, the concentration of economic life in the center of industrial cities is to be explained only in small part by a presumed necessity of commodity exchange to pass through the city center; it presupposes a radical transformation in the ownership of the means of production in city and country, in the way production is organized, and limits to working-class mobility, among other things. And finally the real history of this transformation, and the urbanism it begot, is much less idyllic than the harmonious order of Von Thünen-type location models would have us believe.

Urbanization and suburbanization have, of course, come a long way from the age of the classic nineteenth-century industrial city. This story goes beyond the purposes at hand.[189] Briefly, the most significant reorientation of urban structure occurred as a result of the profound transformation to modern corporate capitalism around the turn of this century. The tumult and reforms of the Progressive era focussed, to a large extent, on the problems of the industrial city of the second stage of accumulation and the effort to redirect city growth along the new lines of the twentieth-century city. This meant, in contrast to the nineteenth century, things such as a radical decentralization and multinucleation of manufacturing, retailing, and wholesaling; more spatially extensive configurations made possible by the automobile and truck; and the movement of the working class, especially the growing strata of white-collar workers, to the suburbs. It also has meant permanent political separation from the central city of ever more numerous suburban jurisdictions; the breakdown of the grid street system and a generalization of the curvilinear pattern; the entry of large-scale mortgage finance into urban-suburban investment; and the direct support of the federal government for suburbanization. And it has included mass consumption of consumer durables; mass homeownership; greater community-level collective consumption; and a qualitative jump in the degree of discontinuous "sprawl-type" development. The central business district has, at the same time, shifted almost exclusively to office buildings devoted to finance capital, corporate administration, state functions, and professional services. Rents have continued to go up at the center, while the density gradient of the city has continued to decline. But, unlike the nineteenth century, the suburban "ring" has increasingly become the focus of productive life, and the suburban explosion has proceeded so rapidly, the "zone of transition" around the central business district has given way to something nearer to a zone of abandonment.

The sheer volume of suburbanization since World War II has fooled many people into believing that it represented an entirely new phenomenon. But the continuity with the past is strong. It goes back even to the early nineteenth century, when the capitalist development process began to force rapid urbanization, new patterns of production, and new divisions of social life; and when the American bourgeois patterns of affection for the urban periphery were established, putting space between themselves and the city's problems and bringing rural landscapes into the city.

Notes

1. William Alonso, *Location and Land Use* (Cambridge: Harvard University Press, 1964); Richard Muth, *Cities and Housing* (Chicago: University of Chicago Press, 1969); Edwin Mills, *Studies in the Structure of the Urban Economy* (Baltimore: The Johns Hopkins University Press, 1972).
2. David Harvey, *Social Justice and the City* (London: Edward Arnold, 1973), p. 168.
3. Richard Walker, "Urban Ground Rent: Building a New Conceptual Framework," *Antipode* 6, no. 1 (1974): 51–58; idem, "Contentious Issues in Marxian Value and Rent Theory: A Second and Longer Look," *Antipode* 7, no. 1 (1975): 31–54.
4. Alonso, *Location and Land Use*, p. 18. For a systematic critique of neoclassical consumer theory, see Herbert Gintis, "Consumer Behavior and the Concept of Sovereignty: Explanations of Social Decay," *American Economic Review* 62, no. 2 (1972): 267–78.
5. Edward J. Nell, "Economics: The Revival of Political Economy," in *Ideology in Social Science*, ed. Robin Blackburn (London: Fontana, 1972), pp. 76–95.
6. See the critical essays in E. K. Hunt and Jesse G. Schwartz, eds., *A Critique of Economic Theory* (Harmondsworth, Middlesex: Penguin Books, 1972); Joan Robinson, *Economic Heresies* (New York; Basic Books, 1973).
7. For a critique of the ideology of social harmony in location models since Von Thünen, see Joern Barnbrock, "Prologomenon to a Methodological Debate on Location Theory: The Case of Von Thünen," *Antipode* 6, no. 1 (1974): 59–65.
8. See, for example, John F. Kain, "The Distribution and Movement of Jobs and Industry," in *The Metropolitan Enigma*, ed. James Q. Wilson (Cambridge: Harvard University Press, 1968), pp. 1–39; refs. to pp. 2–4.
9. For a more comprehensive introduction to Marxist method and theory, see Richard Walker, "The Suburban Solution: Urban Reform and Urban Geography in the Capitalist Development of the United States" (Ph.D. diss., The Johns Hopkins University, 1977), chap. 1, pp. 15–122 and refs. cited therein.
10. Neither cities nor capitalism change cleanly from one era to the next. The problem of distinguishing a new urban era from a past one is obviously complicated by considerations of diffusion of innovation, differing economic roles of cities, local quirks, differing rates of growth, and so forth.
11. David Harvey, "Urbanization Under Capitalism: Part I" (Unpublished manuscript, 1975), p. 16; see also idem, "The Geography of Accumulation," *Antipode* 7, no. 2 (1975): 9–21.
12. See Simon Kuznets, *Capital in the American Economy* (Princeton, N.J.: National Bureau of Economic Research, 1961); Moses Abramowitz, "The Nature and Significance of Kuznets Cycles," *Economic Development and Cultural Change* 9 (1961): 225–48; Brinley Thomas, *Migration and Economic Growth* (Cambridge: Cambridge University Press, 1973).
13. N. D. Kondratieff, "The Long Wave in Economic Life," *Review of Economic Statistics* 17 (1935): 105–15; see also George Garvy, "Kondratieff's Theory of Long Cycles," *Review of Economics and Statistics* 25, no. 4 (1943): 203–20; Ernest Mandel, *Late Capitalism* (London: New Left Books, 1975); Bob Rowthorn, "Late Capitalism," *New Left Review*, no. 98 (1976): 59–83; Joseph Schumpeter, *Business Cycles*, 2 vols. (New York: McGraw-Hill, 1939).
14. David Harvey, *Social Justice and the City*, pp. 41–43.
15. Ibid., pp. 57–73; Abramowitz, "Kuznets Cycles," p. 240.
16. The best discussion of this phenomenon is Homer Hoyt, *One Hundred Years of Land Values in Chicago* (Chicago: University of Chicago Press, 1933), especially pp. 368–422. Hoyt had discovered the Kuznets cycle about the same time as Kuznets, but did not know what he had stumbled on.
17. See Gregory Singleton, "The Genesis of Suburbia," in *The Urbanization of the Suburbs*, ed. Louis Masotti and Jeffrey K. Hadden (Beverly Hills, Calif.: Sage Publications, 1973), pp. 29–50; Kenneth T. Jackson, "Urban Deconcentration in the Nineteenth Century: A Statistical Inquiry," in *The New Urban History*, ed. Leo Schnore (Princeton: Princeton University Press, 1975), pp. 110–42.
18. For an account of the evolution of twentieth-century suburbanization, see Walker, "Surburban Solution," chaps. 4–7, pp. 293–615.
19. For more on the petty commodity stage of capitalist production, see Maurice Dobb, *Studies in the Development of Capitalism* (New York: International Publishers, 1963).
20. See, for example, Paul Gates, *The Farmers' Age* (New York: Holt, Rinehart, and Winston, 1960).
21. Jackson T. Main, *Social Structure in Revolutionary America* (Princeton: Princeton University Press, 1965), pp. 66–67.
22. They were also marked in the South, whose economy was built around the supply of raw materials to England. The pressures of this linkage had much to do with the distinct evolution of the South as a slave mode of production within the world capitalist order. Southern development and urbanism require a treatment separate from the heavily northern-biased one given in this article.
23. Roy Robbins, *Our Landed Heritage: The Public Domain, 1776–1970* (Lincoln: University of Nebraska Press, 1976), pp. 3–118; Thomas Le Duc, "History and Appraisal of U.S. Land Policy to 1862," in *Land Use Policy and Problems in the United States*, ed. Howard Ottoson (Lincoln: University of Nebraska Press, 1963), p. 3–27; Gates, *Farmers' Age*; Henry Nash Smith, *Virgin Land* (Cambridge: Harvard University Press, 1970), pp. 123–263.
24. Lance Davis, Richard Easterlin, William Parker et al., *American Economic Growth* (New York: Macmillan

Co., 1972), p. 28. Household production still produced two-thirds of all clothing worn in 1810. Thomas Bender, *Toward an Urban Vision* (Lexington: University Press of Kentucky, 1975), pp. 28–29.

25. Ibid.

26. George Rogers Taylor, "American Urban Growth Preceding the Railway Age," *Journal of Economic History* 27, no. 3 (1967): 321.

27. See, generally, Douglass C. North, *The Economic Growth of the United States, 1790–1860* (New York: W. W. Norton, 1966).

28. On the cyclical movements of this period, ibid.; Carter Goodrich, Julius Rubin, H. J. Cramner and Harvey Segal, *Canals and American Economic Development* (New York: Columbia University Press, 1961); Jeffrey G. Williamson, *American Growth and the Balance of Payments, 1820–1913* (Chapel Hill: University of North Carolina Press, 1964), pp. 89–111; Walker, "Suburban Solution," pp. 176–89.

29. Stanley Lebergott, *Manpower in Economic Growth* (New York: McGraw-Hill, 1964), p. 510.

30. Schumpeter, *Business Cycles*, p. 289.

31. On the conditions of manufacturing in this period, see Walker, "Suburban Solution," pp. 189–94; North, *Economic Growth*, pp. 156–77, especially; Allen Pred, "Manufacturing in the American Mercantile City: 1800–1840," *Annals of the Association of American Geographers* 56, no. 2 (1966): 307–38; David Montgomery, "The Working Classes of the Pre-Industrial American City, 1780–1830," *Labor History* 9, no. 1 (1968): 3–22; George Rogers Taylor, "The National Economy Before and After the Civil War," in *Economic Change in the Civil War Era*, ed. David Gilchrist and David Lewis (Greeneville, Del.: Eleutherian Mills-Hagley Foundation, 1965), pp. 1–22; Schumpeter, *Business Cycles*, pp. 285–92; various essays in Harold F. Williamson, ed., *The Growth of the American Economy* (New York: Prentice-Hall, 1944).

32. The shortage of free labor was most crucial. Early spokesmen for domestic manufactures had to argue that the demand for labor would not draw it off from agriculture or trade, and they tried in vain to resist the flow of labor to the West. In practice, factory owners had often to resort to marginal forms of labor, such as unmarried women, children, or occupants of asylums and poorhouses. Montgomery, "Pre-Industrial American City," p. 18; cf. Sidney Pollard, *The Genesis of Modern Management* (Cambridge: Harvard University Press, 1965), pp. 160–208, on English practices.

33. Pred, "American Mercantile City," p. 307.

34. George Rogers Taylor, "The Beginnings of Mass Transportation in Urban America," *Smithsonian Journal of History* 1, nos. 2, 3 (1966): no. 2: 35–50; no. 3: 31–54; ref. in pt. 1, p. 38.

35. Pred, "American Mercantile City," p. 336.

36. Taylor, "Beginnings of Mass Transportaion," pt. 1, p. 38.

37. Martyn J. Bowden, "Growth of the Central Districts in Large Cities," in *The New Urban History*, ed. Leo F. Schnore (Princeton: Princeton University Press, 1975), pp. 75–109; ref. to pp. 83–86. See also David Ward, *Cities and Immigrants* (New York: Oxford University Press, 1971); pp. 85–103.

38. Ward, ibid.

39. Montgomery, "Pre-Industrial American City," pp. 20–22.

40. Ibid., pp. 13, 21.

41. Sam Bass Warner, *Streetcar Suburbs* (Cambridge: Harvard University Press, 1962), p. 19.

42. Ira Katznelson, "Community Conflict and Capitalist Development" Paper prepared for the 1975 annual meeting of the American Political Science Association, San Francisco, Calif., September 2–5; ref. to p. 6 et passim.

43. Jackson, "Urban Deconcentration," pp. 126–27.

44. Ibid., p. 126.

45. Taylor, "Beginnings of Mass Transportation," p. 38.

46. Warner, *Streetcar Suburbs*, p. 134.

47. Walker, "Suburban Solution," pp. 253–70; David Rothman, The *Discovery of the Asylum* (Boston: Little, Brown & Co., 1971); Raymond Mohl, *Poverty in New York, 1789–1825* (New York: Oxford University Press, 1971); Robert H. Bremner, *From the Depths* (New York: New York University Press, 1956), pp. 3–123; Clifford S. Griffen, *The Ferment of Reform: 1830–1860* (New York: Thomas Y. Crowell, 1967); Roger Lane, *Policing the City: Boston* (Cambridge: Harvard University Press, 1967), pp. 26–38; Montgomery, "Pre-Industrial American City."

48. Hans Huth, *Nature and the American* (Lincoln: University of Nebraska Press, 1972), p. 123.

49. For a brief history of the omnibus, see Taylor, "Beginnings of Mass Transportation," pt. 1, pp. 40–48.

50. Jackson, "Urban Deconcentration," pp. 113–17. See generally, Ralph H. Brown, *Historical Geography of the United States* (New York: Harcourt, Brace & Co., 1948); Aaron M. Sakolski, *The Great American Land Bubble* (New York: Harper and Bros., 1932); Homer Hoyt, *Land Values in Chicago*; Richard Wade, *The Urban Frontier* (Cambridge: Harvard University Press, 1959); Charles Glaab and Theodore Brown, *A History of Urban America* (New York: Macmillan Co., 1967), pp. 25–51.

51. It also contrasts with the compact, socially controlled settlements of colonial New England, which had given way to a free land market and scatteration by the mid-eighteenth century. See Brown, *Historical Geography*, pp. 49–56. Add-on urban development guided by private property, profits, and the market seems so natural to us today that we may forget to comment on this aspect of the urbanization/suburbanization process.

52. This is clear from reading any of the works referred to in nn. 23 and 50, above.

53. Jackson, "Urban Deconcentration," pp. 115; Taylor, "Beginnings of Mass Transportation," pt. 1, p. 36. Both authors have worked up tables for city and suburban growth in selected large cities.

54. Kenneth T. Jackson, "Metropolitan Government versus Political Autonomy: Politics on the Crabgrass Frontier," in *Cities in American History,* ed. Kenneth T. Jackson and Stanley K. Schultz (New York: Alfred Knopf, 1972), pp. 442–52.

55. Jackson, "Urban Deconcentration," pp. 126–27; Warner, *Streetcar Suburbs,* p. 19; Taylor, "Beginnings of Mass Transportation," pt. 1, pp. 36, 37, 40.

56. Jackson, "Urban Deconcentration," p. 118; Warner, *Streetcar Suburbs,* pp. 15–21; Pred, "American Mercantile City," p. 325.

57. Jackson, "Urban Deconcentration," pp. 120–25; cf. Taylor, "Beginnings of Mass Transportation," pp. 35–40. However, the innermost wards invariably lost population owing to the expansion of the nonresidential business district; it was the next ring of wards, occupied by the working class, usually immigrants, that became, in most cases, more crowded than anything previously known.

58. Jackson, "Urban Deconcentration," p. 122.

59. The phrase is due to Warner.

60. Compare with Taylor, "Beginnings of Mass Transportation," pt. 1, pp. 44–45; and Walter Isard, "A Neglected Cycle: The Transport-Building Cycle," in *Review of Economics and Statistics* 24, no. 4 (1942): 149–58.

61. Taylor, "Beginnings of Mass Transportation," pt. 2, p. 47; K. H. Schaeffer and Eliot Sclar, *Access for All: Transportation and Urban Growth* (Baltimore: Pelican, 1975), pp. 20–21; Gareth Stedman Jones, *Outcast London* (Harmondsworth, Middlesex: Penguin Books, 1976), pp. 207–8.

62. The best source on mill towns other than Lowell is James E. Vance, Jr., "Housing the Worker: The Employment Linkage as a Force in Urban Structure," *Economic Geography* 42, no. 4 (1966): 294–325.

63. Ibid., pp. 304–6.

64. On Lowell, see: ibid., pp. 312–17; Bender, *Urban Vision,* pp. 32–51; Norman Ware, *The Industrial Worker, 1840–1860* (Chicago: Quadrangle Books, 1964), pp. 71–105 et passim; Herbert Gutman, "Work, Culture, and Society in Industrializing America, 1815–1919," *American Historical Review* 78, no. 3 (1973): 531–88; ref. to pp. 550–53.

65. Vance, "Housing the Worker," p. 314.

66. ". . . in Lowell there was hardly an hour of the day or a relationship of any sort that was not covered by the regulations, written or understood, of the corporations." Ware, *Industrial Worker,* p. 78.

67. Bender, *Urban Vision,* p. 110.

68. Ware, *Industrial Worker,* pp. 125–153.

69. On Pullman and its lessons for other capitalists, see Stanley Buder, *Pullman: An Experiment in Industrial Order and Community Planning, 1880–1930* (New York: Oxford University Press, 1967), p. 131; Edward Greer, "Monopoly and Competitive Capital in the Making of Gary, Indiana," *Science and Society* 40, no. 4 (1976–77): 465–78; ref. to pp. 468–69.

70. See the essays in David T. Gilchrist and W. David Lewis, eds., *Economic Change in the Civil War Era* (Greeneville, Del.: Eleutherian Mills-Hagley Foundation, 1965).

71. North, *Economic Growth,* p. 205.

72. Ibid., pp. 205, 210.

73. Ibid., p. 204.

74. Ibid. The broadening market is North's chief causal factor, as we would expect from a theorist heavily steeped in exchange-based economics.

75. Contrary to the "take-off" theory of Walt W. Rostow, *The Stages of Economic Growth* (Cambridge: Cambridge University Press, 1971), p. 61, or the "age of railroads" interpretation of Joseph Schumpeter, *Business Cycles,* p. 326, the railroad boom from 1849 to 1854 actually *lagged* behind the progress of manufactures and gave little impetus to American capital goods industries, the industrialization of the Northeast, or lowering freight rates before the middle of the 1850s. See Albert Fishlow, *Railroads and the Transformation of the Ante-Bellum Economy* (Cambridge: Harvard University Press, 1965), pp. 55, 160, 260 et passim. In New England, accumulating profits from manufacturing were directed into railroad building in the late 1840s (ibid., p. 244).

76. Taylor, "National Economy," p. 21; North, *Economic Growth,* p. 207; Goodrich, *American Economic Development,* p. 231; Fishlow, *Ante-Bellum Economy,* pp. 293–94.

77. Bender, *Urban Vision,* p. 106.

78. Ware, *Industrial Worker,* pp. 106–24.

79. Ibid., p. 26; Fishlow, *Ante-Bellum Economy,* p. 248.

80. Ware, *Industrial Worker,* pp. 26–70; 198–226. Cf. David Montgomery, "The Shuttle and the Cross: Weavers and Artisans in the Kensington Riots of 1844," *Journal of Social History* 5, no. 4 (1972): 411–46.

81. Ware, *Industrial Worker,* pp. 227–40; Sam Bass Warner, *The Private City: Philadelphia* (Philadelphia: University of Pennsylvania Press, 1968), pp. 76–78.

82. Gilchrist and Lewis, *Civil War Era,* p. 148.

83 David Montgomery, *Beyond Equality* (New York: Knopf, 1967), p.8. The number for Philadelphia is 15.6 per establishment: Warner, *Private City: Philadelphia,* p. 77.

84. Montgomery, *Beyond Equality,* p. 30.

85. Williamson, *Balance of Payments,* p. 307.

86. Pred, "American Mercantile City," p. 314; Ware, *Industrial Worker,* p. 103. An indirect sort of financial rationalization was achieved by several states defaulting on their debts, most of which had financed internal improvements with British and eastern capital.

87. North, *Economic Growth,* p. 257; Taylor, "National Economy," p. 13.

88. Joseph Petulla, *American Environmental History* (San Francisco, Calif.: Boyd and Fraser, 1977), pp. 96–101; Clarence Danhof, "Agricultural Technology to 1880," in *The Growth of the American Economy,* ed. Harold F. Williamson (New York: Prentice-Hall, 1944), pp. 113–140.

89. North, *Economic Growth,* p. 209.

90. Taylor, "National Economy," p. 16.

91. See, generally, Thomas, *Migration and Economic Growth.*

92. Bender, *Urban Vision,* pp. 105–7; Ware, *Industrial Worker,* pp. 149–53.

93. North, *Economic Growth,* p. 170; Taylor, "National Economy," p. 15.

94. Taylor, "National Economy," p. 17.

95. Davis, *American Economic Growth,* p. 601.

96. See, generally, ibid.; Williamson, *Balance of Payments;* Gilchrist and Lewis, *Civil War Era;* Schumpeter, *Business Cycles;* Thomas, *Migration and Economic Growth;* Walker, "Suburban Solution," pp. 206–11 and data, appendix 1.

97. Stephen Hymer, "The Multinational Corporation and the Law of Uneven Development," in *Economics and World Order,* ed. Jagdish N. Bhagwati (New York: Macmillan Co., 1972), pp. 113–40; ref. to p. 118.

98. Davis, *American Economic Growth,* p. 601; Ward, *Cities and Immigrants,* p. 22.

99. Harvey, "Urbanization Under Capitalism," p. 108.

100. Ward, *Cities and Immigrants,* p. 31.

101. Ibid., pp. 85–105; Warner, *Streetcar Suburbs,* pp. 46–66.

102. Montgomery, *Beyond Equality,* p. 37; Warner, *Streetcar Suburbs,* p. 6.

103. See above, n. 92.

104. Taylor, "Beginnings of Mass Transportation," pt. 1, p. 3; Schumpeter, *Business Cycles,* pp. 289–90. Waterpower continued to be used (it still contributed around fifty percent of the supply in 1860), but the age of fossil fuels had been launched. Petulla, *American Environmental History,* pp. 149–54.

105. Pred, "American Mercantile City," p. 317.

106. Rolla M. Tryon, *Household Manufactures in the United States, 1640–1860* (Chicago: University of Chicago Press, 1917). Cities benefited from being nodes of the system, not simply because of the efficiencies of their location in terms of transport and production, but also from forces for economic centralization, such as rate and credit discrimination. The exploitation by the cities of the rural hinterland is a topic in itself. See, for example, Richard Peet, "Rural Inequality and Regional Planning," *Antipode* 7, no. 3 (1975): 10–25; refs. cited therein.

107. Clearly, the demand for urban public services depends on more than urban growth per se; it also depends on changing technical and social definitions of what is necessary for urban production and consumption. Similarly, the supply of services by private enterprise or the state depends on technical and economic conditions (profitability, investible surplus) and decisions as to the appropriate mode of supply, especially the division of labor between private business and the state. In any event, the supply of public (municipal) services increased very fast after 1840; the municipal debt grew twenty-five times between 1840 and 1870. See A. M. Hillhouse, *Municipal Bonds* (New York: Prentice-Hall, 1936), p. 34.

108. Ward, *Cities and Immigrants,* pp. 89, 91.

109. Glaab and Brown, *History of Urban America,* p. 143.

110. Hoyt, *Land Values in Chicago,* p. 104; Ward, *Cities and Immigrants,* p. 100.

111. Ward, *Cities and Immigrants,* p. 101.

112. Later experience (at the end of the century), when a transformation to a new stage of accumulation and a new urban-industrial growth ensemble was under way, reinforces the impression of several factors together being critical, rather than any one alone. The need for a labor pool was a clear barrier to industrial decentralization for a time, as indicated, for example, by George Pullman's need to build a town to house his workers in the 1880s. But the existing urban pool was growing less desirable, owing to workers' increasing intransigence and organization, and this was another reason Pullman wanted to build his model town on the fringe of Chicago. At the same time large factory complexes, such as Pullman's, could internalize most of their essential linkages and economies of agglomeration, so central city location offered less advantage than the cheap land and open spaces outside the city. Factories so large could also attract their own labor force. In addition, the general level of production could not support the cost of a modern, space-extensive city, nor could it solve the technical problems of a transportation system that could integrate such a city. See Walker, "Suburban Solution," chap. 4, pp. 293–428. Cf. Buder, *Pullman;* E. E. Pratt, *The Industrial Causes of Congestion of Population in New York City* (New York: Columbia University Press, 1911); Graham Taylor, *Satellite Cities* (New York: Appleton, 1915).

113. See Ward, *Cities and Immigrants*, pp. 105–25; and David Ward, "The Victorian Slum: An Enduring Myth?" *Annals of the Association of American Geographers* 66, no. 2 (1976): 323–36; refs. cited therein.

114. See David Harvey, "Labor, Capital, and Class Struggle Around the Built Environment in Advanced Capitalist Societies," chapter 1 of this volume.

115. Vance, "Housing the Worker," p. 307.

116. Ibid., pp. 318–25.

117. Ibid., pp. 319–22. The speculative nature of the Hadley Falls Company may well be owing to the fact that capital was moving out of the primary circuit of production in New England by 1847 and into secondary investments and speculations.

118. The motive force here was, of course, the wage-lowering competition of surplus laborers. The capitalists simply let the market take its "natural" course. Industrialists no longer needed housing to attract labor and were happy to be rid of this low-return investment, and the new providers of housing, while probably satisfied with a lower return than was industrial capital, were not willing to accept so low a return as decent housing for low-income workers would have brought. They therefore let workers crowd together as a "market adjustment." Vance, "Housing the Worker," p. 324, says as much, without the critical conclusion. On rates of return to investors in the nineteenth-century housing market, see Warner, *Streetcar Suburbs*, pp. 117–19.

119. There is no direct evidence of what industrialists were thinking about housing and class consciousness at this time. But the comparison to the rather open rejection of direct provision of housing (as in the Pullman experiment) at a later time is suggestive, particularly in light of the advocacy of small property and homeownership put forward by some Lowell burghers in the 1840s as a solution to worker alienation: the "solution" seized upon full scale by Vanderbilt, Gary, and most of the capitalist class by the end of the century. See references in n. 69, above; Bender, *Urban Vision*, pp. 115–16; Joel Tarr, "From City to Suburb: The Moral Influence of Transportation Technology," in *American Urban History*, ed. A. B. Callow (New York: Oxford University Press, 1973), pp. 202–12; Walker, "Suburban Solution," pp. 336–47; 368–90.

120. Vance, "Housing the Worker," p. 319 et passim; Roy Lubove, *The Progressives and the Slums* (Pittsburgh, Pa.: University of Pittsburgh Press, 1962), pp. 38–39 et passim; Warner, *Streetcar Suburbs*, pp. 67–152.

121. Vance observes that there had been crowding in some European cities before the freeing of the housing market and that some small manufacturing towns in the U.S. retained relatively decent housing, but ". . . when we look beyond a small group of often artificially immured cities, overcrowding and debasement of the workingman's home came with the generalized housing market." Vance, "Housing the Worker," p. 324. Yet Vance seems to attribute this debasement to the lag required to gear up a housing industry, rather than to the logic of profits and the market. Lubove frames the correct response in his critique of model tenement reform: "In effect, those who could afford the large capital investment required to build model tenements were not particularly interested; they had better uses for their capital which did not involve the annoyance. . . . On the other hand, the small entrepreneurs, sometimes immigrants themselves, who owned the lion's share of New York tenements, were not prepared to sacrifice their profits for the sake of humanity." Lubove, *Progressives and the Slums*, p. 39.

122. Taylor, "Beginnings of Mass Transportation," pt. 1, p. 39. Again, densities did not ordinarily rise as high as New York's, nor did they rise at all in some cases. See above, n. 57.

123. Karl Marx, *Capital* (New York: International Publishers, 1967), 3:773. See also Harvey, "Labor, Capital, and Class Struggle."

124. E. P. Thompson, *The Making of the English Working Class* (Harmondsworth, Middlesex: Penguin Books, 1968).

125. Warner, *Private City: Philadelphia*, pp. 79–98. Walker, "Suburban Solution," pp. 358–68; 392–400.

126. John Foster, *Class Struggle and the Industrial Revolution* (London: Weidenfield and Nicolson, 1974).

127. Jones, *Outcast London*, p. 14.

128. Walker, "Suburban Solution," pp. 270–81; 328–68 and refs. there.

129. Ward, *Cities and Immigrants*, p. 107.

130. For the theory of spatial entrapment today, see Harvey, *Social Justice and the City*, pp. 170–71. This is illustrated graphically, in that many workers were forced into shanty towns on the urban fringe in the initial stages of the industrial stage of accumulation and the free housing market, and then were forced back into the center city as the middle-class exodus (via streetcars) picked up speed. Ward, *Cities and Immigrants*, p. 106.

131. Gutman, "Industrializing America."

132. See, generally, Ward, *Cities and Immigrants*, pp. 125–45; Jackson, "Urban Deconcentration"; Taylor, "Beginnings of Mass Transportation"; Hoyt, *Land Values in Chicago*, pp. 81–107; Warner, *Streetcar Suburbs*; Joel Tarr, *Transportation Innovation and Changing Spatial Patterns: Pittsburgh, 1850–1910* (Pittsburgh, Pa.: Carnegie-Mellon University Press, 1972); idem, "City to Suburb."

133. Warner, *Streetcar Suburbs*, pp. 46–66.

134. Ward, *Cities and Immigrants*, p. 130; cf. Taylor, "Beginnings of Mass Transportation," pt. 2, p. 33; and Jackson, "Urban Deconcentration," p. 134. Original studies are cited by all of the above.

135. Taylor, "Beginnings of Mass Transportation," pp. 31–38.

136. Jackson, "Urban Deconcentration," pp. 134–39. In the smaller city of Louisville, as we would expect, the separation of work and home among the elite proceeded more slowly through the second half of the century. Ibid., pp. 139–40.

137. Ibid., pp. 131–32. See also Hoyt, Land Values in Chicago, pp. 279–367; and Roger Lotchin, "San Francisco, 1846–1856: The Patterns of Chaos and Growth," in Cities in American History, ed. K. T. Jackson and S. K. Schultz (New York: Knopf, 1972), pp. 151–60. George Rogers Taylor remarks that some wealthy merchants remained in downtown Boston "as late as the 1840s," while Philadelphia's more conservative elite held on, in significant numbers, to their central strongholds until after the Civil War. Taylor, "Beginnings of Mass Transportation," pt. 1, p. 40. The latter may help explain why slums owing to entrapment were slow to form in Philadelphia (Warner, Private City: Philadelphia, p. 56), and why the streetcar mania was also delayed there. See n. 138, below.

138. Taylor, "Beginnings of Mass Transportation," pt. 2, p. 49.

139. Edward S. Mason, The Street Railways of Massachusetts (Cambridge: Harvard University Press, 1932), pp. 1–4.

140. Jackson, "Urban Deconcentration," p. 134 and refs. there.

141. Taylor, "Beginnings of Mass Transportation," pt. 2, p. 47.

142. Alonso, Location and Land Use, p. 18.

143. For the very wealthy, money was probably never the limiting factor, as many owned summer estates long before the suburban era. However, so great was the fad for country estates in the 1830s and '40s that many people overextended themselves financially, trying to realize the ideal. Huth, Nature and the American, p. 123.

144. Singleton, "Genesis of Suburbia," p. 38.

145. See, generally, Marx, Capital, 1:330–35; 359–68; 418–27; Stephen Marglin, "What Do Bosses Do?" Review of Radical Political Economy 6, no. 2 (1974); Herbert Gintis, "The Nature of the Labor Exchange and the Theory of Capitalist Production," Review of Radical Political Economy 8, no. 2, (1976): 36–54.

146. See above, n. 37.

147. Lane, Policing the City; Warner, Private City: Philadelphia, chap. 7, pp. 125–60; Lubove, Progressives and the Slums, pp. 11–12.

148. Lubove, ibid., pp. 11–23; John Duffy, A History of Public Health in New York City, 1625–1860 (New York: Russell Sage, 1968); Nelson Blake, Water for the Cities (Syracuse, N.Y.: Syracuse University Press, 1956).

149. Warner, Private City: Philadelphia, pp. 62; 78; 125–60.

150. Rothman, Discovery of the Asylum.

151. Ibid., pp. 138–41.

152. See, generally, Hoyt, Land Values in Chicago.

153. This has been thoroughly documented for the agricultural sector. See Sakolski, Great American Land Bubble; Robbins, Our Landed Heritage; Robert P. Swierenga, Pioneers and Profits: Land Speculation on the Iowa Frontier (Ames: Iowa State University Press, 1968). And it shows up clearly in Hoyt's classic study of Chicago land history (see n. 16, above).

154. See above, n. 107. Cf. Hoyt, Land Values in Chicago, p. 397.

155. Jackson, "Urban Deconcentration," p. 116.

156. Warner, Streetcar Suburbs, pp. 11–14 et passim.

157. Peter Schmitt, Back to Nature (New York: Oxford University Press, 1969), p. xvii.

158. Ibid., especially chaps. 2 and 4. Smith, Virgin Land, pp. 71–123. An essential part of this complex process of cultural diffusion was the creation of a suburban ideology in terms of the physical environment. The same thing crops up in Olmsted and discussions of the moral influence of rapid transit. See Bender, Urban Vision, pp. 159–88, and further discussion in text; ref. n. 119, above.

159. Warner, Streetcar Suburbs, pp. 58–60.

160. Bender, Urban Vision, p. 162.

161. Ibid., p. 175

162. Ibid., p. 181.

163. Raymond Williams, The Country and the City (London: Chatto and Windus, 1973), pp. 124–25.

164. Richard Sennett, Families Against the City: Middle-Class Homes of Industrial Chicago, 1872–1890 (Cambridge: Harvard University Press, 1970).

165. Tryon, Household Manufactures; Mary Patricia Ryan, "American Society and the Cult of Domesticity: 1830–1860" (Ph.D. diss., University of California at Berkeley, 1972).

166. See refs. under nn. 11, 12, 16, 60, above.

167. Taylor, "Beginnings of Mass Transportation," pt. 1, pp. 44–45; pt. 2, p. 39 et passim. For later waves of streetcar building see Mason, Street Railways of Massachusetts.

168. Warner, Streetcar Suburbs, p. 49.

169. Warner, ibid., pp. 29–34 et passim. Hoyt, Land Values in Chicago, chap. 7, pp. 368–423, especially.

170. A good theoretical discussion of horizontal subsidization of suburbanization through nonmarginal cost pricing and hyperextension of the utility-transport network is Mason Gaffney, "Land and Rent in Welfare Economics," in Land Economics Research, ed. Marion Clawson, M. Harris, and J. Ackerman (Baltimore: The Johns Hopkins University Press, 1962), pp. 141–67. See also Walker, "Urban Ground Rent," pp. 51–59.

171. Taylor, "Beginnings of Mass Transportation," pt. 2, p. 50. Charles J. Kennedy, "Commuter Services in the Boston Area, 1835–1860," *Business History Review* 36 (1962): 153–70.
172. Taylor, "Beginnings of Mass Transportation," pt. 1, p. 47.
173. Ibid., pt. 2, p. 37, concerning profitability.
174. Mason, *Street Railways of Massachusetts,* pp. 1–13; 41–70. See also Walker, "Suburban Solution," pp. 388–90; Ward, *Cities and Immigrants,* pp. 130–31.
175. Homer Hoyt, *The Structure and Growth of Residential Neighborhoods in American Cities* (Washington, D.C.: Federal Housing Administration, 1939), map, p. 110; idem, *Land Values in Chicago,* pp. 53–74; 82–107; 132–41; 142–59; 184–96; Ward, *Cities and Immigrants,* p. 100; Pred, "American Mercantile City"; E. J. Hobsbawm, "The 19th Century London Labour Market," in *London: Aspects of Change,* Center for Urban Studies (London: McGibbon and Kee, 1964), pp. 3–28, ref. to pp. 7–9. Warner, *Private City: Philadelphia,* p. 59. For example, Warner describes the movement of workers to different employment loci in Philadelphia in 1860: the central business district, the northwestern locomotive and metalworking center, the Kensington textile center, and the Southwark mills (ibid., pp. 60–61).
176. Ward, *Cities and Immigrants,* pp. 87–89; 94–101; Bowden, "Districts in Large Cities"; Hoyt, *Land Values in Chicago.*
177. Walker, "Suburban Solution," chaps. 4, 5.
178. See above, n. 145.
179. David Harvey, "Class-Monopoly Rent, Finance Capital, and the Urban Revolution," *Regional Studies* 8, no. 3 (1974): 239–55; David Harvey and Lata Chatterjee, "Absolute Rent and the Structuring of Space by Financial and Governmental Institutions," *Antipode* 6, no. 1 (1974); 22–36.
180. See, generally, Ward, *Cities and Immigrants,* pp. 105–25; idem, "Victorian Slum."
181. Ward, *Cities and Immigrants,* p. 121; Warner, *Streetcar Suburbs,* p. 46; idem, *Private City: Philadelphia,* pp. 56–57.
182. The tendency of different groups of immigrants to specialize in their employment (with consequent locational impacts) was marked. Ward, *Cities and Immigrants,* p. 107.
183. Immigrants were greatly overrepresented near the central business district as a result, chiefly, of their being unskilled (or having skilled positions closed to them); the variety of occupations of the central business district served the unskilled better. Ibid. We have also seen how the Irish, as common day laborers in construction, were relegated to the shanty town of Lowell.
184. See above, n. 147.
185. Montgomery, "Kensington Riots of 1844." These ethnic tensions were certainly important in encouraging people to seek out their "own kind" in residential location, for mutual defense and support.
186. Warner, *Private City: Philadelphia,* pp. 62, 78; cf. Ware, *Industrial Worker,* pp. 26–71; on the origins of conflict, ibid., pp. 149–54.
187. Ware, *Industrial Worker,* pp. 227–40.
188. Taylor, "Beginnings of Mass Transportation," pt. 2, p. 50. Warner also notes the tendency for poor laborers to concentrate on the south side of Philadelphia in 1860, and that of the skilled workers to live to the north. Warner, *Private City: Philadelphia,* pp. 60–61.
189. My effort to complete the story can be found in Walker, "Suburban Solution," chaps. 4, 7.

Chapter 9

SEGREGATION IN A FRAGMENTED CONTEXT: 1950–1970

OLIVER P. WILLIAMS
KENT EKLUND

One of the most characteristic features of metropolitan areas in the United States is their jurisdictional fragmentation. Since urban areas always have uneven spatial distributions of population as described by most sociologically significant attributes, it follows necessarily that the local municipalities in metropolitan areas will differ in terms of the compositions of their respective populations. This paper is concerned with changes which may be taking place in these compositions; that is, with whether social distances between municipalities within a single metropolitan area are increasing. Two models, one predicting increases in social distances and another predicting decreases, can be constructed from contemporary observations about urban life in the U.S. Any change in either direction has important implications for public policy.

Concepts of Inter-Municipal Social Composition

The Lifestyle Model
The basic premise of the lifestyle model is that families with similar beliefs, norms, and habits with regard to their daily living patterns will tend to seek residences near one another.[1] This tendency is assumed to characterize all urban areas, but because of the particular properties of American local government organization and structure, municipal boundaries, increasingly, also define the boundaries separating socially different populations: the local American municipality is not only responsible for a

The authors are particularly indebted to John A. Williams for his helpful criticisms, advice, and last minute data analysis. In addition, Richard Greenfield and James Riberio provided individual assistance in data processing.

bundle of socially meaningful services, but, more important, it exercises regulatory authority in the area of land use and urban development. This aggregation of authority, combining control over land use and development with the capability for providing essential public services, points to a local governmental arrangement that can strongly influence the structuring of alternative lifetyles.[2] Varieties of police practices, overt and covert racial discrimination, selective interaction between municipal officials and local realtors, the style and manner of recruiting public officials and public efforts to enhance local identity—all are among the practices which guide businesses and households in selecting locations.[3]

The lifestyle model does not insist that people consciously choose housing according to municipal boundaries. They may choose residences based on the attributes of dwellings, including their price; but they also seek to avoid conflicts, minimize fears, allay anxieties, and generally achieve a feeling of well-being through the selection of a residence. The generalized feelings may well be enhanced by the belief that the house to be selected is in an area where the likelihood of adverse environment or social change is minimal. Municipal power acts as a kind of "unseen hand" which, by controlling structures and providing symbols, influences the residential choices of urban populations. The result is that, over time, people like one another become sorted out by municipality.

The well-known Tiebout models can be easily subsumed by the lifestyle model, but they contain more stringent assumptions.[4] The Tiebout models hypothesize that people buy entitlement to public services through their residential choices. Thus, municipal fragmentation makes possible many different market baskets of public services, and these, in turn, lead to people sorting themselves along municipal lines in terms of shared preferences for particular service packages.

The implications of the lifestyle model can be given both malignant and benign interpretations. The former view argues that territorial decentralization leads to inequality in the distribution of social goods. The rich become separated from the poor, the better educated from the less well educated, the upper status from the lower status, etc. Regardless of municipal revenue redistribution schemes, such as revenue sharing, the end result is undesirable for a democratic nation. The more benign interpretation is suggested by the Tiebout models, which say, in a way, that people get what they pay for and that decentralization provides a system where more people can pay for what they want. If some prefer fewer public services as a trade off for more personally disposable income, that option is also provided for. Thus, regressivity in public finances is muted by relieving some lower-income populations of the necessity of paying taxes to finance services they do not want.

The Technology Model

This model asserts that modern conditions continually undermine the traditional significance of the residential location choice; and, therefore, social segregation is unlikely to increase. There are two components to the argument.

The first is technological in the literal meaning of the term. Modern communications and transportation technology is seen as freeing urban man from spatial dependencies. Technology reduces the cost of overcoming space friction, thereby laying the basis for a new spatial order.[5] Both social and economic exchanges are less and less structured through spatial propinquity. Thus, a wide range of alternative locations is equally capable of satisfying individual needs. The automobile allows friendship groups, employment linkages, church congregations, or kinship relationships to operate successfully with members widely scattered over the metropolitan area. As access becomes less and less a function of propinquity, we should anticipate decreasing areal specialization.

The second component is comprised of the enlarged social institutions which have developed as a result of general modernization. Where once the local community coordinated most of the functions supporting daily family life, now this is less frequently so. Education, socialization, social control, employment, consumption, and distribution are increasingly coordinated and controlled by institutions which are trans-community. This development has been described as the replacement of horizontal integration by vertical integration.[6] Thus, policies like court-ordered busing, state-mandated educational standards, environmental impact studies, and federally financed highways, which vitally effect social access opportunities, emanate from vertical organizations, rather than from horizontal local governments. It therefore makes less and less difference as to which municipality one lives in within the metropolitan area.

Thus, the technological model extrapolates from the facts that social institutions are increasing in scale and complexity and concludes that local level institutions are declining in importance. As this process takes place, residential choice will be a less and less critical decision and tendencies toward spatial forms of social segregation will decline.

Municipal Differentiation: Operationalization

The basic concept used to test the two models is *differentiation*, the degree to which municipalities have dissimilar characteristics. Census data are used as indicator variables and include occupation, income, education, rent, and value of residential property. Limits to refinement in the use of these indicators are set by the earliest census used, which is that of 1950.

Changes in differentiation are measured over the intervals 1950 to 1960 and 1960 to 1970.

The models are tested on the urbanized portion of the Philadelphia Standard Metropolitan Statistical Area.[7] We define the urbanized area for each year as those municipalities with more than 300 persons per square mile, contiguous with others of a similar or greater density radiating out from the core city, Philadelphia.[8] This definition yields 128 units in 1959, 168 in 1960, and 202 in 1970.[9] The size of the municipalities in the urbanized area varies enormously, ranging from Philadelphia's approximately 2,000,000 inhabitants, to a few places under 1,000.[10] It is recognized that in a statistical sense a small municipality is more likely to have highly specialized characteristics than is a large one. Of course, the association of smallness and specialization is the whole point of creating independent suburbs. The issue is: Are the many municipalities, regardless of size, becoming more differentiated over time?

The concept of differentiation is measured by the *index of segregation* derived by the Duncans.[11] The index identifies the percentage of a subpopulation which would have to move from one municipality to some other one in order for all municipalities to contain the same percentage of that specified subpopulation. The measure was originally developed to describe the distribution of subpopulations, such as racial or ethnic groups. Here, it will be used to measure the distribution of persons with a certain level of educational attainment, occupation, etc. The advantage of using the segregation index here is that it yields a single, metropolitan-level indicator, which can be used to compare distributions across the three points in time: 1950, 1960, and 1970. Increases in the size of the index will give support to the lifestyle model; decreases will suggest the appropriateness of the technology model.

There are, however, several disadvantages to the index of segregation.[12] In a statistical sense, the smaller a subpopulation, the greater the probability of its having a high index of segregation. Thus, if we are observing a subpopulation, such as adults with an elementary education, declining relative to the whole population, it is likely that the index value will increase. It is difficult to decide whether such a finding would support the lifestyle model. However, if a subpopulation is increasing relative to the total population, and its index of segregation is also increasing, then the evidence in support of the lifestyle model is strong. Appendix A furnishes the changing percentages across levels for the education and occupation variables so that the reader may evaluate the findings with regard to this consideration.

The second shortcoming of the index of segregation is that it is only a metropolitan-level statistic. It does not allow us to say where the segregation is taking place or how great the concentration is in particular municipalities. Thus, it is not possible to relate the segregation findings across sets of variables. A limited exploration into these municipal-level considerations will be undertaken, however, and, for this purpose, a second measure of differentiation is introduced: the *location quotient*.[13] This yields a score for each municipality and represents the degree to which the municipality has a proportionate share of the subpopulation being observed. When a municipality's subpopulation proportion is equivalent to the proportion in the entire metropolitan area, then it may be said that the municipality has its "fair share."

The index of segregation and the location quotient are applied to various subpopulations defined in terms of categories of the variables education, occupation, income, housing values, and rent. The categories or levels were established in several different ways. It was the objective to have them accord with some measure of social distance, preferably of an ordinal nature. This was relatively easy except for the occupation variable (see discussion below). The selection of break points was largely arbitrary, but designed to show sufficient intervals along a social dimension so that comparisons could be made.

The break points used for income, housing values, and rent turned out to be determined largely by the constraints of the census categories. We started with the assumption that the top fifth of the population in income, for example, would have the same social meaning in the three decades; the problem was operationalization. As it turned out it was neither possible to have the same number of levels for all variables, nor the same proportions in each level for a given variable. What we tried to do, then, was to make each named level (lowest, second, third, etc.) equivalent across the three years, in terms of its proportion of the total population. Our success (and lack of success) in doing this is displayed in appendix B. Following this procedure we had eight levels for income, six for housing values and seven for rental values. Each level is designed to have a similar social meaning across time.

The subpopulations for education and occupation are objectively defined: the degree to which the proportion of the population in each subpopulation varied across time was not subject to control or manipulation, therefore.

Testing the Models

Education and Occupation. Education and occupation, together with income, are the traditional census indicators of status. Income has the last ambiguity, but may be most subject to reporting error. On the other hand, occupation titles may be accurately reported, but their status connotation is subject to great variance. The census of occupations was never designed for research on social status; but, for lack of a better alternative, social researchers have used it. Some attempts will be made to deal with this problem; yet, certainly, the ambiguity of census occupation groupings must be kept in mind.

Table 9-1. Index of Segregation: Education and Occupation

	1950	1960	1970
Education	%	%	%
Elem. under 6 yrs.	14.3	*	25.8
Elem. 7–8 yrs.	8.2	*	15.5
H. school 1–3 yrs.	3.1	7.2	13.6
H. school 4 yrs.	10.8	11.9	11.0
College 1–3 yrs.	18.4	20.4	21.7
College 4 or more yrs.	25.7	30.9	32.0
Occupation			
Professional	16.1	18.3	17.8
Managerial	12.7	17.4	21.7
Sales	7.6	7.6	14.1
Clerical	5.4	10.3	7.0
Craftsmen	6.6	10.6	11.0
Operatives	11.8	15.2	17.0
Service	10.9	14.3	14.6
Labor	9.3	14.5	17.9

*Comparable data not available.

Table 9-1, which gives the segregation indices for educational levels and occupational groupings, indicates that there is an overall tendency towards greater segregation over the twenty-year period.[14] However, as the pattern of change differs between the educational and occupational portions of the table, and as they are both, supposedly, indicators of status, the question is, Why are the results different?

With regard to education, one of the chief characteristics of the overall pattern is that the highest values are for the educational extremes. However, it should be pointed out that the increasingly segregated subpopulation with only elementary education constitutes a *declining* proportion of the overall population, while this is not the case for the college educated. Indeed, the latter is *increasing* as a proportion of the overall population at the same time that it is becoming increasingly segregated. The form which this separation of the most educated takes can be clarified if we look at the municipal level. Through the use of location quotients, we find that in

1970 there were 38 municipalities which had double their proportional share of persons with four or more years of college, while in 1950 there were 30. Given the fact that the number of metropolitan municipalities increased from 128 to 202, between 1950 and 1970, this means that in 1970 there was a smaller percentage of municipalities which had double their "fair share" of the college educated. The same pattern of distribution is found among municipalities for those with one to three years of college. However, rarely does one encounter a case of a municipality with double its share of any of the rest of the other educational subpopulations, including the least educated. Underlying the increasing segregation of the college educated is a high degree of concentration in relatively few municipalities. The tendency for the segregation of the college educated to be manifested by concentrations in a limited number of municipalities is a pattern that is maintained throughout the twenty-year period.[15]

Returning to the issue of occupational classification, consider that the order in which the occupational groups appear in table 9-1 is designed to form a social hierarchy. In 1960, at least for the United States as a whole, that is the way the occupational groups ranked in terms of mean income.[16] However, aggregations at the national scale are likely to differ greatly from those at the municipal level. In addition, occupational categories are dynamic; the classifications have undergone substantial changes. The most rapid change is taking place among professionals. Thus, in table 9-1 the findings on occupation must be taken advisedly. Changing patterns of segregation may reflect changes in the occupations included in each category or may, indeed, reflect changing patterns of spatial distribution. Analysis of the income distributions should aid in clarifying this dilemma.

Income. The evidence in table 9-2 on changing distributions of subpopulations defined in terms of income levels generally gives support to the lifestyle model. The indices increase at all levels across the three time periods. However, the subpopulation in the highest income category, as can be seen by reference to appendix B, is proportionally smaller in 1970 than it is in the previous decades. This suggests caution in concluding that there is increasing segregation of the rich. The data are much more workable for the other extreme, as it is possible to construct subpopulations for the lower two income levels which are approximately equivalent in proportional terms across the three censuses. Increased segregation of the poor, therefore, seems more strongly documented by the evidence at hand.

However, as the segregation index yields only an overall statistic on the total number of people who would have to be moved to achieve proportionality in all municipalities, it does not tell us the degree of concentration of any subpopulation in terms of the number of very specialized local governmental units. Again, we must turn to the location quotients.

Table 9-2. Index of Segregation: Family Income

	1950	1960	1970
Family Income Level	%	%	%
Lowest	8.6	21.6	24.2
2nd	8.4	19.1	18.9
3rd	7.1	16.5	14.2
4th	7.2	7.5	8.5
5th	8.6	8.0	10.9
6th	11.4	9.9	14.9
7th	14.3	16.1	22.4
Highest	23.5	35.5	39.7

Table 9-3 pertains only to those municipalities which have more than double their proportional share of income subpopulations defined in terms of a particular level. It is rare for any municipality to contain double its proportional share of the middle-income subpopulations, but, as table 9-3 indicates, municipalities with overrepresentations of the extreme income subpopulations are more commonplace. Furthermore, concentration is more likely to occur for the highest income subpopulations than for the lower-income ones. By 1970, thirty-six municipalities, or about eighteen percent of the total, had double their fair share. Not only is this concentration greater at the top end of the scale, but also there the percentage of municipalities in the "double-fair-share" category has increased. There are eight municipalities in 1970 with double their share of the very poor, but this does not represent an increase in the percentage of municipalities with high concentrations of the very poor.

At this point we may conclude that, of the three sets of status variables we have examined so far (income, occupation and education), the most extreme segregation indices are manifest in income. Is the entire segregation pattern, therefore, simply a reflection of income differences with the values for the latter two representing partial correlations among the indicators? The concept "lifestyle" is not simply a synonym for income, for it connotes value differences among urban populations which may be independent of income. We know that many well-educated, professional persons have incomes comparable to that of some blue-collar workers. The lifestyle theory could be tested more accurately; therefore, if we could hold one variable, such as income, constant, while varying another, such as occupation, we might more accurately test the lifestyle hypothesis. The 1970 census permits a move in this direction, though comparable data are not available for 1950 and 1960.

Location quotients were computed for two occupational groups,

Table 9-3. Municipalities with Double a "Fair Share" of Subpopulations at Levels of Family Income

Family Income Level	1950 number	1950 percentage	1960 number	1960 percentage	1970 number	1970 percentage
Lowest	6	4.7	1	.6	8	4.0
2nd	2	1.6	0	.0	0	.0
3rd	0	.0	0	.0	0	.0
4th	2	1.6	0	.0	1	.5
5th	0	.0	1	.6	1	.5
6th	3	2.4	0	.0	0	.0
7th	6	4.7	1	.6	20	9.9
Highest	16	12.6	27	16.5	36	17.8
	N=128		N=168		N=202	

professionals and craftsmen, subdivided by income level. Professionals and craftsmen were selected because they represent white- and blue-collar categories in which there are some significant income overlaps. The selection, therefore, allows observation of what happens when members of different occupational groups with comparable family incomes bid for the same housing stock. If the price of housing alone determines where people live, everything else being equal, one would expect to find in a given municipality the same location quotients for professionals and craftsmen of a given income level.

If professionals and craftsmen of similar incomes are equally attracted by the housing within their economic means, without regard to the municipality in which it lies, then each group should locate identically. This does not mean that an equal number of professionals and craftsmen of a given income level will be found in each municipality, but rather that each municipality would have the same share of the metropolitan population of professionals and craftsmen from the given income group. Table 9-4 displays a correlation matrix among the location quotients for various income groups of both professionals and craftsmen. A high positive correlation indicates a propensity for the two populations to live in the same municipalities. A high negative correlation indicates that the two groups appear to avoid living in the same municipality.

Note that the correlations among income levels within occupational categories (upper-left and lower-right boxes) tend to be positive, while the correlations across occupations, even when incomes are held constant, tend to be negative (the lower-left box). This indicates that for these two groups similarity of occupation, rather than similarity of income, generally dictates the choice of municipality in which to live. The only positive correlation between categories across occupational lines involves craftsmen in the highest income group and professionals in income groups in a somewhat more intermediate bracket. That income does play a role in the distribution of subpopulations across municipalities is indicated by the within-occupational-group correlations across income levels. Generally, the closer the income categories, the higher the positive correlation. The insight we gain from table 9-4 is that both occupation and income provide cues as to where people are likely to live, but also that the interaction between the two attributes is complex. There is some indication that a trade off occurs whereby persons with higher status occupations, but lower incomes, will tend to live with those with lower occupational status, but higher incomes.

Table 9-4. Correlation Matrix of Location Quotients: Municipalities by Occupation and Income, 1970

Occupation Income	P/ 7	P/ 7–10	P/ 10–15	P/ 15–25	P/ 25 +	C/ 7	C/ 7–10	C/ 10–15	C/ 15 +
Professional									
$ 7,000 & under	1.000								
7–10,000	.350	1.000							
10–15,000	.082	.208	1.000						
15–25,000	.122	.024	.664	1.000					
25,000 +	.280	.054	.217	.669	1.000				
Craftsmen									
$ 7,000 & under	—.219	—.085	—.373	—.493	—.423	1.000			
7–10,000	—.260	—.186	—.571	—.706	—.607	.358	1.000		
10–15,000	—.200	—.009	—.065	—.395	—.515	.153	.463	1.000	
15,000 +	—.028	—.029	.250	.144	—.044	—.085	—.037	.262	1.000

Rents and Housing Values. Housing values and rent levels are highly correlated with income. Here, we use them as a check on the income findings. Housing value is more subject to municipal influence than are income levels; after all, it is primarily through local housing policies that municipalities can effect a population screening process. Thus, housing values and rent levels measure more accurately than any other of our indicators, those municipal differences resulting from municipal actions.

Table 9-5. Index of Segregation: Value of Owner-occupied Dwellings and Rent Levels

	1950	1960	1970
Value, owner-occupied			
dwellings	%	%	%
Lowest	32.2	37.9	50.4
2nd	24.5	*	42.8
3rd	27.8	*	27.4
4th	29.6	26.2	28.1
5th	42.4	49.1	48.5
Highest	64.6	65.2	65.7
Rent per month			
Lowest	20.7		21.3
2nd	24.6		31.1
3rd	21.5	data	20.0
4th	17.8	not	18.7
5th	16.3	comparable	36.5
6th	16.4		39.6
Highest	20.2		39.3

*Comparable levels cannot be computed.

The description of the distribution of house values and rents (table 9-5) adds several new dimensions to the previous profiles of change in the metropolis. In the first place, these indicators, which reflect property values, have higher segregation indices than those for any of the other variables. Again, the highest index values tend to be at the extremes.

The highest house value level in 1970 is for those houses valued at $35,000 and above. While this category included only 4.5 percent of the owner-occupied stock, the degree of segregation for this small category is extreme, as fully 65 percent of these houses would have to be "moved" across municipal lines in order to achieve equal distributions. The next highest level represents 15 percent of the housing stock (1970 value of $20,000 to $35,000); and, here, nearly one-half would have to be "moved" to achieve proportionality. Perhaps this second figure is even more revealing with respect to the degree of segregation of the housing stock because it represents so substantial a number of dwellings.

American municipalities are usually described as oriented toward exclusionary policies; that is, they wish to keep problems away from their door. One way is to keep out the poor or, more specifically, to keep out cheap housing which, it is commonly thought, yields little in tax revenue and may produce much in the way of expenses. Thus, it makes sense to reverse our earlier procedures here by looking at the location quotients as measures of concentration. Table 9-6 describes the distribution of municipalities that have one-half or less their fair share of each of the six levels of owner-occupied housing divided according to price. (Again, appendix B should be consulted to see how the break points were defined.) An increasing number and proportion of the suburbs are succeeding in not providing much lower-priced housing. By 1970, 158 municipalities out of the 202 managed to have less than half their fair share of the cheapest housing; and 130, or 64 percent managed the same with respect to the second-lowest category. This pattern may well reflect the process of aging in the housing stock of the inner suburbs, as much as it does the success of exclusionary zoning policies. But, regardless of how it happens, a comparison of the percentage columns in table 9-6 reveals that a polarization with respect to the housing stock is taking place.

Table 9-6. Municipalities with One-half "Fair Share" of Housing by Value

	1950		1960		1970	
	number	percentage	number	percentage	number	percentage
Housing value						
Lowest	72	57	126	77	158	78
2nd	68	54	*	*	130	64
3rd	50	39	*	*	65	32
4th	32	18	15	9	25	12
5th	18	14	36	22	49	24
Highest	50	39	90	55	112	55
	N = 128		N = 168		N = 202	

*Comparable levels cannot be computed.

An examination of the results on rental properties in table 9-5 reveals a pattern similar to that for owner-occupied dwellings. A computation of a table on rents similar to table 9-6 would also yield similar results.

Conclusions

The most general conclusion to be drawn from the evidence is that the segregation which existed within the metropolitan areas in 1950 has become more pronounced as the metropolis has expanded. Furthermore, measured in terms of the five indicators selected here, the extremes are generally the most segregated and are becoming increasingly more so. Assuming that the bounding categories for the scales refer respectively to lower and higher social status vis-à-vis education, occupation, income, and property values, segregation manifests itself by a greater concentration at the top end of the scale. That is, the high segregation index for the well educated, the rich, and the occupationally well placed results from extreme concentrations in a relatively few municipalities. Segregation indices for the lower ends of the scales reflect the accumulation of lesser degrees of malapportionment across all municipalities.

The fact that segregation indices are increasing and that some higher status categories are becoming more concentrated lends support to the lifestyle model as the model most aptly describing the dynamics of metropolitan population changes. The population that is most capable of selecting its location and is most aware of the implications of locational choices is, in fact, becoming politically more isolated from the rest of the population.

Yet this evidence may not mean that the technology model is unsound; its assumptions may be correct. But the very technology that allows people to be less dependent, in general, on location for structuring their interactions produces some urbanites who are now freer than ever before to use location with exquisite precision to achieve their lifestyle values.

Notes

1. Oliver P. Williams, *Metropolitan Political Analysis, A Social Access Approach* (New York: The Free Press, 1971), chap. 1.
2. Frederick M. Wirt et al., *On the City's Rim* (1972), provides a good review of some of these suburban characteristics. Also see Michael Danielson, *The Politics of Exclusion* (1976); and Richard F. Babcock, "Exclusionary Zoning," in "The Urbanization of the Suburbs," ed. Louis H. Masotti and Jeffrey K. Hadden, *Urban Affairs Annual Review* 7 (1973), chap. 12.
3. James Q. Wilson, *Varieties of Police Behavior: The Management of Law and Order in Eight Communities* (New York: Atheneum, 1968), documents the many subtle and overt patterns of police discretion at the local level.
4. See Bruce Hamilton, "Property Taxation's Incentive to Fiscal Zoning," in *Property Tax Reform,* ed. George E. Peterson (Washington, D.C.: The Urban Institute, 1973), for references to Tiebout models.
5. The most forthright statement of this model may be found in Melvin Webber et al., *Exploration in Urban Structure* (Chicago: Rand McNally, 1964), pp. 79–137.
6. Roland Warren, *The Community in America* (Chicago: Rand McNally, 1963).
7. The counties in the SMSA are, in Pennsylvania: Bucks, Chester, Delaware, Montgomery, and Philadelphia; in New Jersey: Burlington, Camden, and Gloucester.
8. Pennsylvania and New Jersey have township systems of local government into which all counties are divided. Townships were thus judged to have been urbanized when they reached a density that indicated the presence of subdivision activity; hence, the selection of the 300 persons per square mile criterion.
9. For certain statistical procedures, one or two extreme cases are excluded so *N* may vary slightly. Missing data may also reduce *N* slightly.
10. The mean populations of municipalities are 24,585 (1950); 23,754 (1960); and 22,143 (1970).
11. Otis Dudley Duncan and Beverly Duncan, "Residential Distribution and Occupational Stratification," *American Journal of Sociology* 60 (March 1955): 493–519.
12. An additional disadvantage is that a large city could affect the index disproportionately if it had a highly atypical population. Actually, this was not the case, since Philadelphia, the largest city in our study, had a moderating effect on the index. The Duncan segregation index would have been higher had we excluded Philadelphia and examined only the suburbs.
13. Brian J. L. Berry and Frank E. Horton, *Geographic Perspectives on Urban Systems* (Englewood Cliffs, N.J.: Prentice-Hall, 1970), p. 389.
14. In an attempt to simplify the occupational indices of segregation, the managerial and professional occupations were collapsed into one white-collar category, and all the rest were collapsed into a blue-collar category. The educational categories were collapsed to include two extremes: those with an elementary education and those with at least some collegiate experience. Results of this collapsing simplify the results of table 9-1 while merely reenforcing them.

| | Index of Segregation | | |
	1950	1960	1970
White-Collar Occups.	17.0	23.5	26.9
Blue-Collar Occups.	11.9	16.3	17.6
College Education	24.2	28.6	30.1
Elementary Education	13.0	18.2	20.7

15. The municipalities are not the same ones throughout the time span in question, however. New municipalities replace some inner suburbs as the place of residence for the educated elite.
16. Peter M. Blau and Otis Dudley Duncan, *The American Occupational Structure* (New York: Wiley and Sons, 1967).

Appendix A. Percentages of Subpopulations by Levels for Education and Occupation: 1950, 1960, 1970

	1950	1960	1970
Education[a]	%	%	%
Elem. under 6 yrs.	19.6	5.0	10.7
Elem. 7–8 yrs.	26.8	32.8	15.9
H. school 1–3 yrs.	20.4	23.1	22.9
H. school 4 yrs.	21.9	24.4	31.8
College 1–3 yrs.	4.9	6.8	7.9
4 or more yrs.	6.4	7.9	10.8
Total	100.0	100.0	100.0
Occupation[b]			
Professional	10.0	12.3	15.8
Managerial	9.3	8.2	8.0
Sales	7.8	8.2	7.8
Clerical	16.1	18.5	21.1
Craftsmen	16.3	15.3	13.6
Operatives	25.5	21.2	17.6
Service	8.4	9.1	10.7
Labor	8.8	7.0	5.1
Total	100.0	100.0	100.0

[a]All persons 25 years old or older.
[b]Males, 14 years old or older.

Appendix B. Percentages in Subpopulations by Level for Family Income, Value of Owner-occupied Dwellings and Rental Units: 1950, 1960, 1970.

Variable	1950 Definition	%	1960 Definition	%	1970 Definition	%
Family income level						
Lowest	$ 0.0–500	12.5	$ 0–2,000	7.6	$ 0.0–2,000	13.2
2nd	0.5–1,500	11.1	2–3,000	5.6	2.0–4,000	10.2
3rd	1.5–2,500	15.4	3–5,000	18.2	4.0–7,000	15.4
4th	2.5–3,000	9.1	5–6,000	13.3	7.0–9,000	12.1
5th	3.0–4,000	18.9	6–7,000	12.2	9.0–12,000	17.1
6th	4.0–5,000	11.8	7–9,000	19.0	12.0–15,000	12.4
7th	5.00–7,000	12.5	9–15,000	19.3	15.0–25,000	15.1
Highest	7,000 +	8.7	15,000 +	5.7	25,000 +	4.4
Value, owner-occupied dwellings						
Lowest	0.0–4,000	8.3	0–5,000	6.3	0.0–7,500	12.6
2nd	4.0–5,000	8.1	5–10,000	37.1	7.5–10,000	12.4
3rd	5.0–7,500	29.9	10–15,000	35.1	10.0–15,000	26.7
4th	7.5–10,000	25.7	15–25,000	16.6	15.0–20,000	19.8
5th	10.0–15,000	18.6	25,000 +	5.0	20.0–35,000	21.4
Highest	15,000 +	9.4			35,000 +	7.0
Rent per month						
Lowest	0–19	8.3	0–39	7.1	0–50	8.5
2nd	20–29	22.7	40–59	26.9	50–70	21.3
3rd	30–39	23.0	60–79	32.3	70–90	22.4
4th	40–49	18.5	80–99	17.9	90–120	17.2
5th	50–59	10.8	100–150	12.5	120–150	14.8
6th	60–75	8.5	150 +	3.4	150–200	10.3
Highest	75 +	8.2			200 +	5.5

Chapter 10

LOCAL EXCLUSIONARY POLICIES IN BRITAIN: THE CASE OF SUBURBAN DEFENSE IN A METROPOLITAN SYSTEM

KEN YOUNG

JOHN KRAMER

In recent years a number of academic analysts have called for greater equity in metropolitan land use.[1] Recent years have also produced an unambiguous record of failure in the attempts to achieve it. Much of the advocacy and many of the failed policies have a common root in false or simplistic typifications of the nature of local politics and, in particular, of the ways in which suburban leaders go about the business of protecting their communities against unwelcomed change. Ultimately, the identification of feasible strategies for "opening up the suburbs" in the interests of the inner-city poor can proceed only from a sympathetic understanding of the nature of territorial defense in a suburban setting.[2]

We argue in this paper that the covert creation and maintenance of local exclusionary policies is a feature of allocative decision making in English local government. Being covert, these processes go largely unremarked and may indeed seem unremarkable when set against the scarcely disguised racial aversions and the debates over local autonomy and zoning prerogatives which characterize American urban politics. But a more searching analysis of politics in the English metropolitan areas uncovers equally striking exclusionary practices. In the first section of the paper we argue that patterns of socio-spatial access[3] and changes in these patterns via locational decisions are controlled both by public policy and by social norms; some of the English evidence on this score is reviewed.

This paper arose from two closely related research projects carried out at the University of Kent at Canterbury, England, from 1974 to 1976. Ken Young's project, "Political Integration in the London Metropolitan Region" was financed by the Social Science Research Council; John Kramer's "Local Suburban Political Change" was financed by the Centre for Environmental Studies. The authors are grateful to the two foundations for their generous support. The full account of our findings, which this paper summarizes, will appear as *Strategy and Conflict in Metropolitan Housing* (London: Heinemann, 1977).

In the next section we pose the question of whether areawide metropolitan authorities on the English model have the capacity to induce changes in the patterns of access, specifically via policies to "open up the suburbs." The past decade of political experience in the Greater London area is briefly recounted, and we conclude that the failure of a powerful metropolitan authority to bring about a substantial reallocation of suburban space is rooted in the imperatives of suburban territorial defense. In the final section we argue that the public maintenance of suburban exclusionary policies is best understood as a process of environmental management; specifically, of *social area* management.

Defending Social Space: Exclusivity and Separatism

A number of features distinguish British urban politics from those of the U.S.[4] Foremost among them is the regularity and centralism of the British governmental system. Many fewer, relatively large authorities encompass a narrower range of resource variation; relatively strong bodies are responsible for metropolitan policy making; and a strong and authoritative central government is readily inclined to proclaim "the national interest" against the prerogatives of localism. Also distinctive is the urban authorities' relative immunity from public feeling. Representative linkages are comparatively weak; major parties control recruitment and selection for elective competition; the prevailing norms of government in many areas are paternalistic and unresponsive; the local press is ordinarily a quiescent and submissive reflector of official views.[5] In sum, English urban governments enjoy a high degree of insulation from a characteristically inert political environment.[6]

Another distinctive feature of the British scene, and one crucial to the argument of this paper, is the very broad scope of public policy. With a complex and comprehensive system of land-use controls, and with a very large and active public authority sector providing homes to rent, the question of "Who gets where, when, and how?" is more readily answerable from the analysis of public policies than from the analysis of market forces. And those public policies are frequently generated and negotiated within a network of intergovernmental relations.

If, as we shall argue, intergovernmental politics in the English metropolitan areas often center on the issue of social access and suburban exclusivity, they reflect in such instances the underlying social forces that maintain the boundaries and integrity of distinct social areas. For, although the direct representative linkages between elites and the mass populace may be weak, they are characterized by strong value congruence on certain issues. The locality images of suburban elites harmonize with a strong and active grass-roots support for territorial exclusivity.[7]

The quintessential case of a grass-roots response is that of the famous Cutteslowe walls.[8] In 1932 the Oxford City Council introduced a slum clearance program and decanted the inner-city displacees into a suburban site north of the city, directly adjacent to a new, privately developed, middle-class estate. The desire of the private residents to maintain their social distance from their proletarian neighbors led, in this bizarre instance, to the construction of a formidable and unscalable wall as a physical obstacle to the interpenetration of the two communities. As a middle-class respondent put it: "We are private owners and pay a lot of money, especially with increased rates. And there is a lot of riffraff on the other side."[9]

The social force behind this exclusionary response was, as readers of Williams, Mumford, Suttles, and a host of other writers might expect, the desire to minimize interaction between the children from the two distinct social milieux. "At present children on the other side of the wall fight those from this side. If the walls were taken down the fighting would be much worse, and as a mother I feel strongly about this."[10] The notoriety which this particular case received served, perhaps, to obscure the prevalence and typicality of the Cutteslowe response. In the case of a single south London suburb alone, there are two recorded instances of similar physical barriers demanded by private residents to exclude public authority tenants from their territory.[11] Similarly, the location of public housing estates, town expansion and development schemes, and New Towns is characteristically accompanied by protest from existing residents fearing status loss.[12]

Intercommunity conflict is, of course, more commonly expressed through social barriers than through physical ones. Even contiguous working-class areas in Britain maintain cognitive boundaries between the "rough" and the "respectable" areas; the "respectable" group shuns interaction, demarcates territory, stereotypes and stigmatizes its lower-status neighbors.[13] The British studies support what Meyerson and Banfield's classic study of Chicago indicates, that class, not race, provides the cutting edge of social exclusivity.[14] Sensitivity to social boundaries is perhaps most acute when the status gaps are narrow.[15] This commonly occurs between the inner-city working class and the white-collar, lower middle-class population that has achieved a precarious status via social and geographical mobility.[16] These low-status, suburban populations are inherently insecure; if the "Principle of Stratified Diffusion"[17] holds good, the class from which they have recently emerged will soon clamor for access to their advantages. If they themselves cannot move up, they will be reabsorbed into a class from which their fathers may have struggled to escape. Maintaining the sanctity of social space, therefore, becomes the prerequisite of survival in so fluid and delicately stratified a society.

These forces are clearly discernible in London's Essex suburbs, which fan out from the East End of London, an area unremittingly working class in character and symbolic of England's urban industrial proletariat. Here, more than elsewhere in the London region, the suburbs represented social mobility; but here, also, the physical proximity of the urban working class heightened the vulnerability of the new salariat. Willmott and Young capture its spirit exactly:

> Although people talk about travelling "up to town" in this social context, "out" means "up," "up the ladder," up "in the social scale," up "in the world" ... deep down in the lowest strata were Bethnal Green and Stepney and there at the top Woodford and Wanstead. To clamber up the slope was success, to remain at the bottom, failure. Once you had clambered up, you wanted to be distinguished as clearly as possible from those who had given up or never tried.[18]

These social antagonisms underpin the politics of exclusion. They are clearly apparent in the emergence from the late nineteenth century of a definite and politically potent spirit of suburban separatism that colored the politics of metropolitan growth and consolidation in Greater London.

Political separatism, on the one hand, and the policies of exclusion, on the other, were generated by the "new suburbans" of Greater London. Their spirit, an amalgam of fear, loathing, and apprehension, was never more vividly summarized than by Charles Masterman, social critic and Liberal politician, writing in 1909:

> The rich despise the Working people; the Middle Class fear them. Fear, stimulated by every artifice of clever political campaigns, is the motive power behind every successive uprising. In feverish hordes, the suburbs swarm to the polling booth to vote against a truculent Proletariat. The Middle Class elector is becoming irritated and indignant against working class legislation.... Every day, swung high upon embankments or buried deep in tubes underground, he hurries through the region where the creature lives. He gazes darkly from his pleasant hill villa upon the huge and smoky area of tumbled tenements which stretches at his feet. He is dimly distrustful of the forces fermenting in this uncouth laboratory. Every hour he anticipates the boiling over of the cauldron. He would never be surprised to find the crowd behind the red flag, surging up his pleasant pathways, tearing down the railings, trampling the little garden; the "letting in of the jungle" upon the patch of fertile ground which has been redeemed from the wilderness.[19]

Such was the spirit which characterized the politics of metropolitan London over many decades, and which manifested itself in two ways: resistance by suburban leaders to the inclusion of their territories within the metropolitan area; and resistance by suburban leaders and citizens to the "decanting" of a working-class population to the suburbs.

Yet, however much the suburban citizen feared the prospect of working-class neighbors, suburban political leaders seemed to fear working-class voters and the imperialistic ambitions of the inner-London regime even more.[20] Resistance to annexation, on the one hand, and to "overspill"—planned out-migration of the working class—on the other, were to become major issues. The first of these, the proposal for an areawide authority for London, first mooted by H. G. Wells in 1903, aroused suburban antipathy in the years before World War I. Definite proposals for the extension of the London County Council (LCC) boundary to the outermost suburbs engendered fierce and unanimous opposition from 1919 to 1923, and proved sufficient to defeat the jurisdictional integration of the metropolis.[21]

The same spirit smoldered through the years of weak intergovernmental collaboration from 1927, erupting from time to time whenever suburban interests were threatened. In 1961 the national government itself proposed to consolidate the metropolitan area, merging inner city and outer suburbs under a new Greater London Council (GLC). The feasibility of the government's plan depended on buying off the outer suburbs; the price was to guarantee them almost unchallengeable local autonomy as the "primary authorities" within the new metro-system. The national objective of an integrated land-use and transportation network for the metropolis enabled them, in effect, to dictate their own terms for cooperation in the consolidation plan: the maintenance of local prerogatives in the pursuit of exclusionary allocation policies.[22]

Although metropolitan unity had been achieved, the new division of power augured well for suburban exclusivity. From 1919 to 1964 the politics of exclusion had been successfully maintained by the suburbs against the "overspill" of the urban poor. The location of the London County Council's suburban estates of working-class housing after 1919 became a contentious issue, and the LCC struggled to acquire large sites for development against the opposition of the suburban local and county governments, an opposition that grew more intense as the Labour party rose to power in inner London.[23]

The suburbs struggled with a variety of tactics to impede and delay the LCC's land acquisitions until the point at which they were saved by the new policy developments of the wartime and postwar years: a "Green Belt" restriction on further suburban sprawl; a land-use master plan based on the concentric decline of residential densities; and a framework for the creation of New Towns and later for the expansion of existing towns at some distance beyond the Green Belt.[24] All these developments eased the pressure on the suburbs after World War II, and with the passage of the London Government Act in 1963 the vexing and long-standing metropolitan issues seemed to have been resolved, for the foreseeable future, in the suburbs' favor.

"Opening Up the Suburbs" in a Metro-system

The initial optimism of the new London suburban governments was rudely and immediately shattered, first by the election of a Labour majority on the new Greater London Council in April, 1964, and then by the election of a Labour government at the national level, six months later.[25] Suburban fears that metropolitan and national authorities might combine against them were rearoused by the government's commitment to give whatever support seemed necessary to the GLC's Labour leaders against the London boroughs. The new government also gave high priority to a massive public housing drive centered on the larger cities, and, under ministerial pressure, local governments were required to make substantial increases in their public housing programs. The new GLC's aspiration to the role of areawide reallocator of housing opportunities was almost immediately endorsed by a committee of inquiry into the conditions of London housing; its report both revealed the magnitude of the London housing crisis and identified the GLC as the appropriate authority to aid, by redistribution, the decaying inner areas.[26] Overcrowding in the decayed inner area of London ensured that some out-migration would be necessary if slums were to be redeveloped at tolerable densities. New sites for new development had, therefore, to be sought. Thus, the striking disparities in the allocation of space to the various "housing classes," and, in particular, the continued low density development of "luxury homes" in the outer suburbs, emerged afresh as major issues for public policy.

The Labour GLC's first response to the situation was to emulate its predecessor, the LCC and attempt to acquire suburban sites for its own housing construction program. These intentions were immediately frustrated. The suburbs promised a determined resistance. The precise executive powers of the GLC were not clear. The political costs of a direct confrontation with the suburbs were high, for this action would be, predictably, unpopular. Moreover, the outcome of such a confrontation, being subject to ministerial adjudication, was by no means certain. Faced with pressure to produce quick results, the GLC policy changed rapidly from site acquisition to the less-threatening strategy of negotiating access to a share of the small, but recently augmented, public housing programs of the independent and individual suburbs.[27]

The tactics of conciliation produced fewer returns than had been expected. By the time the Conservatives deposed Labour in the GLC 1967 election, the policy of negotiated access to the suburbs' own housing stocks had made only minimal and temporary headway. For the next three years the suburbs enjoyed their expected hegemony in London politics. No attempts were made to "open the suburbs" to the inner-city working class, for the main thrust of Conservative GLC policy from 1967 to 1970 was to promote privatization and social diversity. But by 1970 the very extent of the suburbs' success in maintaining their exclusivity was to count against them. GLC housing officials, fretting under unaccustomed Conservative control, succeeded in sponsoring a study of the pattern of metropolitan housing needs.[28] The study was carried out by an intergovernmental body chaired by a senior civil servant from the Ministry of Housing and Local Government and drew heavily upon data collated by the GLC itself.[29]

The report indicated that the disparities in the housing conditions between the suburbs and the central city were *widening*, for suburban conditions were improving more rapidly than were those of the inner area.[30] Its completion in early 1970 coincided with another unexpected development, the election of a Conservative national government. Paradoxically, while Conservative regimes at London's County Hall and in the suburbs had maintained exclusionary policies that favored the middle-class, owner-occupier, the new Conservative Ministers were reformist and interventionist in outlook. The new Secretary of State adopted and published the housing needs report. The County Hall leadership, in tune with developments in the national party and aware of the explosive potential of the housing needs report, had meanwhile anticipated the changing political climate and switched the housing chairman for another who was more easily persuaded of the necessity for a major campaign to acquire suburban space.

The next two years saw a critical struggle as the GLC, with strong central government backing, sought to acquire suburban land for working-class housing, and as the suburbs sought to deflect those demands. By 1972 the issue was resolved in the suburbs' favor. The Conservative suburbs had worked within their own party to defuse the threat. In a series of stormy meetings at Conservative Central Office in central London, suburban leaders mounted a revolt and totally repudiated the policies of their national and GLC colleagues. The Ministers withdrew from the "political mine field" of London politics having achieved little; the GLC leadership, shaken by the display of suburban *force majeure*, reverted to the previous policies and dismissed its interventionist housing chairman. Once again, the suburbs had successfully maintained their exclusivity; and their intransigence was vindicated by a series of secretly negotiated "nonagression pacts" in which the GLC renounced its future rights to bid for suburban space. These guarantees—legally worthless but morally advantageous to the suburbs—were barely ratified by the local and metropolitan leaders before the control of the GLC fell once again into the hands of the Labour party.

With a Labour majority at County Hall, the recurrent threat to suburban amenity was once again renewed. The Labour party had moved toward a more interventionist stance during its six years of opposition, and the new housing chairman immediately advocated a strong, areawide drive to "open the suburbs." The campaign was, however, unexpectedly delayed by internal political wrangles among the new Labour administration. Not until eighteen months had passed, and Labour had returned to power nationally, was it announced that the GLC had formulated a *Strategic Housing Plan* for the metropolis.

The plan took the form of a thoroughly researched analysis of the London housing situation and a package of proposals to remedy its deficiencies within ten to fifteen years.[31] For the suburbs, the most threatening aspect was the promulgation of building targets for each sector of London; the outer suburbs were faced with a demand for massive increases in building. As London's *Evening Standard* perceptively commented:

> ... the implication is that leafy suburban boroughs with relatively few problems must build homes to rent for the families trapped in the overcrowded, twilight areas of inner London.[32]

But the advertised confrontation between the GLC planners and the defended suburbs never materialized. Economic crisis overtook the hopes of the plan's supporters. A political upheaval within the ruling GLC Labour party led to massive cuts in the GLC housing program, the apparent renunciation of the plan, and the dismissal of the housing chairman who had sponsored it. These developments ensured that, for the third time in ten years, the threat of large-scale public housing in the suburbs was lifted.

The failures of metropolitan policy to challenge suburban exclusivity, and the reasons for these failures, emerge clearly enough from this bare narrative of events. In the first place, the initial metropolitan leaders experienced major role uncertainties. There were no prototypes for England's first metropolitan authority; its objectives and modes of operation were nowhere spelled out and were only gradually and haltingly defined.[33] Furthermore, the leading politicians and officials of the first GLC had previously run the London County Council; and, despite their drastically reduced formal powers, they continued to look to that body for their role models. For these reasons it took a notionally "strategic" authority ten years to evolve an explicitly strategic housing plan.

The metropolitan system also experienced marked political discontinuities in a policy area where the overall objectives—the redistribution of "life chances" among the metropolitan population—were necessarily very long term. While the most affluent suburbs remained securely Conservative, control of the GLC changed from Labour to Conservative and back again in the first nine years. Thus the elections of 1967 and 1973 removed two housing chairmen from their posts and put in others with antithetical policies. Intraparty politics also contributed to the policy discontinuities. Political disputes within the ruling party removed the remaining chairmen from office at the peak of its policy commitment. Metropolitan housing policy from 1965 to 1975 thus alternated between opposite poles of challenging and reinforcing suburban exclusivity. And in the context of London's overall political marginality, the imperatives of party management—keeping party unity and taking no electoral risks for the sake of dubious returns—ensured that policies to "open up the suburbs" enjoyed the support of only a few, policy-oriented leaders in each party.

Ultimately, however, the GLC failed, even in its short-term and transitory objectives, and failed because it lacked the resources to implement its policies. These resource deficiencies were not primarily formal or statutory in nature. Rather, they were *political* in the sense that the exercise of formal power would entail gross penalties in interorganizational cooperation and public support.

Moreover, GLC leaders repeatedly failed to understand the origins and strengths of suburban opposition to their policies. In our view, public policy making in suburbia is best understood as a process of environmental management. The problematic environment has two aspects: On the one hand, the local socio-political environment and the valued characteristics of the local community; on the other hand, the interorganizational environment consisting of a shifting nexus of public agencies, most of which are concerned with bringing about unwelcomed changes in the socio-political environment of the suburban policy makers. The delicate business of manipulating a dual environment under conditions of mutual interdependence we term *social-area management,* and it is to the explication of this concept that we now turn.

The Dynamics of Exclusion: A Social-Area Management Approach

The essence of the social-area management approach is that it views local policy making as a process of environmental management. It can be said to operate wherever local policies are influenced by the simultaneous need: (a) to promote, maintain, or enhance certain characteristics of the local environment in accordance with local elite images of its present and possible future states; and (b) to manage the competition with, and dependencies upon, other official bodies acting as an interorganizational environment, under conditions where the latter have the capability to induce stress and change in the local environment. In this final section we briefly sketch the three key components of the social-area management paradigm: elite images of the locality; the policy nexus of local management; and tactics for managing the interorganizational environment.

Elite Images of the Locality

The focus of this approach, which we developed in order to explain the conflicts between a metropolian authority and its suburbs (but which has a wider application), is upon local political leaders as environmental managers. Local governments, while by no means the sole agencies acting to maintain or change community characteristics, nevertheless have a pervasive and inescapable impact upon them. As Professor Stewart has remarked:

> The local authority is, or can be, the main instrument of urban management. Our cities and towns can today be regarded as in part the creation of the local authority. The local authority may own a third of the property, may have built a third of the buildings; it will have built the road system and allocated the land. It educates the children and deals with the problems of the elderly, handicapped and deprived. It licenses, it approves, it controls, it governs many activities.... The local authority cannot evade its responsibilities for urban management. It has inherited them and it maintains them. True, it shares them with many other organisations. The local authority, because it is a multi-purpose authority impinging on the urban environment at many points, has a special role in urban management. The role can be identified, recognised, and planned for. Or it can merely be allowed to happen. The local authority is playing a key role in urban management, even where it does not recognise it.[34]

The consequences of policy do not, of course, expire at local boundaries, for the policy role is not enacted within a self-contained theater. Nor is the locality immune to the wider social and economic forces for change. Nevertheless, local policy makers, for the most part, act *as if* their localities were self-contained. They perceive their environment as bounded, though rarely as impermeable. It is for them a field of vision, expectation, and action, akin to what field theorists in psychology termed the "life space" of the individual.[35]

The ways in which the properties of this bounded environment are imagined by suburban leaders is central to the explanation of their actions. The roots of exclusionary tactics and of the complementary local policy nexus both lie in the local policy makers' understandings of their local world. Those understandings we shall term the *assumptive world*.[36] The assumptive world is multidimensional; it includes perceptions of the world, evaluations of its aspects, a sense of relatedness to them, and recurrent demands that they be acted upon. These dimensions interact to generate preferred states of the world and "calls to action":

> A man is tied to his assumptive world. By learning to recognise and act appropriately within his expectable environment a man makes a life space his own . . . the assumptive world not only contains a model of the world as it is . . . it also contains a model of the world as it might be [these models may represent probable situations, ideal situations, or dreaded situations].[37]

The most readily apparent and accessible aspect of the assumptive world of suburban politics is the "image" of the locality to which its policy makers subscribe. No image can adequately capture the entire social and spatial "reality" of so large a locality, though it may express its central values and perceptions. As Anselm Strauss has written in a pioneering work, "Certain stylized and symbolic means must be resorted to in order to 'see' the City," using a form of shorthand characterization. Moreover, argues Strauss, these stylized and symbolic constructions arise from membership in particular social worlds; they are embedded in particular milieux shared and, thereby, taken for granted.[38] So defined, they correspond closely to the sentiments of the wider suburban populace.

What is taken for granted in London's outermost suburbs is a lingering rurality, symbolized by wildlife, trees, agricultural remnants, and the immediacy of the protected countryside: the symbolically potent "Green Belt."[39] The officially sanctioned "image" of a suburban locality is frequently expressed in borough guides or in observations submitted to government agencies on matters affecting the character of the area. Frequently, the outer suburbs are presented almost as free-standing towns, linked, in a single dimension, to the metropolis by easy and rapid rail access. Their social atmospheres are prized as safe, middle class, privatized and familistic; they are "favoured residential areas."[40] *The function of suburban policy making is to give expression to these images.*

The assumptive world of the suburban elite incorporates more than a simple image of the locality itself and of its properties. It also embodies typifications of social groups and unquestioned premises as to their motives. It is characterized by implicit theories as to the nature of society, the springs of human behavior, and the scope of government.[41] Insofar as it provides the predicates of action, the overriding concern is to manage, maintain, and enhance the social, physical, and fiscal characteristics of the locality and its populace *as presently imagined.* The interplay of wider social and economic forces operating locally ensures that the image is continually strained by changing realities. Policy making is, therefore, a *dynamic* response, and the impetus behind suburban policy is the *mismatch* of the "models of the world" as perceived by local policy makers: specifically, between models of the local world as it is and was, and models of the local world *as it might become* in both preferred and dreaded situations.

Managing the Local Environment:
The Policy Nexus of Suburban Conservatism

Proposals for the planned migration of a population of lower-status outsiders into a suburban area trigger a preexisting response to a future dreaded in the imagination and are seen to pose a profound threat to the locality. The nature of the threat is precisely delineated within the assumptive world of suburban leaders. The newcomers would be "different" in a number of important dimensions. They would not "look after" their homes. Their children would be rowdy and violent. The parents would be dependent upon locally provided social services. They would not, in any case, be "happy." Their presence would cause the existing population to flee, thus encouraging a greater influx of inner-city dwellers. These migrants would be Labour voters and would so alter the political balance of London as to enable the abhorrent policies of welfarism to be pursued even more effectively.[42]

Yet, for the suburban policy makers the perceived impact of the loss of exclusivity is not only social: it is also physical and fiscal. On the *physical* side, making room for inner-city dwellers would necessitate development of the open spaces, of which borough guides often speak so proudly, as well as of redevelopment of the grander areas of large, detached houses at far higher densities. Moreover, these developments would inevitably be in the dreary and visually offensive style thought common to public sector architecture. The aim of suburban physical policy—the protection of amenity in the natural and built environments—would, as a consequence, be frustrated.

On the *fiscal* side, the new population would lack the spirit of independence that motivates the existing inhabitants to look after themselves. The newcomers would generate greater demands on costly social welfare services. Their relatively low incomes would qualify them for rent rebates, thereby augmenting the costs of public housing. Further, the newcomers would be insensitive to the increases in residential property taxes which the needs-meeting policies would generate. As they became a political force in the locality, they would thereby threaten the existing leaders' policies of financial stringency and prudence. To a limited extent, these changes in demographic character would be compensated for by the equalization effects of the British local financial system. But some proportion of the load would fall upon the local exchequer. However, the formal realities of such a situation are distorted in the rhetoric and in the imagination of suburbia's defensive leadership.

Just as resistance to migration from the inner city is a major plank in the management of the local environment, so also is local housing policy an important instrument of environmental management. In order particularly to restrain the growth of what is seen as a dependency-creating form of housing tenure, the suburban leaders have increasingly shifted the emphasis in housing policy away from municipal housing towards novel and ingenious measures designed to promote owner-occupation. The benefits of public tenancy have diminished; those of ownership have increased; and access to the private ownership sector is greatly facilitated for the moderate-income citizen. The launching of one borough's "sponsored development" program, a public authority/private enterprise partnership to provide "homes for the needy, not the greedy," epitomized this trend.[43] Other innovations include various forms of assisted house purchase, while the considerable attention given to the sale of council houses to their tenants at well below market price similarly represents the articulation and development of the policy nexus of suburban conservatism. By reducing the size of local public sector housing stocks, these "domestic" policies also contribute indirectly to the exclusionary goal, for they reduce the pool of public housing and thereby diminish the scope for rehousing inner-London families.

The policy nexus of suburban defense may be more or less conscious or contrived, more or less developed. From the image of the "favored residential suburb" derive the broad lines of policy in the social, physical, and fiscal spheres (see figure 10-1). Complementary to these local "policy outputs" are the responses made to pressures emanating from the interorganizational environment. These pressures, which, in the case of "opening the suburbs," ran counter to local policy, call for a similar degree of ingenuity if they are to be successfully managed.[44]

Tactics for Managing the Interorganizational Environment
Local policy makers are faced with a wide variety of pressures and stimuli from their external environment. To engage with (for example) regional, national or international, social, political, or economic forces is beyond the capabilities of any single local council, although collective action through the Local Government Associations can often work to promote or to prevent social and economic change. To some extent, land-use controls may enable local elites to maintain preferred environmental states, but local public policy is characterized by negative constraints upon change, rather than by positive incentives to change. Exogenous changes

```
                    ┌─────────────────────┐
                    │    IMAGERY :        │
                    │  The  Favoured      │
                    │ Residential  Suburb │
                    └─────────────────────┘
```

FISCAL CONSERVATISM	SOCIAL CONSERVATISM	PHYSICAL CONSERVATISM
LOW TAX RATES, LIMITED EXPENDITURE	OTHER SOCIAL POLICIES HOUSING POLICIES	PROTECTION OF AMENITY IN BUILT & NATURAL ENVIRONMENT

Specific policies on e.g. rents policy, housing finance,
building programmes, co–operation with private developers,
mortgage opportunities, assisted purchase schemes,
disposal of public housing stock.

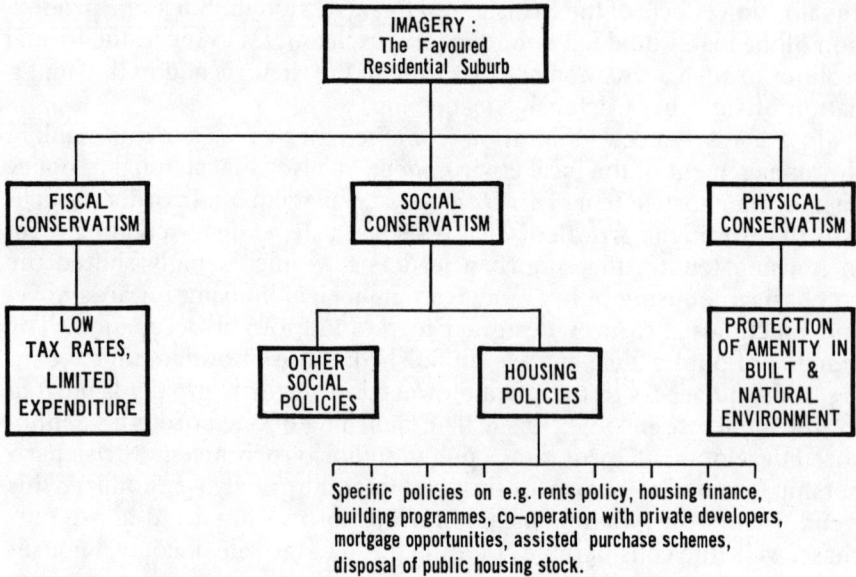

Figure 10-1. The Policy Nexus of Suburban Conservativism

in population, migration, the labor market, or tastes may defy a purposive response; the external world is notoriously intractable. However, in the case of the external governmental environment (the network of other agencies in the public policy sphere), a more direct and reciprocal relationship exists.[45]

This configuration of outside forces may be seen by a local suburban political elite as a series of irksome constraints and interferences (which are to be bypassed or ignored whenever possible); or, in some instances, as a set of overwhelmingly pervasive exogenous factors to which they must uncomplainingly submit. In the case of the more ingenious and aware suburban leaders, however, the activities of other governmental agencies are seen as a further aspect of the total environment to be managed. External governmental agencies and powerful private corporations may act either to promote or to undermine local policy. Sometimes the activities of these external agencies may be subverted to local advantage. Sometimes political or other devices exist through which local leaders can influence the direction of external pressures. For these leaders the management of the interorganizational environment is an exercise in creativity: less an enterprise to be shunned than a challenge which may possibly be exploited to local advantage.

The necessity of managing the external environment arises most clearly when other governmental organizations attempt to *sponsor* local change.

This was most crucially the case in the politics of London suburban defense, when the suburbs faced pressure from the central government, the GLC, and neighboring inner-London boroughs to accommodate inner-city dwellers or release land to meet their needs. These demands were augmented by other, subsidiary, governmental agencies and legitimized by a series of official committees of inquiry. The pattern of pressure, while variable, steadily increased until 1972, when the central government came more closely into the arena and abandoned its traditional posture of unaligned arbitrator between contesting authorities.[46]

The local policy makers engage with each of the other organizational actors, and their skills are severely tested in the business of deflecting external demands. (See figure 10-2.) Yet, of those actors, only the GLC has the *direct* power to violate local territory by acquiring and developing land and decanting an inner-city, working-class population into the dwellings it constructs there. In the ten-year period which we studied, the GLC failed to do so on any significant scale whatsoever. Its land acquisitions were minuscule, despite its own projections that the outermost suburbs could accommodate a massive increase in public sector building.[47]

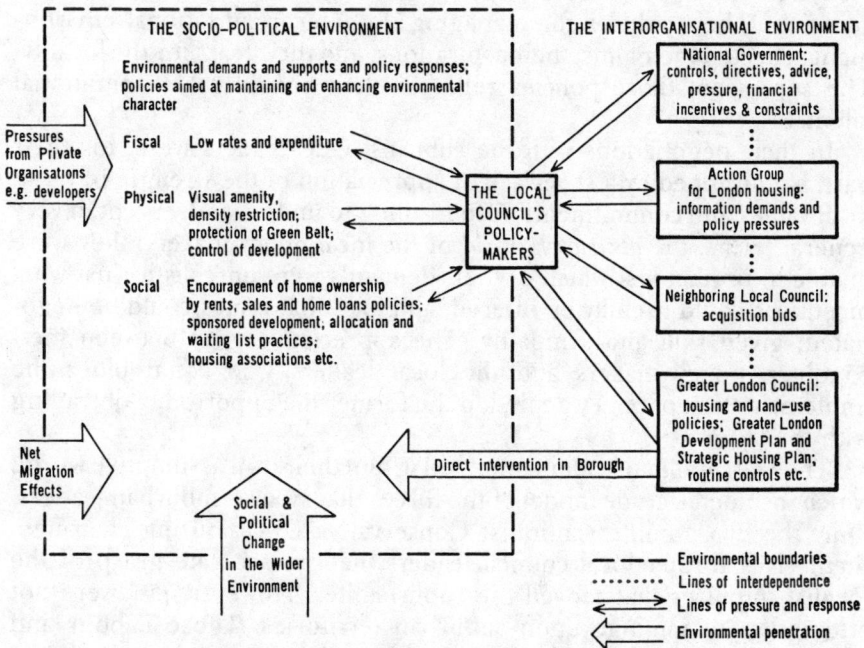

Figure 10-2. The Policy Problem: Managing Two Environments

This recurrent metropolitan failure is a measure of suburban success.

The GLC was limited only in part by its uncertainties, discontinuities, and electoral preoccupations. It also lacked the capability of winning. For a metropolitan leader, "opening up the suburbs" is but one of a number of policy options. His career will not falter if he fails to accomplish so intractable a task. Moreover, a salient clientele for such a policy is hard to identify. The real gains of the inner-London poor seem remote and intangible. The improvement in the "life chances" of any single family would be marginal. An elaborate sequence of "rippling out" families to the *next outermost* location precluded the sudden arrival of the inner-city homeless in leafy suburbia. Nor were job opportunities so distributed as to make these dramatic relocations feasible. GLC housing policy was, therefore, scarcely one of radical populist appeal. Nor did "opening up the suburbs" enjoy a wide constituency among the policy makers themselves, beyond the few committed politicians and the characteristically interventionist professionals.

For the suburban leaders, by contrast, the defense of their territory and the maintenance of its character is their *prime rationale*. They cannot afford to lose the battle for the suburban future. Their strategies in intergovernmental relations derived directly from their understanding of their local situation. Their policies for managing the interorganizational environment reflected their aims, their aspirations, and their fears for the locality. The success of those policies reflected their considerable operational talents.

In their negotiations with the suburbs, GLC leaders were, for their part, handicapped by a sheer ack of appreciation of the strength of these local values and commitments. Often failing to understand, except in very general terms, the *assumptive world* of the local policy makers, they were unable to predict just which of their demands were unrealistic, just what incentives could usefully be offered, and just what issues could be negotiated, given skill and sympathy. The appreciative gaps between metropolitan policy makers and the local leaders who could block the implementation of policy denied to the former the opportunity of trading with the latter.[48]

The metropolitan leaders operated within their own assumptive world, which included a crude model of the forces that swayed suburban leaders. Only the two noninterventionist Conservative GLC housing chairmen, themselves former local council leaders, had an accurate grasp of the localist impulses that moved the suburbanites. However, *they* were not attempting to impinge upon suburban territories. Those Labour and renegade Conservative GLC chairmen who were pursuing interventionist policies had the greatest need to understand their opponents' positions. As pure "metro-politicians," their careers provided them with the least opportunity to have gained that understanding.[49] Their relations with the borough leaders were distant, and their characterizations of the local political situations in which they were attempting to intervene were often colored by the myth of the monolithic opponent. They could neither see the divisions within suburban councils where they existed, nor appreciate the ideological congruity between suburban leaders and their followers. The policy of "opening up the suburbs" resembled, in this respect, the abortive federal land release program in the United States, where failure to grasp the realities of local politics in a number of diverse settings led to the formulation of idealized policies that were easily deflected.[50]

From the metropolitan leaders' inability to appreciate the texture of suburban politics arose the suburban politicians' major tactical asset. A reliance upon procrastination, disguised as protocol, could enable local leaders to outwit and outmaneuver most of their intergovernmental opponents. They could delay and protract the bargaining process while operating quickly and flexibly on the home policy front, for example, by placing Compulsory Purchase Orders on sites for which the GLC was negotiating or by making rapid policy decisions on specific site usage.

In some suburbs, the decision system had undergone a process of modernization and change, leading to a considerable centralization of policy making. Here the local leaders, confident of political support, could introduce new policies at short notice, channel resources toward them, and develop them rapidly. In the case of domestic policies which impeded the metropolitan policy makers—accelerated land assembly for use by private developers, for example—this flexibility gave the local leaders a distinct edge on the GLC and national government.

At the same time, the unwelcomed pressure from higher-level agencies could be treated with excessive and unreal formality. A local leader, conscious of his real local power, could pretend a show of deference to his council and initiate a lengthy process of formal committee and council consideration and reconsideration, a process that would move yet *more slowly* where management reforms had extended the cycle of committee and council meetings.[51] The niceties of protocol—indispensable when, as in this case, the protagonists were independent and constitutionally established governmental bodies—were not lightly violated by either partner, and this formalism operated as a distinct disadvantage to the demanding body. Any direct and personal appeal could be brushed aside with reference to the protocols of policy making, and metropolitan or national policy makers had no way of penetrating this ponderous process. Moreover, when the metro-politicians tried to break the deadlock by unilateral action, the local leaders proved themselves to be capable of swift and decisive response.

Uncertainties, partisan conflicts, political change, and policy discontinuities ensured that no serious and sustained attempt to "open up the suburbs" was made during the first decade of London's metropolitan experiment. Moreover, the suburban leaders showed great tactical resourcefulness in deflecting challenges to their exclusivity and in wresting concessions from fatigued national and metropolitan leaders. Exclusionary policies scored easy victories. Neither the institutional arrangements nor the policies which might undermine the hegemony of the suburbs have yet evolved.

The argument of this paper is that these institutions and policies must be tailored to the reality of suburban politics: in short, to the realities of social-area management. This perspective on the politics of exclusion at least provides a framework for the fuller understanding of the constraints that operate upon public policy in this field. Such an understanding is a precondition of effective action. But the social-area management paradigm is specific neither to suburban locales, nor to two-tier governmental systems. Wherever independently governed territories face threats to their character, scope exists for the purposive manipulation of the dual environment.

Notes

1. Anthony Downs, *Opening Up the Suburbs: An Urban Strategy for America* (New Haven, Conn.: Yale University Press, 1973); Leonard Rubinowitz, *Low-Income Housing: Suburban Strategies* (Boston: Ballinger, 1974); Edward M. Bergman, *Eliminating Exclusionary Zoning* (Boston: Ballinger, 1974); Michael M. Danielson, *The Politics of Exclusion* (New York: Columbia University Press, 1976); Michael Harloe, Ruth Issacharoff, and Richard Minns, *The Organization of Housing: Public and Private Enterprise in London* (London: Heinemann, 1974); see also Kevin R. Cox, *Conflict, Power, and Politics in the City: A Geographic View* (New York: McGraw-Hill, 1973), chap. 5.

2. Studies which take the defended area itself as the unit of analysis include Gerald Suttles, *The Social Construction of Communities* (Chicago: University of Chicago Press, 1972). For a discussion of fiscal incentives to exclusivity, see Mason Gaffney, "Tax Reform to Release Land," in *Modernizing Urban Land Policy*, ed. Marion Clawson (Baltimore: The Johns Hopkins University Press, 1973), pp. 115–52. Two relevant micro-analyses are Oscar Newman, *Defensible Space: People and Design in the Violent City* (London: Architectural Press, 1972); and Nicholas Taylor, *The Village in the City* (London: Temple Smith, 1973). At the level of the individual, see Edward T. Hall's *The Hidden Dimension* (New York: Doubleday, 1966) is the classic study of "proxemics." Hall's work regards animal behavior as analogous to human behavior, a position which might be extended to include the "instinctual" analyses of the animal ethologists, Konrad Lorenz and Robert Ardrey. Suttles, *Social Construction of Communities,* argues cogently against the relevance of such portrayals of animal territoriality to the understanding of social action.

3. The term "socio-spatial access" is used here to denote the availability of locationally specific benefits and disbenefits, in particular those arising from propinquity (as in neighborhood quality), those arising from delivery (as in public services), and those arising from the environment (pollution, crime, and accident levels). For a discussion of spatial accessibilities, see Oliver P. Williams, *Metropolitan Political Analysis: A Social Access Approach* (New York: The Free Press, 1970).

4. For general discussion, see Kenneth Newton, "Community Politics and Decision Making: The American Experience and Its Lessons," in *Essays in the Study of Urban Politics,* ed. Ken Young (London: Macmillan & Co., 1975).

5. David Murphy, *The Silent Watchdog: The Press in Local Politics* (London: Constable, 1976).

6. See, in particular, Stephen L. Elkin, *Politics and Land-Use Planning* (London: Cambridge University Press, 1974), for an argument, now of somewhat diminished validity, about the inertness of the environment of urban government in England. See also John Dearlove, *The Politics of Policy in Local Government* (London: Cambridge University Press, 1973).

7. For a discussion of theories of representative linkage, see Norman Luttbeg, *Public Opinion and Public Policy* (Homewood, Ill.: Dorsey, 1968); and Dearlove, *Policy in Local Government.*

8. The story of the Cutteslowe walls is fully recounted in Peter Collison, *The Cutteslowe Walls: A Study in Social Class* (London: Faber and Faber, 1963).

9. Ibid., p. 140.

10. A survey of families leaving a council estate revealed dislike of neighbors as the major factor in the decision to move. The author's comment: "One objection was the difficulty of bringing up children decently when those of neighbours are completely uncontrolled and have quite different and often unmentionable standards of behaviour and language." In Rosamond Jevons and John Madge's study, *Housing Estates* (Bristol: For the University by J. W. Arrowsmith, 1946), p. 69. For an important argument on the primacy of child-rearing considerations in residential selection, see Oliver P. Williams, "Life Style Values and Political Decentralisation in a Metropolitan Area," *Southwestern Social Science Quarterly* (December 1967), pp. 299–310. For some rather sceptical remarks and the child-centeredness of suburbia, see Ernest Mowrer, "The Family in Suburbia," in *The Suburban Community,* ed. William Dobriner (New York: G. P. Putnam and Sons, 1958), p. 157 ff.

11. In the London borough of Bromley, an affluent and Conservative area, a wall was erected to close access from a London County Council (LCC) housing estate in 1926. The wall stood for years embodying a dispute between the LCC and the borough council as to its legality. The details are on file at County Hall, Minutes of the LCC Housing Committee, 1926–1928. In the southern part of the borough local residents unsuccessfully demanded a substantial fence in 1963. A resident was quoted as claiming: "I think the council owe[s] us this fence. When our houses were built seven years ago we had no idea council houses were to be built there. I grew up in a council house and saved hard to get away to a place of my own when I married." J. Tucker, *Honourable Estates* (London: Gollancz, 1966), p. 20.

12. For opposition to the location of local council housing, see: ibid.; Terence Young, *Becontree and Dagenham* (London: Becontree Social Survey Committee, 1934); J. H. Nicholson, *New Communities in Britain: Achievements and Problems* (London: National Council of Social Service, 1961); Ruth Durant, *Watling: A Survey of Social Life on a New Housing Estate* (London: P. S. King & Son, 1939). Harold Orlans describes the opposition to the location of the first New Town built under the 1946 act in *Stevenage: A Sociological Study of a New Town* (London: Routledge and Kegan Paul, 1952). Local authority resistance to "overspill" is featured in Leslie P. Green, *Provincial Metropolis* (London: Allen and Unwin, 1959); and John K. Friend, C. J. L. Yewlett, and John M. Power, *Public Planning: The Intercorporate Dimension* (London: Tavistock, 1974).

13. See, especially, a study of two contiguous communities in Leicester: one old, established, and "respectable"; the other a "rough," white immigrant group that moved into a cheap private rental estate: Norbert Elias and John L. Scotson, *The Established and the Outsiders* (London: Cass, 1962). See also John Mogey, *Family and Neighbourhood* (London: Oxford University Press, 1956).

14. Martin Meyerson and Edward C. Banfield, *Politics, Planning, and the Public Interest: The Case of Public Housing in Chicago* (Glencoe, Ill.: The Free Press, 1955). See also Edward C. Banfield and Morton Grodzins, *Government and Housing in Metropolitan Areas* (New York: McGraw-Hill, 1958). Alvin Boskoff notes that the urban class system focusses around "the issue of impersonal but informal exclusion." Alvin Boskoff, *The Sociology of Urban Regions* (New York: Appleton-Century-Crofts, 1962), p. 199. A more thorough review and analysis of territorial exclusion is given in David Harvey, *Social Justice and the City* (London: Edward Arnold, 1973), pp. 65–73.

15. The responses of residents and public officials to questions about maintaining the quality of residents and keeping "undesirables" out indicate the universality of status-based exclusion in Oliver P. Williams et al., *Suburban Differences and Metropolitan Policies* (Philadelphia: University of Pennsylvania Press, 1965), p. 219.

16. D. Chapman, *The Home and Social Status* (London: Routledge and Kegan Paul, 1955). Raymond E. Pahl, *Patterns of Urban Life* (London: Longmans, 1970), pp. 118–19. The classic study is Peter Willmott and Michael Young, *Family and Class in a London Suburb* (London: Routledge and Kegan Paul, 1960). George Grossmith and Weedon Grossmith's *Diary of a Nobody* (Bristol: J. W. Arrowsmith, 1892) is a gentle satire on the problems of maintaining a precarious status in the North London suburbs of the late Victorian era.

17. Michael Young and Peter Willmott in *The Symmetrical Family* (Harmondsworth, Middlesex: Penguin Books, 1973) elaborate the "Principle of Stratified Diffusion," a concept of lagged social equality. See, particularly, chapter 1: "The Slow March."

18. Ibid., p. 5. See, more generally, James H. Johnson, "The Suburban Expansion of Housing in London, 1918–1939"; and J. T. Coppock, "Dormitory Settlements Around London," in *Greater London*, ed. John T. Coppock and Hugh C. Prince (London: Faber and Faber, 1964). See also Chapman, *Home and Social Status*; and Mowrer, "Family in Suburbia."

19. C. F. G. Masterman, *The Condition of England* (London: Methuen, 1909), pp. 58–59. The best account of the rise of London's outer suburbs is Alan Jackson, *Semi-Detached London: Suburban Development, Life, and Transport, 1900–1939* (London: Allen and Unwin, 1973).

20. The boundaries of metropolitan London were first defined in 1855, when the Metropolitan Board of Works was established as London's first areawide authority. With a population of 2.4 million, the nation's capital was compact and self-contained, with less than one-seventh of the area's total population lying beyond the boundary. The population had already increased rapidly during that century; it was to continue to grow, progressively radiating out beyond the limits of administrative London. By 1891 a third as many "Londoners" resided outside as inside the 1855 boundary; by 1931, nine-tenths. And by 1937, the majority of the capital's population lived in the newer suburbs of the Edwardian and interwar years. In 1889 the powerful London County Council replaced the Board of Works. A pioneer of municipal initiative, the LCC was controlled by left-wing parties from 1889 to 1907 (by the Progressives) and from 1934 to 1965 (by the Labour party). During those two periods the LCC leaders pursued expansionist policies and sought to dominate the political life of the growing metropolis. For the partisan conflicts over that object, see Ken Young, "The Conservative Strategy for London, 1855–1975," *The London Journal* 1, no. 1 (May 1975): 56–81. For a general view of the political stresses engendered by metropolitan growth, see Ken Young and John Kramer, *Strategy and Conflict in Metropolitan Housing* (London: Heinemann, 1977), chap. 2.

21. Beyond the LCC area the new suburbs expanded within the territories of the "Home Counties," the County Councils of Kent, Essex, Hertfordshire, Middlesex, and Surrey. These counties had lost territory to London when the Metropolitan Board of Works was created in 1855, and were acutely sensitive to the losses of property tax, authority, and prestige that would follow upon any further expansion of the LCC. The local councils which governed the individual suburbs shared power with their county councils, and in the interwar period unanimously preferred to maintain that arrangement. Thus, LCC proposals to annex the suburbs encountered solid opposition from all the other local and county jurisdictions in the metropolitan region.

22. In framing the precise legislative proposals for the division of power between the new Greater London Council (GLC) and the new London borough councils, considerable concessions were made to the suburbs. Most significant for this story was the limitation of the powers which were given to the GLC in the fields of housing and land-use planning. Concessions made between 1960 and 1963 were sufficient to swing the suburbs behind the reorganization plan, and so ensure both that their Conservative representatives in the House of Commons would support the legislation, and that the officials of the existing suburban governments would cooperate in planning the transition to the new system of government. For the details, see Young and Kramer, *Metropolitan Housing*.

23. The steady rise of Labour representation on the LCC between 1919 and 1934 alarmed the Conservative suburbs. The Conservative party mounted elaborate antisocialist campaigns, but the exodus of the middle-class voters to the new suburbs led inexorably to a permanent Labour majority on the LCC. The repeated failures of the Conservative electoral challenge led the Conservatives to adopt a policy of metropolitan unification, for it seemed at that stage that the suburbanites would provide a solid majority on any areawide

council. At the same time, they sought a localization of power, whereby the local units of government would enjoy almost untrammeled autonomy. After 1956 these goals complemented the Whitehall civil servants' own goals of rationalizing land-use and transportation planning via metropolitan unification. For the political considerations, see Ken Young, *Local Politics and the Rise of Party* (Leicester: Leicester University Press, 1975).
24. See P. J. O. Self, *Cities in Flood* (London: Faber, 1961). See also the definitive account of British urban policy, Peter Hall, *The Containment of Urban England* (London: Allen and Unwin, 1973).
25. For the reorganization of London government, see Gerald Rhodes, *The Government of London: The Struggle for Reform* (London: Weidenfeld and Nicolson, 1970); Gerald Rhodes, ed., *The New Government of London: The First Five Years* (London: Weidenfeld and Nicolson, 1972); Donald Foley, *Governing the London Region* (Berkeley and Los Angeles: University of California Press, 1972); and Frank Smallwood, *The Politics of Metropolitan Reform* (Indianapolis, Ind.: Bobbs-Merrill, 1965). For the distribution of political support in the 1964 GLC election, see Gwyn Rowley, "The Greater London Council Elections in 1964: Some Geographical Considerations," *Tijdschrift voor Economische en Sociale Geografie* (May/June 1965), pp. 113–14.
26. Report of the Committee on Housing in Greater London, cmnd. 2605 (London, 1965).
27. The essence of this scheme was that the GLC bid for the right to nominate families to vacancies created both by new building and by re-lets in the local public housing stocks. A percentage of vacancies, varying from ten to fifteen percent, was chosen as a reasonable initial target, and comparable proportionate help was sought from each independent suburb. The local governments of the inner area were thus to obtain relief from their own local housing stress by drawing, via the GLC, on this central housing pool. The "nominations scheme" proved a source of considerable initial conflict between the GLC and the suburbs. Strenuous diplomatic efforts resulted in the establishment of a very modest pool of vacancies, which thereafter declined over a seven-year period to an inconsequential level. See Young and Kramer, *Metropolitan Housing*, chaps. 3–6.
28. The chief salaried officials of the LCC housing department had long records of service with the Council in its era of Labour control. Only the Director of Housing J. P. Macey had any experience of the policy reversals which normally follow changes in partisan control in English local government. In addition, these officials were committed by their professional ideology to a major role for public housing in a program of social reform. Although constitutionally nonpartisan, several of them have expressed a private allegiance to the Labour party. While they were not—at least at the higher levels—disloyal to their new political masters, they were distressed by some of the new policies and sought a reversion to the traditional objectives of their organization.
29. The study was nominally carried out by the Standing Joint Working Party on London Housing, a body composed of salaried public officials from Whitehall, the GLC, and the London borough councils. It appeared as *London's Housing Needs Up to 1974* (London: Ministry of Housing and Local Government, 1970).
30. The report revealed that the level of housing deficiency—that is, the excess of potential households over available accommodation—ran at twelve percent for Greater London as a whole in 1966. The degree of deficiency varied from seven percent in the southern suburbs to twenty percent in Inner North London. The pattern of generally substandard housing reinforced the pattern of numerical deficiency. Current trends revealed a faster rate of improvement in the suburbs than in the inner area. The projections to 1974 indicated that some outer suburbs would be in a notional surplus situation by that year, while shortfalls and vast tracts of inadequate housing would remain in the inner area. The report called for "a new initiative" to tackle these growing inequities.
31. *A Strategic Housing Plan for London* (London: Greater London Council, 1974). For an analysis of the plan, see Della A. Nevitt, "Towards a Greater London Housing Strategy," *The London Journal* 1, no. 1 (May 1975): 135–42.
32. *Evening Standard*, 8 July 1974.
33. Some U.S. parallels to this leadership uncertainty are to be found in Edward Sofen, *The Miami Metropolitan Experiment* (Bloomington: Indiana University Press, 1963). See also Walter A. Rosenbaum and Thomas A. Henderson, "Explaining the Attitude of Community Influentials Toward Government Consolidation: A Reappraisal of Four Hypotheses," *Urban Affairs Quarterly* (December 1973), pp. 251–75.
34. John D. Stewart, *The Responsive Local Authority* (London: Charles Knight, 1974), p. 95.
35. Kurt Lewin, *Resolving Social Conflicts* (New York: Harper and Row, 1948); idem, *Field Theory in Social Science: Selected Papers*, ed. D. Cartwright (London: Tavistock, 1952); Harold Mey, *Field Theory: A Study of Its Application in the Social Sciences*, trans. Douglas Scott (London: Routledge and Kegan Paul, 1972).
36. The concept and scope of the assumptive world is formulated and discussed in Ken Young, "Values in the Policy Process," *Policy and Politics* 5, no. 3 (March 1977). The term is adapted from C. Murray Parkes, "Psychological Transitions: A Field for Study," *Social Science and Medicine* 5 (1971): 101–15. It is also used by Cantril et al. in a paper on the transactional view in psychological research, quoted in Clyde Kluckhohn, "Value Orientations in the Theory of Action," in *Toward a General Theory of Action*, ed. Talcott Parsons and Edward Shils (Cambridge: Harvard University Press, 1952).
37. Parkes, "Psychological Transitions," p. 104. Parkes' insight is also treated imaginatively in Peter Marris' study of bereavements, *Loss and Change* (London: Routledge and Kegan Paul, 1974).
38. Anselm Strauss, *Images of the American City* (New York: The Free Press, 1961), pp. 6, 67. There is today a massive literature on environmental perception, much of it stimulated by Kevin Lynch's pioneering study

of "imageability," *The Image of the City* (Cambridge, Mass.: M.I.T. Press, 1960). However, unlike Strauss' work, it is almost entirely unsociological. A good, general review of the field is Peter Gould and Rodney White, *Mental Maps* (Harmondsworth, Middlesex: Penguin Books, 1974). The images of elite policy makers have not yet been studied; for some remarks on this see Ken Young, "Values in Urban Politics: The Case of 'Localism,' " European Consortium for Political Research, 1975.

39. Proposals to surround cities with a protected ring of agricultural and recreational countryside have a considerable antiquity, being found as early as the thirteenth century B.C. The LCC took an initiative in the interwar years to halt suburban sprawl by means of an agreed Green Belt. The proposal had featured prominently in the regional plans of that era, and was endorsed in the Greater London Plan of 1943, a master strategy that provided the framework for regional planning until the 1970s. "Garden Cities," or New Towns, located beyond this belt, provided for urban growth and were a complement to Green Belt policy. Successive national and local governments in Britain continue to affirm the sanctity of the Green Belt. Few public policies receive so widespread and unquestioning endorsement. See Frederic J. Osborn, *Green Belt Cities* (London: Evelyn, Adams, and Mackay, 1969); and Peter Hall, *Containment of Urban England.*

40. These remarks are based on: the results of interviews with political leaders in a range of London suburbs; the scrutiny of borough guides; a survey of replies to government proposals for London government from 1960 to 1963; and an in-depth case study of policy making in a single London suburb, reported in Young and Kramer, *Metropolitan Housing.*

41. For comments on some of these several aspects of the assumptive worlds of local policy makers, see Dearlove, *Policy in Local Government*; and Janet Lewis, "Local Authority Social Service Provision in Four London Boroughs: An Examination of the Sources of Variation" (Ph.D. diss., University of London, 1975). Robert Putnam's *The Beliefs of Politicians* (New Haven, Conn.: Yale University Press, 1973) is a pioneering work on the tapping of beliefs as to the nature of society. Apart from the work of Parkes, our position demonstrably owes much to Kenneth Boulding's seminal work, *The Image* (Ann Arbor: University of Michigan Press, 1956).

42. These are not impressions, but the summarized responses from interviews with London suburban politicians carried out from 1974 to 1975. We are, of course, not concerned here with the "validity" of these projections; they are real enough for the suburban leaders. Certainly the process of residential displacement, most familiar in a racially mixed context, is not less apparent in the genteel, yet bitter, antagonism of London's suburbanites:

> On both sides they're recent and on both sides from the East End. That's what really made us decide to retire to Worthing. You can't talk to these people, we just don't speak the same language. Some of the old residents down the road asked me who was coming after us. We've sold the house to a young architect and his wife, so we were able to assure them that *we* hadn't let them down. (Quoted in Willmott and Young, *London Suburb,* p. 21.)

These citizen sentiments were very closely reflected in our interviews with suburban leaders. See also remarks made by Gerald Suttles, *Social Construction of Communities,* pp. 235–41.

43. Under mounting pressure from Ministers and the GLC to make a contribution to London housing needs and bring into use sites acquired for public housing, at least two suburbs (and a number of other authorities in southeastern England) proposed "sponsored development" as a compromise solution. This involved entering into a contract with a major private construction firm to build cheap housing for sale to chosen moderate-income families. The houses and apartments in one case were built on sites reserved for public rental housing to a lower and cheaper standard than that mandatory for orthodox "council houses." Moreover, the final sale price was well below market rates, for the suburban leaders applied a discount to the notional site value, ultimately including it in the sales package at about half its open market rate. Buyers for the houses were to be nominated from among the existing local tenants or housing applicants, with some limited nominating rights conceded to the GLC. See Young and Kramer, *Metropolitan Housing,* chaps. 5 and 6.

44. The *tension* between the demands of the two environments may be seen as the crucial factor in domestic policy development. An arch-Conservative and "traditionalist" area, unremittingly "localist" in many dimensions, may nevertheless prove highly innovative. For clues to the resolution of this apparent paradox, see Peter Marris, *Loss and Change;* and Donald Schon, *Beyond the Stable State* (London: Temple Smith, 1971). The social-area management paradigm presents as essentially similar suburban exclusionary policies, the inner-city's demolition response to the threat of "gentrification," and the rural local authority's eviction action against intellectual squatters in a mining village—all of which are contemporary events in England. The positive policies employed by inner-city councils to retain their indigenous working-class populations by enhancing their local housing opportunities are similarly explicable, if not precisely paralleled in the suburbs. The threat to locality structure may be posed by *inflow* or *outflow* of population. It is the presence of this threat that provides the incentive to innovation and becomes the key to the localist-innovative paradox.

45. The classic study of the complex "intercorporate network" is J. K. Friend, J. M. Power, and C. J. L. Yewlett, *Public Planning.* A concise summary is given by John Friend in "Planners, Policies, and Organizational Boundaries: Some Recent Developments in Britain," *Policy and Politics* 5, no. 1 (September 1976): 25–46.

A rather different approach, and one which emphasizes the conflicting aspects of interagency relations, has been developed within organization theory. A general review of the applicability of this perspective to urban politics is given by Stephen L. Elkin, "Comparative Urban Politics and Interorganizational Behaviour," in *Essays on the Study of Urban Politics,* ed. Ken Young (London: Macmillan & Co., 1975), pp. 158–84. Harloe, *Organization of Housing,* explores the complexities of the network of public and private agencies engaged in housing provision in Greater London.

46. The unwillingness of the first GLC leaders to force a confrontation with the intransigent suburbs lay in the Ministers' power to decide acquisition issues when the two levels of local government could not reach agreement, and in the customary unwillingness of Ministers to make such unpopular decisions. However, under the Conservative government of 1970–74, considerable cabinet concern was felt about the adverse electoral consequences of a poor housing record. In 1972 the Secretary of State for the Environment established the Action Group on London Housing, a body of key politicians from the GLC and the inner and outer boroughs, chaired by the Undersecretary of State. Thereafter, the Action Group played a major role in challenging the suburbs' defensive posture and throwing ministerial weight behind the drive to "open up the suburbs."

47. Between 1965 and 1970 the GLC acquired around 175 acres per year for housing purposes in the *whole* of Greater London. The figure rose to an average of around 230 acres per year for 1970 through 1973.

48. Vickers' concept of "appreciative behaviour" closely parallels the postulated relations between perception, evaluation, cathexis, and action elaborated in Young, "Policy Process." See also Geoffrey Vickers, *Value Systems and Social Processes* (London: Tavistock, 1968).

49. Interventionist Labour Chairmen Evelyn Denington and Gladys Dimson had political experience only from the LCC and GLC. The Conservative interventionist Geoffrey Chase-Gardener was a real estate agent with minimal political experience, and that solely on the GLC. All three fell far short of their aims. The two Conservative chairmen who sympathized with the "localist" sentiments of the suburbanites were: Horace Cutler, a landlord and builder who formerly had led suburban Harrow Borough Council; and Bernard Perkins, formerly leader of the Lambeth Borough Council. Both conceded autonomy to the suburbs during their chairmanships.

50. Martha Derthick, *New Towns In-Town: Why a Federal Program Failed* (Washington, D.C.: The Urban Institute, 1972).

51. Since 1967 local governments in England have been exhorted to reorganize, streamline, and centralize their decision-making systems. For a general review of these developments, see Peter G. Richards, *The Reformed Local Government System,* 2nd ed. (London: Allen and Unwin, 1975).

ABOUT THE AUTHORS

JOHN A. AGNEW is Assistant Professor of Geography, Maxwell Graduate School, Syracuse University, where he has taught since 1975. A native of Cumbria, England, he received his B.A. from the University of Exeter, and his M.A. and Ph.D. from the Ohio State University. His major research and teaching interests are in urban political geography and the geography of development.

KEVIN R. COX, originally from Warwick, England, was educated at Cambridge University and at the University of Illinois. Professor of Geography at the Ohio State University, his primary research interest is the social and political geography of the city. His articles have appeared in professional journals in geography, sociology, and political science. He is co-editor of *Behavioral Problems in Geography: A Symposium* (Northwestern University Press, 1969), co-editor of *Locational Approaches to Power and Conflict* (Sage Publications, 1974), and author of *Conflict, Power, and Politics in the City: A Geographic View* (McGraw-Hill, 1973).

MICHAEL J. DEAR received his doctorate from the University of Pennsylvania after practicing as a planner for the Greater London Council, in England. He is presently Assistant Professor of Geography at McMaster University, Hamilton, Ontario. His research interests include locational conflict over planning decisions, and public sector planning.

KENT EKLUND was educated at Augustana College and at the University of Pennsylvania. He is now Assistant Professor of Political Science at St. Olaf College in Northfield, Minnesota. His major research interests include urban politics with particular emphasis on the interrelations of policy and location. He has served as consultant to the state of Minnesota on problems of urban growth and on the social impacts of public facilities.

DAVID HARVEY was born in England, where he attended Cambridge University. His major current interests are in urban social geography, and he has done extensive research on urban housing markets. He is the author of *Explanation in Geography* (Edward Arnold, 1969) and *Social Justice in the City* (Edward Arnold, 1973). His papers have appeared in geography, political science, and regional science journals. Serving now as Professor of Geography and Environmental Engineering at the Johns Hopkins University, he has also taught at Bristol University and at Pennsylvania State University.

REX HONEY, a native of San Diego, California, was educated at the University of California at Riverside and also at the University of Minnesota. His major research interest is jurisdictional organization, and he has done extensive work on this topic in both the U.S. and the United Kingdom. He is currently Associate Professor of Geography at the University of Iowa.

JOHN KRAMER is Professor of Sociology at the State University of New York College at Brockport and has also taught at the University of Missouri at St. Louis. He was born in Philadelphia and educated at Dartmouth College and Yale University. His major research interest is urban politics, on which he has written a number of papers. He edited *North American Suburbs: Politics, Diversity, and Change* (Glendessary Press, 1972) and co-authored *Strategy and Conflict in Metropolitan Housing* (Heinemann, 1977).

JONATHAN LONG is a research associate in the Tourism and Recreation Research Unit attached to Edinburgh University. Originally from Calcutta, he was educated at Bristol University and at McMaster University. He has recently been involved in the Scottish Tourism and Recreation Study and in a research project, Recreational Provision in the Highlands and Islands of Scotland.

KENNETH NEWTON serves as a Research Fellow of Nuffield College, Oxford. He is author of *The Sociology of British Communism* (Penguin Books, 1969), *Second City Politics* (Oxford University Press, 1976), and a variety of articles on urban politics in Britain and the United States. He has taught at the University of Birmingham, the University of Pittsburgh, and has held an ACLS Fellowship at the University of Wisconsin. He is chairman of the Local Politics Workgroup of the European Consortium for Political Research, and is currently engaged in research on the spending patterns of towns and counties in England, and the financial problems of western European cities.

DAVID R. REYNOLDS, whose articles have appeared in many books and professional journals in geography, sociology, political science, and quantitative history, is Professor of Geography and Research Associate, Institute of Urban and Regional Research at the University of Iowa. He is also associate editor of *Geographical Analysis* and co-editor of *Locational Approaches to Power and Conflict* (Sage Publications, 1974). His research interests are primarily focussed upon collective decision making in locational contexts, the spatial organization of political systems, and electoral behavior.

SHOUKRY T. ROWEIS was born in Egypt and educated at Cairo University, Purdue University, and the Massachusetts Institute of Technology. His major current interest is in the dynamics of urbanization in advanced capitalist societies. In 1976 he received the Ontario Confederation of University Faculty Associations award for outstanding contributions to university education. He is presently in the Department of Urban and Regional Planning at the University of Toronto.

ALLEN J. SCOTT is currently Professor of Urban and Regional Planning and Geography at the University of Toronto. Originally from England, he attended Oxford University and Northwestern University. From 1974 to 1975 he was a visiting professor at the University of Paris. He is the author of numerous articles and books in the areas of urban and regional planning, theoretical geography, and regional science.

RICHARD A. WALKER, originally from Manhattan, Kansas, has spent most of his life in the San Francisco Bay area, where he is currently Assistant Professor of Geography at the University of California at Berkeley. His research interests include urban problems with particular emphasis on suburbanization, and environmental and land-use problems. His papers on these topics have appeared in the *Ecology Law Quarterly, Water Resources Research*, the *Coastal Management Journal*, and *Antipode*.

OLIVER P. WILLIAMS, who has taught at Michigan State University and Wesleyan University, is now Professor of Political Science at the University of Pennsylvania. A native of McPherson, Kansas, he attended Reed College and the University of Chicago. His major research interest is comparative urban politics. His papers have appeared in serials such as the *American Political Science Review, Urban Affairs Quarterly*, and the *Public Administration Review*. He is co-author of *Suburban Differences and Metropolitan Policies* (University of Pennsylvania Press, 1965), *Four Cities* (University of Pennsylvania Press, 1963), and he is author of *Metropolitan Political Analysis* (The Free Press, 1971).

KEN YOUNG obtained his doctorate, as well as his bachelor's and master's degrees, at the London School of Economics (LSE). He spent two years with the Greater London Group there, leaving to teach in the Sociology Department at Goldsmiths' College, London. In 1969 he returned to LSE as research officer in the Department of Government. Since 1974 he has been research fellow at the University of Kent at Canterbury, and joint editor for *Policy and Politics*. He is author of *Local Politics and the Rise of Party* (Leicester University Press, 1975), co-author of *Strategy and Conflict in Metropolitan Housing* (Heinemann, 1977), and editor of *Essays on the Study of Urban Politics* (Archon Books, 1975).